THE FORGOTTEN KINGDOM

Society of Biblical Literature

Ancient Near East Monographs

Number 5

THE FORGOTTEN KINGDOM

The Archaeology and History of Northern Israel

THE FORGOTTEN KINGDOM

THE ARCHAEOLOGY AND
HISTORY OF NORTHERN ISRAEL

By

Israel Finkelstein

Society of Biblical Literature
Atlanta

THE FORGOTTEN KINGDOM
The Archaeology and History of Northern Israel

Library of Congress Cataloging-in-Publication Data

Finkelstein, Israel.
    The forgotten kingdom : the archaeology and history of Northern Israel / by Israel Finkelstein.
        p. cm. — (Ancient Near East monographs ; number 5)
    Includes bibliographical references and indexes.
    ISBN 978-1-58983-910-6 (paper binding : alk. paper) — ISBN 978-1-58983-912-0 (hardcover binding : alk. paper) — ISBN 978-1-58983-911-3 (electronic format)
    1. Galilee (Israel)—Antiquities. 2. Galilee (Israel)—History. 3. Excavations (Archaeology)—Israel—Galilee. I. Title.
    DS110.G2F56 2013
    933'.03—dc23
                                                    2013022948

CONTENTS

Acknowledgments

The seeds of this book were sown in a series of lectures I gave at the Collège de France in February 2012. The series, delivered at the invitation of my colleague and friend, Prof. Thomas Römer, was entitled "The Emergence of the Northern Kingdom of Israel." I wish to thank Thomas for his kind invitation, for his hospitality while I was in Paris, and for initiating the publication of this book. The book was first published in French under the title *Le Royaume biblique oublié* (Paris, 2013) by Odile Jacob for the Collège de France.

This book is also based on many articles that I have written over the course of several years, some of them in collaboration with colleagues. I am indebted to four of them who have granted me permission to summarize parts of our articles in this book: Alexander Fantalkin (article on Khirbet Qeiyafa published in *Tel Aviv* 2012), Oded Lipschits (article on Jahaz and Ataroth published in *ZDPV* 2010), Nadav Na'aman (article on Shechem of the Late Bronze Age and the northern kingdom published in *IEJ* 2005), and Benjamin Sass (article on the spread of scribal activity in the Levant in the Iron I-IIA, to be published in *Hebrew Bible and Ancient Israel*).

The preparation of this book was supported by the Chaim Katzman Archaeology Fund at Tel Aviv University. I am grateful to Myrna Pollak for her highly professional editing of the manuscript and to Alexander Pechuro and my student Maayan Mor for the preparation of the figures.

ABBREVIATIONS

AB   Anchor Bible
ABD   *Anchor Bible Dictionary*. Edited by D. N. Freedman. 6
              vols. New York: Doubleday, 1992.
ABS   Archaeology and Biblical Studies
AJA   *American Journal of Archaeology*
AASOR   Annual of the American Schools of Oriental Research
AOAT   Alter Orient und Altes Testament
BA   *Biblical Archaeologist*
BASOR   *Bulletin of the American Schools of Oriental Research*
Bib   *Biblica*
BJS   Brown Judaic Studies
BN   *Biblische Notizen*
CBQ   *Catholic Biblical Quarterly*
EI   *Eretz-Israel: Archaeological, Historical and Geographical
              Studies*
HBAI   *Hebrew Bible and Ancient Israel*
IEJ   *Israel Exploration Journal*
JAS   *Journal of Archaeological Science*
JBL   *Journal of Biblical Literature*
JHS   *Journal of Hebrew Scriptures*
JNES   *Journal of Near Eastern Studies*
JNSL   *Journal of Northwest Semitic Languages*
JSJ   *Journal for the Study of Judaism*
JSOT   *Journal for the Study of the Old Testament*
JSOTSup   Journal for the Study of the Old Testament Supplement
              Series
NEA   *Near Eastern Archaeology*

NEAEHL	*The New Encyclopedia of Archaeological Excavations in the Holy Land.* Edited by E. Stern. 4 vols. Jerusalem: Israel Exploration Society and Carta; New York: Simon & Schuster, 1993.
OBO	Orbis biblicus et orientalis
OLA	Orientalia Lovaniensia Analecta
OTL	Old Testament Library
PEQ	*Palestine Exploration Quarterly*
PJb	*Palästinajahrbuch des deutschen evangelischen Instituts für Altertumswissenschaft des Heiligen Landes zu Jerusalem*
RB	*Revue Biblique*
SBLABS	Society of Biblical Literature Archaeology and Biblical Studies
SBLMS	Society of Biblical Literature Monograph Series
SBLSBL	Society of Biblical Literature Studies in Biblical Literature
SBLSymS	Society of Biblical Literature Symposium Series
SHANE	Studies in the History of the Ancient Near East
SJOT	*Scandinavian Journal of Old Testament*
UF	*Ugarit-Forschungen*
VT	*Vetus Testamentum*
VTSup	Supplements to Vetus Testamentum
ZAW	*Zeitschrift für die Alttestamentliche Wiessenschaft*
ZDPV	*Zeitschrift des Deutschen Palästina-Vereins*

INTRODUCTION:
WHY A BOOK ON THE NORTHERN KINGDOM?

In the first half of the eighth century B.C.E., Israel ruled over the lion's share of the territory of the two Hebrew kingdoms (fig. 1), and its population accounted for three quarters of the people of Israel and Judah combined (Broshi and Finkelstein 1992). Israel was stronger than Judah both militarily and economically, and in the first half of the ninth century and in the first half of the eighth century—almost half the time the two kingdoms co-existed—Israel dominated the southern kingdom. Nonetheless, Israel has lingered in the shadow of Judah, both in the story told in the Hebrew Bible and in the attention paid to it by modern scholarship.

1. HISTORIOGRAPHY AND HISTORICAL MEMORY

The history of ancient Israel in the Hebrew Bible was written by Judahite[1] authors in Jerusalem, the capital of the southern kingdom and the hub of the Davidic dynasty. As such it transmits Judahite ideas regarding territory, kingship, temple, and cult. Moreover, even what some scholars consider as the early layers of the history of ancient Israel, such as the books of Samuel (e.g., McCarter 1994; Halpern 2001; Römer and de Pury 2000, 123–28; Hutton 2009), were written after the northern kingdom was vanquished by Assyria and its elite was deported. In the late seventh

---

1. In this book "Judahite" is used as an adjective for terms relating to the kingdom of Judah (also described here as the "southern kingdom"), e.g., Judahite pottery. "Judean" is used to refer to geographical regions, such as the Judean Desert. "Israel" generally refers to the northern kingdom, while "ancient Israel" refers to the Iron Age people—north and south combined. In "two Hebrew kingdoms" I ostensibly adhere to the ideology of later Judahite-Judean authors but at the same time acknowledge both the proximities and differences in their material culture and cognitive world (see more in Finkelstein 1999a).

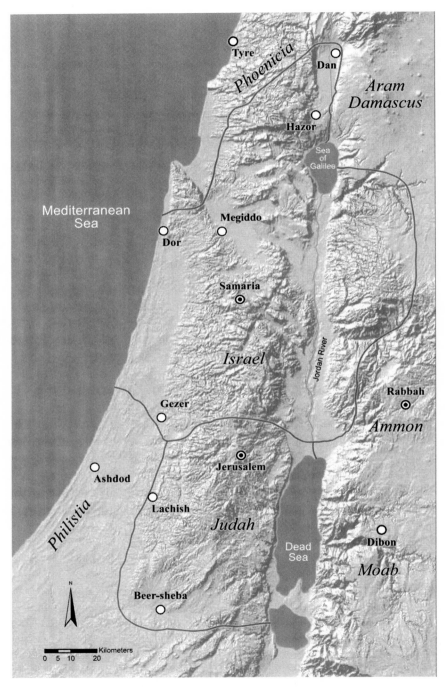

Figure 1. Map of Israel and Judah in the eighth century B.C.E.

century, when the early layer in the Deuteronomistic History was com-
piled (Cross 1973, 274–88; Na'aman 2002b; Römer 2007), the northern
kingdom was already a remote, vague memory over a century old, and
this in a period with no continuity of scribal activity. It is true that Israelite traditions are incorporated in the Hebrew Bible. I refer to blocks such
as the Jacob cycle in Genesis (de Pury 1991), the exodus tradition (van
der Toorn 1996, 287–315), what is known as the "Book of Saviors" in
Judges (Richter 1966), positive traditions regarding King Saul in Samuel,
the Elijah-Elisha prophetic stories in Kings, and the two northern prophets Hosea and Amos (for the impact of northern texts on the Hebrew
Bible, see Schiedewind 2004; Fleming 2012). These traditions could have
reached Judah orally or in a written form.

The original northern texts—or at least some of them—could have
been written as early as the first half of the eighth century B.C.E. in the
capital Samaria or in the temple of YHWH at Bethel, located on the northern border of Judah (also Fleming 2012, 314–21; for a later date of compilation at Bethel, see Knauf 2006; Davies 2007a, 2007b; for the archaeology
of Bethel, see Finkelstein and Singer-Avitz 2009). Both written texts and
oral traditions were probably brought to Judah by Israelite refugees after
the fall of Israel in 720 B.C.E. (Schniedewind 2004; Finkelstein and Silberman 2006b); estimates of demographic growth in Judah from the Iron IIA
to the Iron IIB (ninth to late eighth/early seventh centuries B.C.E.) indicate that in late monarchic times Israelite groups made up a significant
part of the population of the southern kingdom (Finkelstein and Silberman 2006b). The northern traditions were incorporated into the Judahite
canon either because they supported the Judahite ideology or because of
political needs in Judah to absorb the significant Israelite population in
the kingdom. In the latter case the original Israelite traditions were subjected to Judahite needs and ideology, as in the case of the book of Samuel,
which incorporated negative northern traditions about the founder of the
Davidic dynasty but gave them a twist to clear David of all wrongdoing
(McCarter 1980a; Halpern 2001). So even here the genuine, original voice
of Israel is barely heard in the Hebrew Bible.

The political ideology of the Deuteronomistic History in the Bible
depicts the reality after the fall of the northern kingdom. It is Judah-cen-
tric, arguing that all territories that once belonged to Israel must be ruled
by a Davidic king, that all Hebrews must accept the rule of the Davidic
dynasty, and that all Hebrews must worship the God of Israel at the temple
in Jerusalem. The story of the northern kingdom is therefore mostly tele-

graphic and its tone negative;[2] while the individual Hebrews can all join the nation if they accept the centrality of the Jerusalem temple and dynasty, their kingdom and kings are viewed as illegitimate.

Only Jeroboam I and Ahab are given relatively large shares of text, but, needless to repeat, the tone of this text is negative. For example, Jeroboam I, the founder of the northern kingdom, is described as the original apostate, the individual whose sins doomed the north from the outset (Cross 1973, 274–88). The reign of other north Israelite kings is summarized in a few sentences. Only six verses are given to Omri, the founder of the most celebrated dynasty of the north, the king by whose name Israel is known in Assyrian records. Only one of these verses is informative, that is, nonformulative in nature. Seven verses are given to Jeroboam II, one of the most important kings in the history of the two Hebrew kingdoms, who ruled for approximately 40 years (788–747 B.C.E.) and conquered vast territories. Very little is told about the capital Samaria, and relatively little is known about the countryside towns and villages. This is so due to their distance from Jerusalem and the authors' lack of direct knowledge of the landscape. A good example of the latter is the Israelite territory in Transjordan. Only a few towns are mentioned in this area, the size of which is equal to the highlands territory of Judah, of which the Bible mentions the names of about fifty towns.

This situation is amplified by the fact that biblical, archaeological, and historical studies of ancient Israel have been dominated by the Judeo-Christian historical tradition, which has been shaped, in turn, by the Hebrew Bible, that is, the Judahite text. The Bible is what it is, and hence biblical scholarship basically deals with Judah and with the Judahite perspective of Israel, which was formulated a century after the collapse of the northern kingdom.

Archaeological research somewhat balances this picture. Iron Age Judah has been thoroughly studied. Jerusalem is one of the most excavated cities in the world, especially over the last fifty years, and almost all the major sites in its countryside have been excavated: Mizpah and Hebron in the highlands; Lachish and Beth-shemesh in the Shephelah; and Beer-sheba and Arad in the Beer-sheba Valley. Israel has not been deprived of

---

2. In the book of Chronicles, which was written much later than the books of Kings, probably not earlier than the third century B.C.E., and which represents Second Temple theology and political ideology, the history of the northern kingdom is nearly avoided all together.

investigation. Samaria, the capital, has been thoroughly excavated twice in the past, and all major countryside sites have also been explored. I refer to Bethel, Shechem, and Tell el- Far'ah (Tirzah) in the hill country, Gezer in the southwest, Dor on the coast, and Megiddo, Jezreel, Hazor, and Dan in the northern valleys. In addition, the countryside of the northern kingdom—in the highlands and lowlands alike—has been meticulously investigated in archaeological surveys that have enabled the drawing of settlement maps by period. It is field research, then, that enables one to write an archaeology-based, Judahite ideology–free history of Israel, and in the end also to reach a more balanced reconstruction of the history of ancient Israel in general and the two Hebrew kingdoms in particular.

This book tells the story of the northern kingdom mainly in its formative phases. The lead narrative is that of archaeology—results of excavations and surveys alike. Then the story of archaeology is combined with the little that we know from ancient Near Eastern texts and with those biblical texts that can be judged to provide genuine, nonpropagandistic information—even vague memories—of the northern kingdom.

Regarding biblical materials that do not come from northern circles—for instance, information provided by the books of Kings—the question, of course, is how the late-monarchic Judahite author(s) who lived in Jerusalem knew about events that took place centuries before their own time, some in locations far from Jerusalem. The answer is that the Judahite author(s) must have had access to a list of Israelite kings that specified the years of their reigns and some additional pieces of data about their origins and deaths. This list must have provided them with knowledge that enabled the correlation between the Israelite and Judahite monarchs. The information included in the short biblical verses is generally accurate, as it is supported by extrabiblical Assyrian texts. It should also be remembered that northern sources—if, indeed, put in writing in Samaria or Bethel in the early eighth century—were much closer in date to the formative phases in the history of Israel and Judah in the tenth century B.C.E. than the Judahite authors of late-monarchic and later times. Such northern authors were just over a century away from this formative phase, compared to three centuries for the early Judahite authors of the late seventh century B.C.E. An important source of information could have been Israelite refugees who settled in Judah and who could have provided the Judahite author(s) with written materials as well as oral traditions regarding different parts of the territory of the northern kingdom, on both sides of the Jordan River.

My intention in this book is not to give a full account of the material culture and history of the north in the Iron Age. My goal is to deal mainly with the geo-political situation in the southern Levant, territorial history of Israel and what is described in anthropological literature as "state formation," that is, the development of territorial entities with bureaucratic apparatus and institutions. Special emphasis will be given to the impact of the environment on historical developments and to long-term processes that dictated the history of the north in the late second and early first millennium B.C.E.

The chronological scope of this book is from the Late Bronze II to the Iron IIB. In absolute chronology terms this is the period of time between circa 1350 and 700 B.C.E. However, the main discussion concentrates on a shorter period of time: the rise of territorial polity in the central highlands of Israel between circa 1000 and 850 B.C.E. The Late Bronze Age is discussed mainly as a model for which we obtain reasonably good archaeological and historical materials. The last century in the history of the north is mentioned only in passing toward the end of the book. The final chapter deals with Israelite population in Judah after 720 B.C.E., a phenomenon that was crucial for the shaping of the Hebrew Bible.

2. Recent Advances in Archaeology

A clarification about chronology is in place here. Our knowledge of the chronology—both relative and absolute—of the Iron Age strata and monuments in the Levant has been truly revolutionized. In terms of relative chronology, intensification of the study of pottery assemblages from secure stratigraphic contexts at sites such as Megiddo and Tel Rehov in the north and Lachish in the south opened the way to establish a secure division of the Iron Age into six ceramic typology phases: early and late Iron I (Arie 2006; Finkelstein and Piasetzky 2006), early and late Iron IIA (Herzog and Singer-Avitz 2004, 2006; Zimhoni 2004a; A. Mazar et al. 2005; Arie 2013), Iron IIB and Iron IIC (Zimhoni 2004b). In terms of absolute chronology, intensive radiocarbon studies enable accurate dating of these phases in a resolution of fifty years and less. This can now be done free of past arguments, which were based on uncritical reading of the biblical text (e.g., Yadin 1970; Dever 1997). In this book I will be using the dates that result from two studies:

(1) A statistical model based on a large number of radiocarbon determinations: 229 results from 143 samples that came from 38 strata at 18

sites located in both the north and south of Israel (Finkelstein and Pias-etzky 2010, based on Sharon et al. 2007 and other studies; table 1 here[3]). The radiocarbon results from Israel are the most intensive for such a short period of time and small piece of land ever presented in the archaeology of the ancient Near East.

Table 1: Dates of ceramic phases in the Levant and the transition between them according to recent radiocarbon results (based on a Bayesian model, 63 percent agreement between the model and the data)

Ceramic Phase	Date of Phase [B.C.E.]*	Transition between Phases [B.C.E.]
Late Bronze III	−1098	
		1125–1071
Early Iron I	1109–1047	
		1082–1037
Middle Iron I	1055–1028	
		1045–1021
Late Iron I	1037–913	
		960–899
Early Iron IIA	920–883	
		902–866
Late Iron IIA	886–760	
		785–748
Transitional Iron IIA/B	757–	

* The beginning of the first phase and the end of the last phase cannot be determined by the data at hand.

---

3. The model divides the period discussed in this book slightly differently from the six ceramic phases mentioned above. It adds the Late Bronze III, divides the Iron I into three rather than two phases, and ends with the late Iron IIA. The reason for the latter is the Hallstatt Plateau in the radiocarbon calibration curve, which prevents giving accurate dates to samples that come from Iron IIB and Iron IIC contexts.

(2) A statistical model for a single site—Megiddo: circa 100 radio-carbon determinations from about 60 samples for 10 layers at Megiddo, which cover circa 600 years between circa 1400 and 800 B.C.E. (Toffolo et al. forthcoming; demonstration in fig. 2). Megiddo is especially reliable for such a model because the time span in question features four major destruction layers that produced many organic samples from reliable contexts. This, too, is unprecedented: no other site has ever produced such a number of results for such a dense stratigraphic sequence.

The general model (table 1) represents a conservative approach for determining the dates. It creates certain overlaps in the dates of the phases and a fairly broad range for the transition periods. When this model is adapted to historical reasoning (e.g., the end of Egyptian rule in the Late Bronze III), one gets the following dates, which will be used in this book (Finkelstein and Piasetzky 2011):

Late Bronze III: twelfth century until circa 1130 B.C.E.
Early Iron I: late twelfth century and first half of the eleventh century B.C.E.
Late Iron I: second half of the eleventh century and first half of the tenth century B.C.E.
Early Iron IIA: last decades of the tenth century and the early ninth century B.C.E.
Late Iron IIA: rest of the ninth century and the early eighth century B.C.E.
Iron IIB: rest of the eighth century and early seventh century B.C.E.

Several additional developments in the archaeology of the Levant in recent years facilitate the compilation of an archaeology-based history of the northern kingdom of Israel:

(1) The parting from the concept of a great united monarchy in the days of the founders of the Davidic dynasty. According to the Hebrew Bible and the traditional view in biblical and archaeological scholarship, which was founded on an uncritical reading of the biblical story, the united monarchy was ruled from Jerusalem and stretched over the entire land of Israel. According to some biblical references, probably depicting Iron Age realities, it extended from Dan to Beer-sheba (2 Sam 3:10; 1 Kgs 5:5). According to another version, probably inserted in the Persian period, it stretched across a much larger territory (1 Kgs 5:4). On the

Figure 2. The eastern and southern baulks of Area H at Megiddo, showing different layers and their relative and absolute dates.

side of biblical scholarship, it is clear today that the biblical idea of a great united monarchy is a literary construct that represents the terri-torial ideology, kingship concepts, and theological ideas of late monar-chic, Judahite authors (e.g., Van Seters 1983, 307–12; Knauf 1991, 1997; Miller 1997; Niemann 1997; Finkelstein and Silberman 2006a). On the side of archaeology, it has become clear, among other reasons thanks to the radiocarbon studies mentioned above, that the monuments that were traditionally perceived as representing the great united monarchy of the tenth century B.C.E. were in fact built during the rule of the Omride dynasty in Israel in the ninth century B.C.E. (summary in Finkelstein 2010). This development in research brought about a new understanding of the days of the Omride kings—especially their building activities and the demographic structure of their kingdom. The demise of the united monarchy as a historical reality means that the two Hebrew kingdoms emerged parallel to each other, as neighbouring entities independent of each other, in line with the long-term history of the central highlands in the Bronze and Iron Ages.

(2) The advances in the study of relative and absolute chronology of the Iron Age strata in the Levant, as described above, are behind the rec-

ognition that in the northern valleys the Iron I still features "Canaanite" material culture and territorial disposition (ch. 1).

(3) The large scale surveys in the highlands, including the core area of the northern kingdom, make it possible to produce settlement maps for the different phases of the Iron Age and hence open the way for a nuanced understanding of the demographic, economic, and social changes involved in the rise of territorial north-Israelite entities.

3. The Personal Perspective

My involvement in the study of the northern kingdom stems from several stages in my career as a field archaeologist. The intensive archaeological survey that I conducted in the hill country north of Jerusalem in the 1980s brought to my attention the special nature of the highlands from the social and economic perspectives (for background, see Alt 1925b; Marfoe 1979). It also drew my attention to the intensity of Iron Age settlement activity in the areas north of Jerusalem relative to the territory south of it and to the cyclic, long-term nature of the settlement processes in the highlands (Finkelstein 1995). Needless to say, understanding the settlement history of the highlands in terms of cyclic history stands in contrast to a major concept of the biblical authors (followed by many modern scholars), namely, that ancient Israel was a unique phenomenon and that Israelite history was linear in nature, from conquest to settlement, to a period of charismatic leadership (the judges), to kingship and the rise of territorial kingdoms. Acknowledging all this also called my attention to French *Annales* historians (e.g., Bloch 1952; Braudel 1958), according to whom long-term processes and developments in the countryside are no less influential than momentous "events" such as military campaigns or affairs in the corridors of power in palace and temple. In short, the surveys in the highlands illuminated important historical processes such as the paucity of settlement activity in the Late Bronze Age, the nature of the wave of settlement in the Iron I, stability of settlement activity in most areas throughout the Iron Age as opposed to certain abandonment processes in one area (in the plateau of Gibeon) in the early Iron IIA, and settlement decline in southern Samaria after the fall of the northern kingdom in 720 B.C.E.

My excavations at the site of Shiloh in the early 1980s helped me understand the material culture in the highlands and the nature of the Iron I—the period of the emergence of ancient Israel (Finkelstein 1988). In addition, the results of the surveys and the excavation at Shiloh gradually heightened my awareness of the complexity of the biblical sources on the early history of Israel.

Starting in the 1990s I turned to the lowlands and especially to the Jezreel Valley. The excavations I have conducted over the last twenty years together with colleagues and students at Megiddo opened the way for a better understanding of the Iron Age in the northern valleys.[4] First and foremost, preparing for the dig at Megiddo I became aware of the problems in the traditional dating of the Iron Age strata and monuments in the Levant. This led me to propose the "low chronology" for the Iron Age (Finkelstein 1996a), a chronological system that is now supported by radiocarbon studies and that helped revolutionize what we know about the northern kingdom. The dig at Megiddo facilitated my understanding of other issues that are discussed in this book. One of them is the study of the end-phase of the Late Bronze Age in the northern valleys. Another is the exceptional—and until recently not fully understood—prosperity of the late Iron I, especially in the Jezreel Valley. I labeled this "swan song" of Canaanite material culture and territorial disposition "New Canaan," a term that is now prevalent in scholarship. The dig at Megiddo also called for a renewed investigation of the transition from second- to first-millennium traits of material culture in the north (from Canaanite to Israelite, as some scholars refer to this process). Parallel to the dig at Megiddo I conducted—also with members of the Megiddo Expedition—two seasons of archaeological survey in the Jezreel Valley with the aim of understanding the settlement systems that corresponded to the main phases of occupation in the central site of Megiddo. The results of this work indicated the dramatic differences between the settlement history of the northern valleys and the central highlands.

In short, thirty years of fieldwork in both the highlands and lowlands of the northern kingdom paved the way for a new understanding of the archaeology and history of ancient Israel. This new understanding resulted in a series of articles that dealt with many aspects of Iron Age material culture, settlement transformations, and territorial history, which are all embedded (and cited) in this book.

---

4. For topics discussed in this book I am especially grateful to the following members of the Megiddo Expedition (past and present): co-directors David Ussishkin, Eric H. Cline, and Baruch Halpern; and senior team members Matthew J. Adams, Eran Arie, Norma Franklin, Yuval Gadot, and Mario A. S. Martin.

1

SETTING THE STAGE: THE SHECHEM POLITY OF THE LATE BRONZE AGE AND THE FINAL DAYS OF THE CANAANITE CITY-STATES IN THE LATE IRON I

In order to draw a clear picture of the settlement and territorial processes that took place in the highlands and the northern valleys in the late Iron I and the Iron IIA, circa 1050–800 B.C.E., I must start with the previous periods. I refer to the Late Bronze II–III and the early Iron I; in absolute chronology terms they cover the period between circa 1350 and 1050 B.C.E. The Late Bronze is especially instrumental here, as it provides a well-documented case—both archaeologically and textually—for the growth of a territorial polity in the central highlands of Canaan.

1.1. THE LATE BRONZE AGE

Territorially, Canaan of the Late Bronze II was divided into a system of city-states that were dominated by an Egyptian administrative and military system. Each city-state consisted of a main city—the seat of the ruler—and a system of villages around it. The size of the hub-cities, the extent of the territories that they dominated, the number of villages in their hinterland, the volume of their populations, and their nature (for instance, sedentary versus pastoral)—all varied.

Three tools help reconstruct the territorial disposition of the Late Bronze city-states (e.g., Finkelstein 1996c; Naʾaman 1997c). The first is the textual evidence. Here the most important source is the Amarna letters of the fourteenth century B.C.E. (Moran 1992). The approximately 370 Akkadian clay tablets that were found in the late nineteenth century in el-Amarna in Middle Egypt include part of the diplomatic correspondence between Pharaohs Amenophis III and Amenophis IV and rulers of city-states in Canaan—in the area of today's Israel, the Palestinian Authority,

Jordan, Lebanon, and southwestern Syria. It is reasonable to assume that the situation in the Amarna period represents the entire extent of the Late Bronze II–III, from the fourteenth to the twelfth centuries B.C.E. Individuals who wrote to or received letters from Egypt were all rulers of city-states. Although the archive is incomplete—originally the letters must have made up a portion of a much larger archive—I would argue that the material at hand enables a reasonable reconstruction of the territorial map of Late Bronze Canaan. Two factors support this approach:

(1) Most Canaanite city-states mentioned in the archive appear in several letters. This fact diminishes (but does not eliminate) the possibility that additional major city-states are absent from the map because the archive is incomplete.

(2) When mapped, the information provided by the archive does not leave "empty territories." On the contrary, letters that supply detailed information regarding border areas between polities indicate that the territorial boundaries of the major entities mentioned in the correspondence touch on each other. I therefore dispute the notion that certain areas of Canaan, especially in the highlands, were a sort of "no man's land' (contra Na'aman 1997c).

In the area of the future territory of the northern kingdom and its immediate surroundings, the main city-states were: Tyre, Acco, Achshaph, Ginti-kirmil (= Gath Carmel), and Gezer on the coastal plain; Damascus and Ashtaroth in southwestern Syria; Hazor, Rehov, and Pehel in the Jordan Valley; Megiddo, Shim'on, and Anaharath in the Jezreel Valley and vicinity; and Shechem in the highlands of Samaria (fig. 3). The Amarna letters also provide data on the location of Egyptian administrative centers in Canaan. In the fourteenth century, the main Egyptian centers in the area discussed here were Beth-shean in the Jordan Valley and Kumidi in the southern part of the Beqa of Lebanon. Archaeological finds indicate that Beth-shean also continued to play this role in the later phases of the Late Bronze Age.

The second tool that helps us to reconstruct the territorial disposition of Late Bronze Canaan is the petrographic investigation of the Amarna letters (Goren, Finkelstein, and Na'aman 2004). The seat of the sender of a given tablet can be identified according to the mineralogy of the clay. Normally—if the tablet had not been sent from one of the Egyptian centers such as Gaza, the hub of Egyptian administration in Canaan (located outside of the area discussed here)—the mineralogy of the clay should fit the geological formations in the vicinity of the seat of the sender. In the

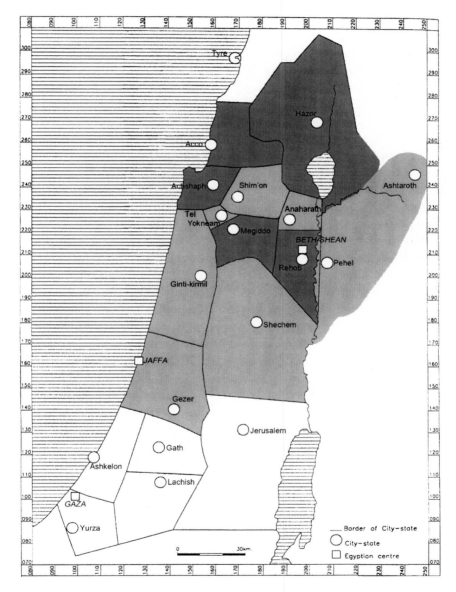

Figure 3. Late Bronze polity in the north, marking the Shechem (light gray) and anti-Shechem (dark gray) coalitions.

northern part of Canaan the petrographic investigation confirmed the status of the city-state known from the tablets and other Egyptian texts and added two unknown centers, only one west of the Jordan River (Tel Yokneam; fig. 3).

The third tool for reconstructing the array of Canaanite city-states is archaeology. The centers of the city-states should usually be identified at the larger Late Bronze sites. If excavated, they must reveal evidence of public architecture such as palaces and temples; Megiddo, Hazor, and Lachish provide the best examples. It is important to note that in most cases the textual evidence of the Amarna archive and the archaeological evidence correspond—yet another validation of the notion that the Amarna tablets give a fairly complete picture of the territorial disposition in Late Bronze Canaan. The territories of the city-states and their populations should be large enough to enable production of agricultural surplus as well as deploy manpower to public works. From the demographic point of view, in order to be able to execute large-scale building activities, the Late Bronze polities each needed a minimal population of several thousand (for this issue, see Bunimovitz 1994).

As observed by Alt (1925b), the Canaanite city-states can be divided geographically into two types. Those located in the lowlands had relatively small territories that were densely populated, while those centered in the highlands, or those that dominated highland areas, stretched over large, sparsely settled territories. Two city-states in the north belong to the latter category: Shechem in northern Samaria and Hazor, dominating the Upper Galilee, in the Jordan Valley. Late Bronze Shechem provides important comparative information for understanding the processes that took place in the northern part of the central hill country in the Iron Age. This is so because the Amarna texts present detailed geographical and historical information about the attempts of Shechem to expand into the lowlands and establish a large highland-lowland territorial entity.

1.1.1. The Shechem Polity in the Amarna Period

The existence of a significant territorial polity at Shechem as early as the Middle Bronze Age is hinted at by the Khu-Sobek Stela, found in Abydos in Egypt. It describes an Egyptian military campaign to the region in the nineteenth century b.c.e. The reference to the "land' of Shechem, and the mention of Shechem as a parallel to Retenu (a title for Canaan), possibly hint that it was a center of a large territorial entity. Only two central hill country sites—Shechem and Jerusalem—are mentioned in the Egyptian Execration Texts of the nineteenth–eighteenth centuries B.C.E., apparently indicating that the entire area was divided between two large political bodies: a northern one centered in Shechem and a southern one centered in Jerusalem. Shechem of that time was apparently a small, unfortified settlement. In the later phase of the Middle Bronze Age it featured impressive monumental stone and earthworks, indicating its ability to control manpower and organize large-scale public construction.

The most notorious figures in the Amarna letters, mainly because of their territorial ambitions and their impact on Egyptian interests in Canaan, are Labayu, the ruler of Shechem,[1] and Abdi-Ashirta and Aziru, the rulers of the kingdom of Amurru, which was located in today's Lebanon and western Syria. Labayu's words, "Who am I that the king should lose his land on account of me" (EA 254:6–9),[2] clearly indicate the kind of accusations directed at him from Egypt—accusations unparalleled in the Amarna correspondence. The territorial situation in the area can be detected by following the maneuvers of Shechem and its allies, on the one hand, and the actions of their opponents, on the other. It is noteworthy that most cities in central Canaan were involved with the two struggling coalitions (fig. 3; see in detail, with more bibliography, Finkelstein and Na'aman 2005; for the letters, see Moran 1992; Na'aman 1975).

1.1.1.1. The Shechem Coalition

The Shechem coalition included city-states on the coastal plain and in the Jezreel and the Jordan Valleys.

Gezer. Located on the international road that led from Egypt to the north, where another road headed east to the highlands near Jerusalem, and controlling the fertile Ayalon Valley, Gezer was one of the most impor-

---

1. The Amarna letters do not specifically mention that Labayu and his sons ruled at Shechem. The only reference to Shechem is in EA 289:18–24, written by Abdi-Heba of Jerusalem, who says: "Are we to act like Labayu when he was giving the land of Shechem to the Apiru?" Petrographic investigation of the Labayu letters confirms that he ruled in the northern part of the central highlands (Goren, Finkelstein, and Na'aman 2004, 262–65), and long-term historical considerations certainly put him in Shechem.

2. The el-Amarna tablets are cited here as EA plus the number of the given letter and lines in the letter.

tant city-states in Canaan. The fact that it was an ally of Shechem is recorded in several places (e.g., EA 250:32–39, 53–56; 289:25–36). At a certain point Labayu entered Gezer and intimidated its ruler, an act taken as a threat to the Egyptian domination of Canaan (EA 253:11–25; 254:6–10, 19–29).

Ginti-kirmil. A place named Ginti-kirmil was most likely the residence of a Canaanite ruler (EA 289:18–20). Petrographic investigation of the Amarna letters has shown that it should be identified with the large mound of the village of Jatt in the Sharon Plain (Goren, Finkelstein, and Na'aman 2004, 256–59). The close relations between its ruler and Labayu of Shechem may be inferred from EA 263:33–34. The alliance of Ginti-kirmil and Gezer with Shechem is referred to in EA 289:18–29.

Tel Yoqneam. A ruler named Balu-mehir was an ally of Labayu of Shechem, as is indicated by the fact that both were about to be handed over together to the Egyptian authorities (EA 245:36–45). Petrographic investigation of the letters sent by this ruler shows that his city, the name of which is not well-preserved, was located at Tel Yoqneam, north of Megiddo (Goren, Finkelstein, and Na'aman 2004, 250–55).

Anaharath. Petrographic analysis identified a seat of an Amarna-period ruler in the eastern Lower Galilee, probably at Tel Rekhesh—most likely the site of the Canaanite and biblical city of Anaharath (Goren, Finkelstein, and Na'aman 2004, 241–43). The author of two letters sent from this place complains that the enemies of Labayu attacked him and conquered his towns—an indication that the two rulers, of Anaharath and of Shechem, were allies.

Pehel. EA 250:35–38 seems to refer to the attempt of Labayu's sons to take over Pihilu (= Pehel in the eastern Jordan Valley, facing Beth-shean). EA 255 reveals that the ruler of Pihilu was the son of Labayu. In EA 256 the ruler of Pihilu discloses that he helped Ashtaroth of the Bashan when all the cities of a land named Garu had become hostile. This may indicate that Ashtaroth cooperated with the Shechem–Gezer–Pihilu axis.

Shim'on. A ruler of Shamuna (= biblical Shimron/Shim'on), located at Tel Shimron at the northwestern tip of the Jezreel Valley, is not mentioned in the letters of the opposing coalitions. This is surprising in view of the fact that Shamuna bordered on the territory of some of the major players in the Labayu-and-sons affair. A look at the map (fig. 3) discloses that Shamuna was the only city needed for the Shechem coalition in order completely to encircle its opponents in the Jezreel Valley. Indeed, the events related to the capture and killing of Labayu (EA 245) may hint that Shamuna acted on his side.

1.1.1.2. The Anti-Shechem Coalition

The following city-states located in the Jezreel and Jordan Valleys opposed Shechem and its allies:

Megiddo. As evident from EA 244–246, Megiddo was a bitter enemy of Labayu and his sons and was physically threatened by them.

Rehob. The sender of EA 249–250 was also an enemy of Shechem. From the content of EA 250 it is quite clear that he ruled in the Jezreel Valley or its vicinity. Since Megiddo dominated the western sector of the valley, it is reasonable to suggest that he governed in the east. Indeed, the petrographic investigation points to Rehob, located at Tel Rehov in the Jordan Valley south of Beth-shean, as the possible seat of this ruler (Goren, Finkelstein, and Naaman 2004, 248–50). After Labayu's death, his sons put strong pressure on this ruler in an effort to persuade him to switch sides and support the Shechem alliance; he refused to join and reported the threats to the pharaoh (EA 250:19–22).

Achshaph and Acco. EA 366 mentions the participation of Acco and Achshaph (also located in the Acco Plain) in an alliance that acted on the side of the pharaoh, probably against Shechem and its allies.

Hazor. EA 364 refers to hostilities between Hazor and Ashtaroth in the Bashan (southwestern Syria). Assuming that the two kingdoms struggled for control over the international road that passed from Beth-shean to Damascus, Hazor—the largest and hence most populous city in Canaan in the Late Bronze Age—might have been involved in the conflict of the two coalitions and confronted the growing power of the Shechem alliance.

1.1.1.3. The Territorial Ambitions of Shechem

The details described above indicate that Labayu attempted to expand—diplomatically and militarily—from the highlands of Shechem in all directions (Finkelsten and Na'aman 2005). At the peak of its maneuvers, the Shechem coalition dominated large and important parts of central Canaan, from the Bashan in the northeast through the central highlands to the Sharon and the coastal plain south of the Yarkon River in the southwest (fig. 3). It controlled important sections of the international road leading from Egypt to Syria and Mesopotamia on the coastal plain and the Bashan, as well as a section of the King's Highway in Transjordan. The Shechem coalition put pressure on the Egyptian stronghold at Beth-shean and threatened to disconnect it from the Egyptian centers of Jaffa and Gaza.

No wonder that the anti-Shechem coalition was consequently supported by the Egyptian authorities.

It is clear from the letters and, of course, from looking at the map, that Shechem needed one more chunk of territory to gain control of much of Canaan: the strategic and fertile Jezreel Valley. This would have given it full command of the international highway to Syria and Mesopotamia, as well as domination over the breadbasket of the country. Shechem's maneuvers are therefore quite transparent: it sought to encircle the two dominating city-states in the Jezreel Valley, Megiddo and Rehob, as well as the Egyptian stronghold at Beth-shean. Its strategy: to win over the city-states to the north of the valley and put direct pressure on the cities of the valley. Regarding the latter, Labayu and his sons assaulted the city-states of Megiddo and Rehob and seem to have managed to gain territories in the southern tip of the valley.[3]

These maneuvers threatened the Egyptian interests in Canaan, and the Egyptian authorities reacted by demanding the arrest of Labayu and his allies and that they report before the pharaoh. Labayu was captured and killed, but his death did not alter the situation. His sons, one of whom must have ruled at Shechem and the other at Pihilu, followed their father's aggressive policies. How the Egyptians finally managed to break the Shechem–Gezer–Pihilu coalition remains unknown.

The "Shechem affair" in the Amarna period sheds light on processes that took place in the same region several centuries later: the rise of the northern kingdom of Israel in the early phases of the Iron Age. Four comments are in place as an introduction to discussing the Iron Age parallels in the chapters that follow:

(1) Had Shechem succeeded in taking over the Jezreel Valley and the territories immediately to its north, it would have established domination over the same areas that were ruled several centuries later by the northern kingdom in its early days (the Tirzah polity, ch. 3).

(2) A thorough study of the remains at Tell Balata—the location of Shechem—shows that the mighty entity of Labayu and his sons was ruled from a modest, unfortified settlement (Finkelstein 2006b).

---

3. A ruler named Yashdata, an ally of Megiddo, was driven from his hometown as a result of the maneuvers of Labayu (EA 248). Scholars have identified his city with Taanach in the southeast of the Jezreel Valley. I do not include it in this discussion because this identification can be disputed. See discussion in Finkelstein and Na'aman 2005.

(3) While the Jezreel Valley featured a dense system of Late Bronze city-states and subordinate towns and villages, the highlands of northern Samaria were sparsely settled by a relatively small number of settlements. On the other hand, Shechem probably controlled a mixed sedentary-pastoral population, which gave it a special strength.

(4) There is no reason why the same phenomena, a strong polity in the northern part of the central hill country, did not continue in the thirteenth to eleventh centuries, yet we have no texts to support or reject this possibility. The only clue may be the biblical story of the strongman Abimelech (Judg 9). This account, which also relates to the area of Shechem, may be based on a memory in the north regarding events that took place before the rise of the northern kingdom (Na'aman 2011b; and see below).

1.1.2. The End of the Late Bronze Age

Hazor, probably the most important city-state in the north, was destroyed in a fierce conflagration probably in the second half of the thirteenth century B.C.E. (Yadin 1972; Kitchen 2002; Ben-Tor 2008). Other city-states, including those located in the Jezreel Valley, as well as the Egyptian center at Beth-shean, continued uninterrupted for almost a century. The system of Canaanite city-states under Egyptian domination in the northern valleys came to an end in a series of destructions in the late twelfth century B.C.E. Radiocarbon results for Megiddo put its violent end at 1193–1113 B.C.E. (68 percent probability). A pedestal of a statue carrying the name of Ramesses VI found at the site indicates that it survived at least until his reign: 1141–1133 B.C.E. Taking this into consideration, the calibrated radiocarbon results can be narrowed to 1141–1113 B.C.E. Nearby Beth-shean yielded several finds from the days of Ramesses IV (summary in Finkelstein 1996b; see discussion of the chronology in A. Mazar 2009) and thus survived at least until his days, that is, 1151–1145 B.C.E. Beth-shean yielded radiocarbon results that seem similar to those from Megiddo (A. Mazar 2009, 25–26).

The destructions in the Jezreel Valley in the late twelfth century B.C.E. were significant (Arie 2011), but in my view the settlement system did not totally collapse. Megiddo was only partially destroyed—the sector of the city that was put to the torch was mainly that of the palace—and several rural sites may have survived devastation (Finkelstein 2003). The destructions in the valley could have been the result of assault by groups of Sea Peoples (Ussishkin 1995) or local unrest: skirmishes between city-states, attacks by gangs of uprooted people (the Apiru of the Egyptian sources), or attempts to expand by sedentary population groups from the hill country.

In the highlands, Shechem was probably destroyed in the later phase of the Late Bronze. The absence of Egyptian or Aegean finds makes it difficult to date this event accurately, whether in the late thirteenth or the twelfth century B.C.E.

1.2. The Iron Age I

1.2.1. The Highlands

The fall of the Late Bronze city-states and the collapse of Egyptian rule in Canaan resulted in two different processes. In the highlands, a wave of settlement that could have commenced as early as the late thirteenth century B.C.E. accelerated in the twelfth and eleventh centuries B.C.E. (Finkelstein 1988). The number of sites grew dramatically, from approximately 30 sites with a total built-up area of circa 50 hectares in the Late Bronze II (thirteenth century B.C.E.) to about 250 sites with a total built-up area of circa 220 hectares two and half centuries later, in the late Iron I (the early tenth century B.C.E.). This means that the sedentary population grew to at least four times its size. The revival of strong sedentary life must have been accompanied by an expansion of agricultural activity, and therefore the share of the pastoral groups probably diminished significantly. Most of these settlements continued uninterrupted to the Iron IIA–B—the time of the northern kingdom—and hence they can be labeled "Israelite" as early as the Iron I. In other words, this wave of settlement gave birth to early Israel (Finkelstein 1988; Faust 2006).

Archaeological and textual clues seem to indicate that the wave of settlement described here brought about the rise of an early territorial entity in the late Iron I (late eleventh and much of the tenth century B.C.E.) in the area north of Jerusalem (ch. 2). For the sake of the discussion here, the question is whether archeology provides clues for the existence of a similar territorial formation in the highlands already in the early phase of the Iron I, in the late twelfth and the early eleventh centuries B.C.E.

Many years ago Martin Noth (1966) suggested that before monarchic times the Israelite population was organized in an amphictyony: a league of tribes whose institutions functioned around a central shrine. This idea was later rejected for both textual and archaeological reasons (e.g., de Geus 1976; Lemche 1977). But could a cult place have served as a center for a territorial entity, even one that stretched over a more limited area in the highlands? The only site where such a theory can be checked is Shiloh, which was excavated intensively in the 1980s (Finkelstein, Bunimovitz, and Lederman 1993) and which is located in an area that was thoroughly examined in archaeological surveys.

1.2.1.1. Shiloh

Shiloh was destroyed in a major conflagration (fig. 4) that Albright dated to about 1050 B.C.E. (1960, 113, 118, 228) by accepting the biblical year-numbers for the reign of the early Davidides and calculating back according to the biblical sequence of events: David circa 1000 < Saul < Samuel < "period of the judges." If one places the beginning of Saul's reign around 1025 and the battle of Eben-ezer at the end of the period of the judges, it is indeed logical to reach a date of roughly 1050 B.C.E. However, calculations of this kind cannot be accepted by modern scholarship. First, the forty-year reign of the early Davidides should be taken as no more than a typological number; second, the biblical sequence of a chaotic period of the judges, followed by the great conquests of David and the golden empire of Solomon, is a theological construct of the late-monarchic author(s) (e.g.,

Figure 4. Destruction of Iron I Shiloh.

Van Seters 1983, 307–12; Knauf 1991, 1997; Miller 1997; Niemann 1997; Finkelstein and Silberman 2006a).

The destruction layer at Shiloh yielded a rich pottery assemblage that can be assigned to a phase later than the very early Iron I (as known, for instance, from the site of Giloh in the south of modern Jerusalem; A. Mazar 1981) and earlier than the late Iron I assemblages (such as that known from Megiddo). Radiocarbon determinations of carbonized seeds and raisins from the Shiloh destruction provided dates in the second half of the eleventh century B.C.E. (Finkelstein and Piasetzky 2006).

The biblical text does not shed light on the history of the highlands in the early Iron I. The conquest and part of the period of the judges narratives should be seen, first and foremost, as a Deuteronomistic construct that used myths, tales, and etiological traditions in order to convey the theology and territorial ideology of the late monarchic author(s) (e.g., Nelson 1981; Van Seters 1990; Finkelstein and Silberman 2001, 72–96; Römer 2007, 83–90). At the same time, the Hebrew Bible (Jer 7:12, 14; 26:6, 9) seems to contain a memory—vague as it may be—about a past devastation of Shiloh. The only devastation of the site known from the thorough excavations is that which took place in the second half of the eleventh century; there was no significant settlement at Shiloh in the later phases of the Iron Age. The late-monarchic biblical references to the destruction of Shiloh seem to constitute a polemic against an early north Israelite shrine. But the primary traditions regarding this shrine could have originated in northern circles in earlier days and could have been brought to Judah with Israelite refugees after the fall of the northern kingdom in 720 B.C.E. So the question arises: Was this memory preserved because of the importance of this place as a cultic focus for the Iron I population of the northern part of the central hill country?

1.2.1.1.1. Was There a Major Sanctuary at Iron I Shiloh?

The answer to this question must first be sought in the finds, and it must be reached through the rules of proto-historic archaeology, that is, without reference to the biblical text, which includes late monarchic and possibly still later polemics.

There is no straightforward evidence in the finds for the existence of a major sanctuary at Shiloh. No architectural trace of a shrine has ever been found at the site. The same holds true for the small finds. The relatively rich assemblage of pottery from the pillared buildings unearthed on the western slope yielded mainly storage vessels, and the entire site produced fragments of a single cult-stand and sherds of two vessels possibly of a cultic nature. This kind of evidence is expected at any Iron I site in the highlands. No *favissa* (pit with cult vessels) or even a modest collection of cult vessels such as the ones found at Late Bronze Shiloh (for the former) or at early Iron II Megiddo and Taanach (for the latter; Loud 1948, fig. 102; Frick 2000, respectively) has been unearthed at Shiloh. The faunal assemblage from the Iron I phase at the site (Hellwing et al. 1993) also provides no evidence. There is nothing in it to point to sacrificial procedures, such as specific preference for certain species, age of slaughter, or body part. On the contrary, the Shiloh faunal assemblage is similar to other Iron I bone assemblages from the Levant.

The circumstantial evidence sheds a somewhat different light on the site. Shiloh does not provide evidence of a typical highlands Iron I settlement, such as nearby Khirbet Raddana and et-Tell (Callaway and Cooley 1971; Callaway 1976; Lederman 1999). Not a single house was found in the several excavated areas (also those dug by the Danish team in the early twentieth century; Buhl and Holm-Nielsen 1969); the buildings unearthed in the west are of public, storage nature, and other areas produced evidence of silos and other installations. The same holds true for Middle Bronze III Shiloh: excavations around the site yielded evidence of a huge stone and earth support-system, fills and storage facilities, but not a single house. Moreover, in the case of the Middle Bronze Age there are indications that the center of the site was also treated with fills and support walls—a possible clue that an important building stood at the summit of the mound (in this case, too, the small finds did not produce clear-cut evidence of the existence of a shrine). There was no settlement at Shiloh in the Late Bronze Age, but the *favissa* found on the northeastern slope hints that cultic-activity did take place at the site at that time. When one attempts to evaluate the nature of Iron I Shiloh, it is impossible to ignore these facts.

To summarize this point, although there is no direct evidence of an Iron I shrine at Shiloh, indirect considerations seem to hint that Iron I Shiloh was not a typical highlands settlement, and the long-term evidence—from the Middle and Late Bronze Ages—seems to hint at the existence of a cult place there.

1.2.1.1.2. Was Iron I Shiloh a Regional Administrative Center?

Shiloh belongs to the group of larger Iron I sites in the highlands, but its size—just over 1 hectare—is not exceptional. The relatively dense concentration of Iron I sites around it can be interpreted as stemming from the favorable environmental conditions in this part of the highlands: fertile valleys amenable to dry-farming, located not far from the pasture areas of the desert fringe to the east and the terraced horticultural land to the west.

The storage facilities at Shiloh—both elaborate pillared houses (fig. 5) and silos—could have served the population of the site and its immediate surroundings. The petrographic investigation of Iron I vessels (Glass et al. 1993) indicates that most of them were produced in the vicinity, except for the collared-rim pithoi, which were manufactured in two workshops to the north: one located near Shechem and the other in Wadi Far'ah, northeast of Shechem. But these data, too, do not shed clear light on the issue under discussion, because collared-rim jars could have regularly been made in specialized workshops (Arie 2006). Hence, with no parallel investigation of other Iron I pithoi assemblages in the highlands, the picture remains somewhat ambiguous.

Moving to the circumstantial evidence, the only clue that Shiloh served as an administrative center comes from the pillared buildings on the western slope of the site; Shiloh is the only Iron I site in the highlands that reveals evidence of public construction. Viewed from this perspective, Shiloh does look like a redistribution facility. One can say no more.[4]

1.2.1.2. Abimelech

As I have already mentioned, the Hebrew Bible may contain a clue for the existence of a territorial entity ruled by a strongman in the area of Shechem in premonarchic times. I refer to the story of Abimelech in Judg 9, which is part of what Richter (1966) described as the "Book of Saviors" in Judges. This is a collection of stories about local northern charismatic military saviors that was probably kept in the north, possibly at Bethel, before the fall of the northern kingdom (on the early nature of the story, see Reviv 1966; Würthwein 1994; Guillaume 2004; Na'aman 2011b). Especially important is Judg 9:26–41, which depicts the activity of a group of Apiru—an uprooted gang that was active in the highlands (Na'aman 2011b). It is impossible to envision an unlawful band performing this kind of activity after the consolidation of the monarchy, thus late-monarchic and later authors could no longer have known of such an early reality. As

---

4. For more on Iron I Shiloh and the traditions related to it, see chapter 2.

Figure 5. Pillared buildings in Iron I Shiloh.

such, the story may preserve a tradition regarding premonarchic times in
the north. The destruction of Shechem in the Iron I, possibly in the late
Iron I, in the tenth century B.C.E., may be related to this memory (Finkelstein 2006b). Therefore, the story of Abimelech in Judg 9 may provide
a clue that the situation depicted in the Amarna letters of the fourteenth
century B.C.E. was in fact prevalent in the northern highlands also in other
premonarchic times, including the Iron I. As I will demonstrate later, the
biblical story of the rise of Jeroboam I may belong to the same genre and
describe a similar reality in the late tenth century B.C.E. (the early Iron
IIA).

To sum up the discussion of the highlands in the early phase of the
Iron I, though there seem to be some indications—archaeological (Shiloh)
and textual (Abimelech at Shechem)—for control of central sites over land
in their vicinity, there is no evidence of the existence of a large territorial
entity similar to Shechem of the Amarna period at that time.

1.2.2. The Lowlands

The processes that took place in the Iron I in the northern valleys were
different from those that characterized the highlands. The main urban

centers of the Late Bronze Age recovered from the destructions at the end of the twelfth century. Megiddo produced evidence of three Iron I layers; other sites with less elaborate stratigraphy, such as Beth-shean, also displayed recovery in the Iron I. Excavations at secondary sites such as Tell Wawiyat and Ein Sephorris in the Lower Galilee (Dessel 1999) indicate similar recovery in the rural sector. Some sites could have continued undisturbed without suffering destruction at all, indicating a demographic and cultural continuity in the Late Bronze-Iron I transition. This can also be seen in the settlement patterns. The northern valleys were densely settled in both the Late Bronze and Iron I, with no sign of a major crisis. In the western Jezreel Valley, for instance, the number of settlements, their location, and the total built-up area did not change much in the transition between the two periods (Finkelstein et al. 2006). The same holds true for the Beth-shean Valley farther to the east and for the northern Jordan Valley (Maeir 1997; Ilan 1999, 162–71, respectively). Hence, the peasants of Canaan, or at least some of them, continued their ages-long routine just a few miles away from the ruined cities.

The recovery of the settlement system in the northern valleys in the early Iron I led to full prosperity at all major sites in the late Iron I, that is, in the late eleventh and early tenth centuries B.C.E. This was accompanied by possible revival of the city-state system and continuity in second-millennium B.C.E. material culture, which means that the collapse in the twelfth century B.C.E. cannot be seen as the watershed in the history of the northern valleys.

1.2.2.1. NEW CANAAN

A few years ago I suggested labeling the late Iron I revival in the northern valleys "New Canaan." The best case study for this is Megiddo. In the early Iron I (late twelfth and early eleventh centuries), after a partial destruction of the Late Bronze city, Megiddo was fully resettled. Over the course of a few decades, this settlement gradually developed into a large, prosperous late Iron I city (late eleventh and early tenth centuries B.C.E.).

The late Iron I city at Megiddo (labeled Stratum VIA by the University of Chicago excavators in the 1930s) is strikingly similar—in almost all its characteristics—to the Late Bronze III city (Stratum VIIA of the twelfth century). No less important, the next city at Megiddo, of the Iron IIA (Stratum V of the late tenth and ninth centuries B.C.E.), is very different in all its features:

- The size of the first two cities (VII and VI) is similar, covering both the upper mound and the lower terrace, an area of about 11 hectares. The Iron IIA city covered the upper mound only.
- Both cities had a palace in the north, near the gate. The Iron IIA palaces are located elsewhere.
- The large "Tower Temple" of Megiddo, which seems to have served as the central shrine of the city, was probably erected in the Middle Bronze and served throughout the Late Bronze Age and the Iron I (e.g., Kempinski 1989, 77–83). During the Iron IIA, Stratum V, the Megiddo cult was not centralized (ch. 5).
- Construction of other Iron I public buildings took into consideration the existence of Late Bronze monuments. This tendency did not continue in the Iron IIA.
- A typical, elaborate late Iron I open-court house in the second millennium tradition was uncovered a few years ago in the southeastern sector of the site. The houses of the Iron IIA use stone pillars, which were not prevalent previously and have a different layout.
- The Iron I pottery indicates a clear cultural continuity of second millennium B.C.E. traditions (fig. 6). The pottery of Stratum V belongs to the very different Iron II repertoire (Arie 2006, 2013).
- The bronze objects of Stratum VI also represent continuity of Late Bronze traditions (Negbi 1974); metal production in the Iron I carries on procedures known in the Late Bronze Age (Eliyahu-Behar et al. 2013).
- The Iron I flint industry, too, retains second-millennium traditions (Gersht 2006).

There can hardly be any doubt, then, that Stratum VI at Megiddo represents a Canaanite city. The previous inhabitants of the city must have returned; others could have come from nearby villages, which gradually recovered from the blow that shook their centers of power in the late twelfth century. It seems that Megiddo continued to serve as the hub of a city-state that dominated the countryside around it. With no written sources at hand, I can hardly prove this assumption. But the analysis of the finds—which points to a large, prosperous city engaged in long-distance trade, with clear indications of social stratification, located at the center of

Figure 6. Pottery assemblage from late Iron I Megiddo, demonstrating strong Late Bronze traditions.

a rural territory, in a region where the old population was not shattered, a region with a tradition of a city-state system—leaves us with no alternative interpretation.

Megiddo was only one link in the "New Canaan" chain. At least in the north, Late Bronze Canaan, which suffered a blow in the late twelfth century, came back to life. Other Iron I city-states can be identified at Tel Kinneret on the northern shore of the Sea of Galilee, Tel Keisan on the coastal plain of Acco, Tel Yokneam in the Jezreel Valley, Dor or Ginti-kirmil (Jatt) on the coastal plain of the Sharon, and possibly Tel Rehov in the Jordan Valley (fig. 7).

Hazor in the upper Jordan Valley came to an end in a devastating destruction in the second half of the thirteenth century B.C.E. Although it was resettled as a small village in the middle of the Iron I, it did not recover its prominence until the late Iron IIA in the early ninth century. The site that took its place as the center of the Jordan Valley north of the Sea of Galilee was Kinneret. A heavily fortified city about 10 hectares in size developed there in the Iron I. It reached its peak of prosperity in the late Iron I and was then destroyed (Münger et al. 2011).

Acco declined at the end of the Late Bronze Age, but Tell Keisan—most probably the location of Late Bronze and biblical Achshaph—continued to prosper in the Iron I (Humbert 1993). It seems that it served as the main center of the northern coastal plain, with its port located at Tell Abu Hawam at the outlet to the Kishon River in the Bay of Haifa. Tel Yokneam was proven by petrographic investigation of the Amarna tablets to have been a center of a Late Bronze city-state. Similar to Megiddo, this site also recovered in the early Iron I and became a prosperous center in the late Iron I. Dor prospered at that time, too, stretching over an area of 7–8 hectares. Its inhabitants engaged in intensive trade with Phoenicia and Cyprus (Gilboa and Sharon 2003). A monumental building excavated in the south of the mound attests to the wealth and urban nature of the Iron I city, which must have dominated the coastal plain of the Carmel ridge. It is possible that Dor replaced Late Bronze Ginti-kirmil as the main center in this region.

Figure 7. "New Canaan," late Iron I city-states in the north.

The excavations at Tel Rehov indicate that the city contemporary to Megiddo VIA probably covered the entire mound—the upper tell and the lower terrace alike—an area of about 10 hectares. Considering that Rehob was a major city-state in the Amarna period and that nearby Beth-shean of the Iron I was a relatively small settlement, one can suggest that Iron I Rehob functioned as a center of a territorial entity that dominated the Beth-shean and eastern Jezreel Valleys.

The pattern of Iron I city-states that emerges from this discussion is quite similar to that which had existed in Late Bronze II–III. Megiddo, Tel Yokneam, Tel Keisan, and Tel Rehov served as hubs of city-states in both periods, and another center was located in the Sharon coastal plain. The only modifications were the demise of Acco and the change in the Jordan Valley north of the Sea of Galilee, where Kinneret replaced Hazor as the center of power in the region.

The prosperity of New Canaan stemmed from the stability of the rural sector and from vibrant exchange with Phoenicia. The northern cities probably traded in secondary products of the horticulture niches in the highlands, serving as gateway communities for these commodities. Copper-production activity is evident in many of the major sites in the Jezreel and Jordan Valleys.

1.2.2.2. Destruction of New Canaan

The urban system of New Canaan collapsed during the late Iron I, when its centers were put to the torch. Violent destructions have been traced in all the main centers. At Megiddo, the entire city was burned to the ground. The conflagration was so intense that mudbricks turned red—which was why the University of Chicago excavators in the 1930s called it "the red-brick city." The accumulation of the collapsed bricks is over 1 meter (fig. 8). Evidence of destruction by fire was unearthed in the other centers mentioned above as well.

This time the fall of the Canaanite system was terminal. Some of the New Canaan sites show evidence of meager activity by squatters on the ruins of the prosperous cities still within the late Iron I, but this was a short-lived, insignificant occupation. In the next settlement phase, in the early Iron IIA, the city-state system was replaced by relatively modest settlements (Megiddo VB and its contemporaries), which can already be assigned to the northern kingdom of Israel. The material culture now changed completely; all features typical of the late Iron I disappeared, and the features of the new phase became characteristic of the material culture of the northern kingdom; they continued undisturbed until the collapse of Israel in the late eighth century B.C.E. and even beyond.

Who destroyed the cities of New Canaan? Since the pottery assemblages from the late Iron I destruction layers in the north look alike, scholars have suggested a single event for the end of this phase: a major earthquake (Lamon and Shipton 1939, 7; Cline 2011), King David's conquests (Yadin 1970, 95; Harrison 2004), or Pharaoh Shoshenq I's campaign (Watzinger 1929; Finkelstein 2002a).

In order to identify the destroyer, one first needs to establish the date of the destruction. The five sites destroyed by fire supplied dozens of radiocarbon determinations (Sharon et al. 2007; Finkelstein and Piasetzky 2009). When absolute dates were established for *each* of the five layers, the results do not support a single event. The sites located in the western Jezreel Valley–Acco Plain seem to give a date in the early tenth century B.C.E.; Tel Hadar on the eastern shore of the Sea of Galilee seems to provide a somewhat later age, and Tell el-Hammah in the Beth-shean Valley gives a seemingly still later date in the mid- to late tenth century B.C.E. (fig. 9). The Megiddo and Tell el-Hammah results are separated by roughly 60 uncalibrated years (3.5 standard deviations); the probability that all these

Figure 8. Destruction of late Iron I Megiddo.

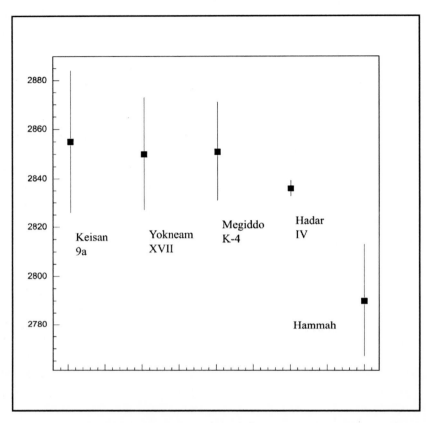

Figure 9. The uncalibrated results for five late Iron I destruction layers in the north, seemingly representing more than one event.

dates represent a single event is therefore low. Indeed, a thorough study of the pottery assemblages seems to point to slight differences between them (Arie 2006). Most likely, then, the late Iron I horizon in northern Israel came to an end in more than one devastation. This conclusion renders the earthquake and single military campaign theories invalid.

The destructions in the north must therefore be understood as representing a period of unrest that stretched over several decades. A reasonable historical explanation would be to associate them with raids on the valley's strongholds by groups from the central highlands.[5] These were either

---

5. Raids by groups from the highlands of the Galilee cannot be taken as an option because this region was only sparsely settled in the Iron I.

assaults by individual bands or the attempts of an early highlands-Israelite territorial entity to expand into areas of the northern valleys bordering on it. It is noteworthy that when these towns were resettled in the early Iron IIA—probably by mixed groups of valley people and highlanders—they continued uninterrupted into the early ninth century, the time of the Omride dynasty. The fact that this later phase in the sites in the northern valleys features north Israelite material culture characteristics strengthens the hypothesis that Israelites from the hill country were responsible for the destructions at the end of the previous period—during the late Iron I.

Needless to say, there is no extrabiblical textual material to shed light on these affairs, and it is impossible to securely connect them to events described in the Bible, since the historicity of episodes that ostensibly took place before the ninth century B.C.E. is questionable. Still, two relatively early biblical accounts may represent memories of stormy events that took place in the Jezreel/Beth-shean Valleys before the emergence of the northern kingdom.

The Song of Deborah in the book of Judges is considered by many to be one of the earliest texts in the Bible (e.g., Albright 1936; Cross 1973, 100). Originally it may have constituted part of a text that recorded traditions about the formative days of northern Israel, a text that was described by Richter (1966) as the "Book of Saviors" in the book of Judges. The Song of Deborah could have been put in writing in the north as early as the early eighth century B.C.E., but it may depict traditions regarding still earlier events that had taken place in the valley over a century before.

The story of the death of King Saul in a battle against the Philistines on Mount Gilboa (1 Sam 31) is so out of geographical context with the rest of the Saul cycle that it may be considered a genuine memory related to the expansion of an early north Israelite polity into the northern valleys in the tenth century B.C.E. This text, too, could not have been put in writing—even in an earlier, north Israelite version—before the first half of the eighth century B.C.E.; the lack of evidence of significant scribal activity in Israel before around 800 B.C.E. (see chs. 4–5) makes it difficult to assign the compilation of these texts to an earlier phase in the history of the northern kingdom.

Still, had there been such traditions regarding possible early events, they must have been transmitted orally for over a century, and hence they can hardly be read as straightforward historical records. I suppose that we need to look at this in a somewhat different way: a period of turmoil and unrest in the tenth century B.C.E. left strong impressions on the people in the north, impressions that could have been expressed in north Israelite oral traditions such as the Song of Deborah and the Saul cycle. They were composed in writing in the high days of the northern kingdom, in the first half of the eighth century.

The destruction of the urban centers of the northern valleys in the late Iron I was the true, decisive watershed in the history of the country. It marks the transition from Canaanite material culture and city-state territorial organization in the second millennium B.C.E. to Israelite material culture and a system of territorial kingdoms in the late tenth to late eighth centuries B.C.E.

2

THE FIRST NORTH ISRAELITE TERRITORIAL ENTITY:
THE GIBEON/GIBEAH POLITY AND THE HOUSE OF SAUL

The gradual destruction of the late Iron I cities in the Jezreel Valley during the tenth century B.C.E., probably by groups from the central hill country, turns the spotlight on the developments that took place in the latter area in the *late* Iron I.[1] The main question for the sake of our discussion is whether at that time the population of the hill country had already been organized into a territorial entity.[2] If the answer is positive, then this would be the earliest attested north Israelite polity. Several clues that come from archaeology, an extrabiblical source, and certain texts in the biblical account seem to testify to the existence of such a polity.

The central hill country—between the Jezreel and the Beer-sheba Valleys—is well known archaeologically from both excavations and intensive survey projects. The surveys, mainly those conducted in the 1980s, revealed a massive wave of settlement that swept throughout this region in the Iron I (Finkelstein 1988; 1995; Zertal 1994; Ofer 1994). The main concentration of sites can be found in the northern part of this region, between Jerusalem and the Jezreel Valley. The settlement process may have started in the final phase of the Late Bronze Age (the late thirteenth or early twelfth centuries B.C.E.), accelerated in the early Iron I (the late twelfth to mid-eleventh century), and reached its peak in the late Iron I (the late eleventh and first half of the tenth centuries B.C.E.). In the late

---

1. To differ from the question asked in chapter 1, regarding the possibility that an *early* Iron I polity existed in the central highlands.

2. The anthropological question of how to describe such an entity (e.g., "kingdom" or "chiefdom") is not my concern here. The emphasis is on the minimal characteristics: a territory larger than that of a typical Bronze Age city-state ruled from a central site.

Iron I there were approximately 250 sites in this area (compared to ca. 30 sites in the Late Bronze Age), with a total built-up area that can be estimated at roughly 220 hectares (ca. 50 hectares in the Late Bronze Age). Using the broadly accepted, average density coefficient of two hundred people living on one built-up hectare in premodern societies, the late Iron I population can be estimated at circa 45,000 people. This population can be identified as indigenous to the southern Levant, composed of sedentary and ex-pastoral groups. The wave of settlement of the Iron I continued undisturbed to the Iron IIA, when the people of the highlands constituted part of the kingdoms of Israel and Judah. This makes it possible to label the Iron I population in the hill country "Israelite."

Most of the Iron I sites in the hill country represent small, isolated settlements that covered an area of up to one hectare. They were not fortified and usually do not reveal any sign of public architecture or prestige items among the small finds. There is no evidence of a developed settlement hierarchy or long-distance trade. No site can be distinguished as a central settlement—the seat of a ruling group. But there is one exception to at least some of these characteristics: a group of sites located in the Gibeon-Bethel plateau north of Jerusalem.[3]

2.1. The Gibeon-Bethel Plateau

A significant concentration of circa thirty Iron I sites is known in the Gibeon-Bethel plateau (ca. 20 × 15 km in size) north of Jerusalem. The data here are significant; the area has been fully and thoroughly surveyed (Finkelstein and Magen 1993), and a relatively large number of sites have been excavated. The latter include Gibeon, Bethel, Tell en-Nasbeh (location of biblical Mizpah), et-Tell (traditionally identified with biblical Ai), Khirbet Raddana, Tell el-Ful, and Khirbet ed-Dawwara (fig. 10).

The sites of the Gibeon plateau display two special characteristics. The first is the appearance of casemate fortifications (fig. 11). The late Iron I–early Iron IIA fortified site of Khirbet ed-Dawwara (excavated by the author), located in the desert fringe northeast of Jerusalem, features

---

3. I am making a distinction here in the names between the geographical unit north of Jerusalem (the Gibeon-Bethel plateau) and the larger territorio-political unit (the Gibeon/Gibeah polity). In the latter I include both place-names because of the difficulty—archaeologically and textually—to locate the hub of the early north Israelite polity described in this chapter (more below).

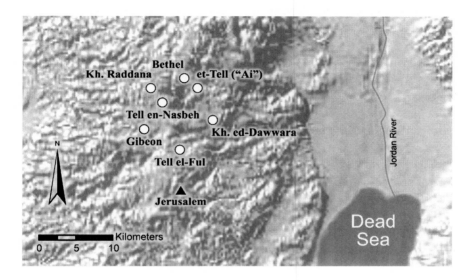

Figure 10. Main archaeological sites in the Gibeon-Bethel plateau north of Jerusalem.

Figure 11. Late Iron I/early Iron IIA casemate fortifications in the Gibeon-Bethel plateau north of Jerusalem: 1. Khirbet ed-Dawwara; 2. Gibeon; 3. et-Tell (Ai); 4. Tell en-Nasbeh (Mizpah).

a strong casemate-like defense wall and pillared houses adjacent to it, some using the casemates as their back broadrooms. The casemate wall at nearby Tell en-Nasbeh was probably constructed in the early phase of the Iron IIA (Finkelstein 2012). Iron I–early Iron IIA et-Tell also seems to feature casemate-like construction on the margin of the settlement. At Gibeon, elements that look like a casemate wall were uncovered in the northwest of the mound (Pritchard 1964, 35, figs. 19, 21; 1963, fig. 1).[4] The pottery from the layers inside the "casemate"—probably coming from make-up fills below the floor—dates to the Iron I, hinting that the fortification should be assigned to the late Iron I or early Iron IIA. Therefore, sites in the Gibeon-Bethel plateau present evidence of public construction of fortifications in the late Iron I–early Iron IIA. In fact, this area features a dense system of such fortifications over a surprisingly small territory; with one exception that will be discussed below, these are the only casemate or casemate-like walls from this period thus far unearthed west of the Jordan River.

The second outstanding characteristic of the Iron I–early Iron IIA sites in the Gibeon-Bethel plateau is the suddenness with which they were abandoned. As I have already noted, excavations and surveys revealed that in the entire central highlands most Iron I settlements continued to be inhabited without interruption in the Iron II. The only exception—a clear *cluster* of Iron I sites (rather than single settlements) that were abandoned (not destroyed) or significantly diminished in size during the early Iron IIA—is found in this relatively small region.

Three cases can be counted under this rubric:

(1) Iron I–early Iron IIA sites that were abandoned and not reoccupied in the later phases of the Iron II: Khirbet Raddana on the outskirts of Ramallah, et-Tell to its east, and Khirbet ed-Dawwara in the desert fringe. The latest pottery retrieved from these sites dates to the beginning of the Iron IIA.

(2) Sites that were abandoned and resettled only in the late Iron II: Tell el-Ful and possibly Gibeon (which may alternatively belong to group 3 below).

(3) Sites that were significantly diminished in size in the Iron II. This group seems to include Khirbet Tell el-'Askar—a large

---

4. I am grateful to my student Omer Sergi, who drew my attention to this find.

Iron I settlement, the survey of which produced a limited
quantity of Iron II sherds—and possibly Gibeon.

At this point of research it is difficult to decide if these sites were all
deserted at the same time or whether they were abandoned gradually. One
way or the other, they present a double riddle: How can we explain their
fortifications, and why were they abandoned?

2.2. Sheshonq I and the Highlands North of Jerusalem

The military campaign of Sheshonq I (biblical Shishak), the founder of
the Twenty-Second Dynasty in Egypt, to Canaan is reported as a list of
conquered towns on a wall in the temple of Amun at Karnak in Upper
Egypt and mentioned in 1 Kgs 14:25–28. The widely accepted dating of the
campaign to 926 B.C.E. is based solely on the biblical reference. However,
the fifth-year-of-Rehoboam datum may have been schematically arranged
to fit the theology of the Deuteronomistic Historian, for instance, his
understanding of sin punished by the assault of a foreign power (Mullen
1992). The complicated chronology of the Twenty-First and Twenty-Second Dynasties in Egypt allows a shift of several years backward or forward in the dates of Sheshonq I (Wente 1976, 276). In addition, it is not
clear whether Sheshonq carried out his campaign in his early years on the
throne or in his later days (Redford 1992, 312). Taking these factors into
consideration, the Sheshonq I campaign could have taken place almost
any time in the mid- to late tenth century B.C.E. One can hardly be more
precise (for an early date in his reign, see Ben-Dor Evian 2011).

The place names mentioned by Sheshonq I clearly represent an Iron
Age reality (fig. 12) in the sense that they differ from the toponyms known
from Egyptian lists that date to the Late Bronze Age. Those that can be
safely identified are located in the Jezreel Valley, along the international
road in the Sharon Plain, in the area of Gibeon north of Jerusalem in the
highlands, in the area of the Jabbok River in Transjordan, and in the Beer-
sheba Valley in the south. Other important regions are missing. These
include the lowlands and highlands of Judah, the fertile and densely settled hill country of northern Samaria (except, possibly, for Tirzah), the
Galilee and the northern Jordan Valley, the central and northern coastal
plain, and much of Transjordan.

A group of places in the Sheshonq I list are located in the highlands
to the north of Jerusalem. Those unanimously identified are Beth-horon,

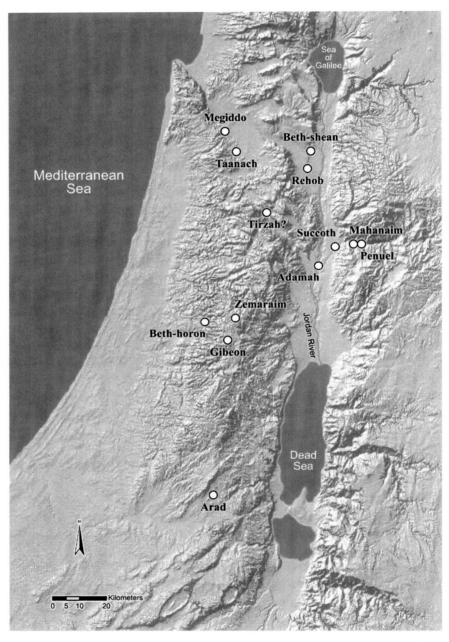

Figure 12. Main places mentioned in the Shoshenq I list engraved on a wall in the temple of Amun at Karnak, Upper Egypt.

Gibeon, and Zemaraim (the latter is located in modern-day Ramallah). It is noteworthy that the Sheshonq I list also mentions a group of sites along the Jabbok River to the east of the Jordan River: Adamah, Succoth, Penuel, and Mahanaim. It is equally important to reiterate that other parts of the highlands—Jerusalem, the entire Judean highlands, and (apart from one possible place) northern Samaria—are missing from the list. Since parts of the list are damaged, one may argue that the name of Jerusalem had originally been included but was not preserved. This is possible but not likely, as rows II and V in the list, which mention places in the highlands to the north of Jerusalem, do not have many damaged place names. Moreover, no Judahite town in the Shephelah appears in the list. Most scholars explain the absence of Judah by adapting the biblical story in 1 Kgs 14 to the reality of the Sheshonq I list: Jerusalem *was* subdued but was saved from destruction by a heavy ransom—the temple treasures that were handed over to the pharaoh at Gibeon (e.g., Kitchen 1986, 447). This interpretation of the events is hardly acceptable. First, why would Sheshonq I receive the surrender tribute at Gibeon and not in the capital of Judah, located only 10 km to the southeast? Second, had the pharaoh subdued the capital of Judah even without conquering it, he would certainly have boasted about it (Knauf 1991, 182). Indeed, new analyses of the archaeological data from Jerusalem have shown that in the tenth century B.C.E. it was no more than a small, poor highlands settlement without monumental construction (summary in Finkelstein 2010, contra A. Mazar 2010). Further, archaeological surveys have revealed that at that time the hill country of Judah to the south of Jerusalem was sparsely inhabited by only a few relatively small settlements (Ofer 1994). No less important, it seems that the expansion of Judah to the territories of the Shephelah and Beer-sheba Valley did not take place before the second half of the ninth century B.C.E. (Fantalkin and Finkelstein 2006; Fantalkin 2008). Indeed, this is the moment when one can detect the first signs of statehood in Judah. In the time of the Sheshonq I campaign, Judah was still a marginal, sparsely settled southern highlands polity made up of a mix of sedentary and pastoral groups and ruled from a small settlement. What has just been said renders the biblical description of the events "in the fifth year of Rehoboam" highly unlikely. First and foremost, the poor material culture of Judah in the tenth century leaves no room to imagine great wealth in the temple—certainly not wealth magnificent enough to appease an Egyptian pharaoh. Indeed, at least some of the repeated references to the looting of the treasures of the temple in the Deuteronomistic

History should probably be seen as a theological construct rather than as historical references (Mullen 1992).

If the absence of Jerusalem and the entire Judahite highlands from the Sheshonq I list seems logical because of the sparseness of Iron I occupation in the southern hill country, this cannot be the reason for the absence of northern Samaria—the most densely settled and economically richest area in the hill country in the Iron I. Shechem, the most important city in that area, is not mentioned, and the same holds true for other principal places, such as Tapuah and Dothan.

It is noteworthy that two regions mentioned in the Sheshonq I list— the highlands to the north of Jerusalem and the area of the Jabbok River— are far from the main international highways and have never been a focus of interest for the Egyptian pharaohs. Moreover, in the time of the New Kingdom, Egyptian pharaohs refrained from penetrating into the sparsely settled, wooded, rugged, and hostile hill country. Indeed, twice in later history—during the Maccabean and First Jewish revolts—large armies of strong empires were destroyed when attempting to enter the heart of the highlands. The march of Sheshonq I against this area is therefore an exception. Having removed the possibility that the target was Jerusalem or the highlands of northern Samaria, one needs to ask what attracted the attention of the Egyptian pharaoh to this relatively remote area that had no real geopolitical importance. The only reasonable answer is that the area around Gibeon, together with the Jabbok region, was the hub of an emerging territorial polity that endangered Egyptian interests in Canaan. Similar to the situation in the Amarna period in the fourteenth century B.C.E., one way in which such an entity could have threatened Egyptian interests was an attempt to expand into the lowlands to its west and north, that is, in the direction of the fertile valleys, the international highway that linked Egypt with the north, and the coastal ports.

In view of all this, it seems logical to suggest that the Egyptian campaign was directed against a tenth-century B.C.E. territorial entity that was centered in the Gibeon-Bethel plateau and that it brought about the decline of this entity and the abandonment of sites in this region. But should this area be considered Israelite or Judahite?

2.3. EXCURSUS: THE LAND OF BENJAMIN: NORTH OR SOUTH?

Na'aman (2009) recently argued that the land of Benjamin—and with it the area of Gibeon-Bethel—belonged to the *southern* territorial entity in the highlands throughout the Bronze and Iron Ages. If so, a major premise in this chapter is undermined. In what follows I wish to explain my opinion on this problem (details in Finkelstein 2011c; for other reconstructions of the role of Benjamin in biblical history, see Davies 2007b; Fleming 2012, 159–61).

Na'aman and I differ on two crucial methodological points. First, Na'aman's view is based mainly on his interpretation of the biblical materials, assisted by ancient Near Eastern texts; archaeology is randomly, in fact, quite seldom used. Second, Na'aman bases his opinion on the state of affairs in late monarchic times (the eighth and seventh centuries B.C.E.) and then retrojects this situation into earlier periods in Judahite history.

My method can be summarized as follows:

(1) Retrojecting the situation of the late eighth and seventh centuries B.C.E. into the past is inadvisable because there is no reason to assume that throughout the centuries the boundary in the central highlands between north and south remained unchanged. In monarchic times oscillations in the Israel-Damascus-Assyria power struggle reflected on small, marginal Judah and could have caused changes in the location of its border with Israel.

(2) One cannot rely on Deuteronomistic texts (in contrast to earlier texts, which the Deuteronomist only redacted) in reconstructing the situation in pre-late-eighth-century times, as they promote late-monarchic (and later) Judahite ideology. As such, disputed situations are presented from a strictly Judahite perspective. Much of this material, therefore, reflects a retrojection to the past of the situation in a relatively late phase in ancient Israelite history. In this, Na'aman falls into the "trap" of Deuteronomistic ideology. Usage of prophetic works is also not advisable, as they also depict the situation in late monarchic and later times.

(3) From the text perspective, the way to overcome the problems specified in points 1 and 2 is to consult pre-Deuteronomistic texts, preferably those that are non-Jerusalem in origin. I refer, for instance, to the "Book of Saviors" in Judges (e.g., Richter 1966; Guillaume 2004, 5–105), pro-Saul and anti-Davidic material in the books of Samuel, material in the Elijah-Elisha cycle in Kings, and to a certain extent eighth-century northern prophetic works (see more in Schniedewind 2004). They may better depict the situation before the eighth century and are free of Judahite territorial ideology.

(4) Archaeology also can help overcome the problems specified in points 1 and 2 above. For late monarchic times, the testimonies of archae-

ology and the Hebrew Bible are generally close. But for cases relating to the formative periods (pre-eighth-century B.C.E.)—remote from the periods of compilation of the biblical texts—the two are contradictory. In such cases there must be a good reason for not following archaeology, which, to differ from the biblical text, provides "real time" evidence of the past.

Following these lines of research, it seems that the land of Benjamin was dominated by the northern kingdom until the decline of the Omride dynasty in 842 B.C.E. It was taken over by Judah in the time of King Jehoash, who may have acted as a vassal of Aram Damascus and hence profited from the Damascene hegemony in the region in his days. Judahite domination in the region is clearly attested starting in the late eighth century and continuing until exilic times (for details, see Finkelstein 2011c).

The perplexity in the biblical text regarding the affiliation of the land of Benjamin stems from conflicting traditions in southern and northern texts. As I have already noted, the Deuteronomistic History and related prophetic works retroject the situation in late monarchic times into the past and promote the idea that the land of Benjamin belonged to Judah at least starting with the fall of the Saulides and the rise of King David to power. Hence 1 Kgs 12:21–24 speaks of Benjamin as part of Judah as early as the secession of the northern tribes in the days of Jeroboam I; 1 Kgs 15:16–22 draws the border with Israel north of Mizpah; and Josh 16:1–2; 18:11–14 follows suit in the description of the tribal boundaries.

When one turns to northern texts, or northern traditions, in various parts of the Hebrew Bible, a different picture emerges. To name the main pieces of evidence:

- In the story of the birth of Jacob's sons, Benjamin is described as the southernmost tribe of the house of Joseph.
- The Ehud story in Judg 3—part of the northern cycle in the Book of Saviors—associates Benjamin, Jericho, and the hill country of Ephraim.
- Judg 4:5—also part of the Book of Saviors—places the northern prophetess Deborah between Bethel and Ramah.
- The Song of Deborah, usually taken to be earlier than Judg 4 (summary of research in Guillaume 2004, 30–35) includes Benjamin among the northern tribes.
- Apologetic materials in the Succession History—in the episodes relating to Shimei the son of Gera and Sheba the son of Bichri—position Benjamin with Israel in opposition to David.

- Hos 9:9 and 10:9 refer to the sin of Gibeah in ostensibly pre-monarchic times in connection to Israel (e.g., Wolff 1982, 158, 184–85).
- And, of course, one cannot ignore the tribal name Benjamin (literally "the son of the south"), indicating its location at the southern end of the territory of Israel.

All this explains why the Saul cycle in 1 Samuel preserves memories of a northern polity in the highlands of Benjamin and Ephraim, with its hub in the area of Gibeon/Gibeah, which was connected to the area of the Jabbok and possibly stretched all the way north to the margins of the Jezreel Valley.

2.4. SHESHONQ I, THE SAULIDE TERRITORY, AND ARCHAEOLOGY

The only possible literary clue for a late Iron I to early Iron IIA territorial formation in the vicinity of Gibeon comes from the biblical account of the days of King Saul (fig. 13). Both the Sheshonq I list and the biblical sources describing the Saulide territorial entity speak about the same geographical niche in the hill country, north of Jerusalem, and both link it with the Jabbok River area; the biblical story specifically connects the Gibeon region with Jabesh-gilead (1 Sam 11; 2 Sam 2:4–7) and Mahanaim (2 Sam 2:12). As I have emphasized above, this geographical combination—of two relatively remote and off-the-beaten-track areas—is unique, and viewing their grouping as a mere coincidence (especially that the two sources seem to describe events that could have been not-too-remote chronologically) seems to me highly unlikely.

But can the biblical story about King Saul, or at least part of it, be historically reliable? Further, how did the information about it reach the author of Samuel several hundred years after the alleged events took place? As far as I can judge, the core of the biblical story reflects, in the main, positive northern traditions on the Saulides that were brought to Judah from the north in the late eighth century B.C.E.

It is widely accepted that 1 Samuel contains pre-Deuteronomistic material that was incorporated into the Deuteronomistic History (Rost 1982; Noth 1981, 77, 86; McCarter 1980b, 26–27). But this old material could not have been put in writing before the expansion of scribal activity in the eighth century B.C.E. (Schniedewind 2004; Finkelstein and Sass forthcoming). It seems to me that northern Saul traditions reached Judah with Israelite refugees in the late eighth century B.C.E., after the fall of the

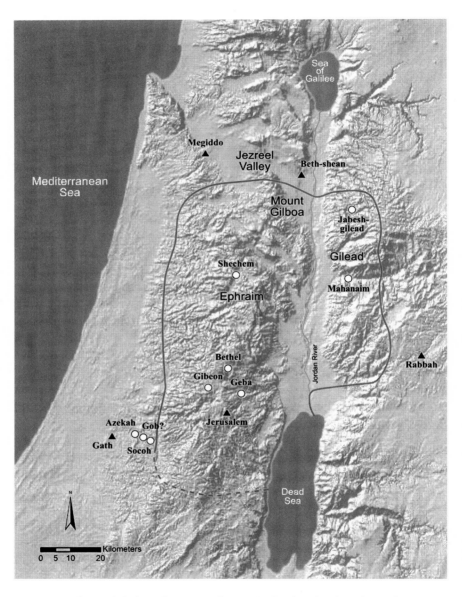

Figure 13. The Saulide kingdom according to biblical and archaeological sources.

northern kingdom (Finkelstein and Silberman 2006b), possibly in oral form. Evaluation of settlement oscillations in the highlands territory of the northern kingdom recorded in archaeological surveys shows a dramatic drop in the number of sites in the area south of Shechem after the eighth century B.C.E. This probably indicates that many of the Israelites who settled in Judah originated from this region, including the hub of the ancient Saulide entity. In late eighth-century Jerusalem these traditions were incorporated into an early, still pre-Deuteronomistic story of the early days of the Davidic dynasty. This served the needs and goals of the dynasty at a time when Judah was revolutionized demographically due to the incoming wave of Israelites and was transformed, almost instantaneously, into a developed kingdom. This suggests that beyond propaganda, Davidic dynasty apologia (McCarter 1980a; Halpern 2001, 73–103), and insertion of later details, at least the germ of the story about the Saulide entity may be taken as a genuine—though vague—northern memory.

But is there another—easier to prove—example of preservation of old memories over centuries of oral transmission?

2.5. PRESERVATION OF EARLY MEMORIES IN SAMUEL: THE CASE OF SHILOH

The books of Joshua, Judges, and 1 Samuel describe Shiloh as a central shrine of the early Israelites, the location of the ark of the covenant. Jeremiah (7:12, 14; 26:6, 9) refers to an ancient temple of YHWH that had stood at Shiloh and that was destroyed because of the wickedness of Israel. Although Shiloh was not an important place in the late Iron II, when most of these texts were put in writing, its location—between Jerusalem and Shechem—was well known, at least to the Deuteronomistic Historian (Judg 21:19).

Archaeology has shown that Shiloh was abandoned after its destruction in the Iron I. Radiocarbon results put this destruction in the second half of the eleventh century B.C.E. (Finkelstein and Piasetzky 2006).[5] There

---

5. It is tempting to see Shiloh as belonging to the late Iron I Gibeon/Gibeah polity discussed here (for the Shiloh-Saul connection in the biblical text, see Miller and Hayes 1986, 133; Schley 1989, 163, 194–97, 201). However, radiocarbon dates—as well as a thorough comparison of the Shiloh V pottery to the assemblages of et-Tell and Khirbet Raddana—seem to show that the destruction of Shiloh took place a century earlier than the abandonment of the Gibeon-Bethel plateau sites.

was no significant settlement there in the Iron II and Persian periods. Remains dating to these periods are meager and of no special importance; they reveal no sign of a cult place or destruction by fire. It is impossible, therefore, to read the Shiloh sanctuary tradition against an Iron II or later background, and for this reason it is unfeasible to associate the destruction of this cult place, as related in the book of Jeremiah, with the conquest of the northern kingdom by the Assyrians in the late eighth century.

Thus, one cannot escape the conclusion that there was a strong memory in late-monarchic Judah of an early devastated cult place at Shiloh. This could have been one more orally transmitted, genuine north Israelite tradition that reached Judah with northern refugees after the conquest of Israel by the Assyrians or a northern etiological tradition that was based on an acquaintance, in monarchic times, with a large ruin at the site. Judahite recognition of the importance of an ancient northern cult place at Shiloh could have catered to those Israelites who seem to have constituted a major element in the population of Judah in late-monarchic times. At the same time, the biblical tradition in Jeremiah takes a strictly Judahite point of view in subordinating Shiloh to Jerusalem (Lemche 1989). The stories of the sinful behaviour of the priests at Shiloh, the defeat of Israel, and the transfer of the ark from Shiloh to Jerusalem could have served the Deuternomistic ideology as a cultic parallel to the rejection of Saul and the election of David (see also Ps 78:60–71; Miller and Hayes 1986, 133).[6]

In the case of Shiloh we have evidence, then, for the preservation in the Bible of certain memories—vague as they may be—of events that probably took place in the second half of the eleventh century. This strengthens the possibility that some memories regarding a north Israelite entity that existed in the tenth century B.C.E. were also preserved and transmitted, first orally and perhaps later in a written form, until they found their way into the late monarchic Judahite text.

---

6. Needless to say, we have no way of identifying the deities worshiped in the highlands in the late Iron I. In the Deuteronomistic History and Jeremiah the Shiloh cult is associated with YHWH. This is probably part of the late-monarchic Judahite theology, aimed at showing that already in the early days the national God of Judah ruled over shrines that were later part of the northern kingdom.

2.6. The Date and Territorial Extent of the Saulide Polity

2.6.1. Dating Saul and the Saulides

I should start by saying that the traditional dating, which puts Saul in the late eleventh century and the Sheshonq I campaign in 926 B.C.E.—almost a century apart—cannot be used as an argument against this historical reconstruction.

The widely accepted date for Saul's reign, circa 1025–1005 B.C.E. (e.g., Cogan 1992), is calculated according to the biblical sequence and numbers: (1) counting back from later monarchs for whom there are extrabiblical synchronisms; (2) accepting the biblical testimony of a forty-year reign for both Solomon (1 Kgs 11:42) and David (2 Sam 5:4); (3) acknowledging the biblical order Saul > David > Solomon; and (4) accepting that the accession formula for Saul in 1 Sam 13:1, which states that he ruled over Israel for two years, is garbled. Assuming that Saul is historical, and reviewing the sequence of events in his reign, especially his military exploits, scholars have come to the conclusion that he must have ruled for a significant number of years. Taking into account the number, which does appear in the text, they have speculated that the original number must have been twenty or twenty-two years (summary in Edelman 1992, 5:992–93).

However, all this cannot serve as solid evidence. The forty-year reigns of Solomon and David should be taken as a symbolic (typological) number (e.g., Handy 1997, 101–2; Ash 1999, 24–25), and the evidence of the length of Saul's rule is highly unreliable. Moreover, setting the three early Israelite monarchs in a sequential order, one after another, may have been the work of a later redactor. From the text itself we cannot know for sure whether David ruled after Saul or whether their reigns overlapped. Edelman rightly argued that "[a] date for Saul cannot be firmly established…. He was associated with Israel, so any attempt to situate him in time needs to be done in relation to other Israelite kings whose existence can be verified by extrabiblical documentation…. It would seem logical to place Saul sometime during the tenth century BC" (1996, 158). In addition, we know from the biblical text that Saul was followed on the throne by his son Eshbaal (= Ishbosheth, 2 Sam 2:8, 10), but we have no way of knowing the actual number of Saulide rulers and the exact length of their reigns. All this means that the Sheshonq campaign, which, as I have shown above, could have taken place any time in the mid- or second half of the tenth century B.C.E., could have coincided with the end days of the house of Saul.

2.6.2. The Territory of the Saulides

The geographical information in the Bible about the Saulide entity is relatively detailed and accurate (fig. 13). This, of course, may stem from the proximity to Jerusalem, that is, to the location of the late-monarchic authors. But the fact that some of the place names (e.g., 1 Sam 9:4) seem to pre-date Deuteronomistic place names (best represented in the tribal lists in the book of Joshua) seems to strengthen the credibility of the story. The fact that the text describes a territorial entity centered in the plateau to the north of Jerusalem, rather than in the traditional centers of such entities (Shechem or Samaria), also lends it trustworthiness.

The biblical text puts Saul in a place named Gibeah of Saul, the identification of which is disputed (summaries in Arnold 1990; Schniedewind 2006). The problem is the appearance in the same region of the place names Geba and Gibeah (as well as Gibeon), which derive from the same root—"hill" (not to mention the longer forms Gibeath Elohim, Gibeah of Saul, Gibeah/Geba of Benjamin). How many sites do they represent, and where should they be located?

Gibeon is securely identified at el-Jib, while Geba near Michmash, probably Geba of Benjamin, is located at Jaba near Mukhmas. Albright identified Gibeah/Gibeah of Saul at Tell el-Ful (1924, 28–43) and interpreted certain remains that he unearthed at the site as the citadel of King Saul. However, this "citadel" is in fact a late Iron II tower, while the Iron I remains at Tell el-Ful are negligible (Finkelstein 2011d). Miller (1975) and Arnold (1990, 54–60) proposed identifying Gibeah at Jaba = Geba mentioned above, a more significant site with Iron I remains. Saul's center of power could have been located there or at Gibeon (Blenkinsopp 1974; Edelman 1996, 155–56; van der Toorn 1993, 520–23).

2.6.2.1. How Far North?

The biblical text is not clear on the extent of the territory that Saul ruled. It tells us that he was a Benjaminite and that the hub of his territory was in the land of his tribe and immediately to its north. The places that play a dominant role in the Saul stories—Ramah, Mizpah, Geba, Michmash, and Gibeon—are all located in the highlands immediately to the north of Jerusalem. When Saul searches for the lost asses of his father Kish (1 Sam 9), he goes to the hill country of Ephraim, to the land of Shalishah, to the land of Sha'alim, and to the land of Benjamin. The first and last names correspond to the tribal territories. The other two are usually sought in the southern flank of the land of Ephraim (Edelman 1988). Finally, as mentioned above, the text emphasizes the connection of the Saulides to Jabesh-gilead and Mahanaim—both located east of the Jordan, on the western slopes of the Gilead.

Another clue for the territory of the Saulides comes from the description of the territory of Eshbaal (Ish-bosheth), the son of Saul, who was made king "over Gilead and the Ashurites and Jezreel and Ephraim and Benjamin and all Israel" (2 Sam 2:9). This description has usually been taken as a genuine historical memory of the territory ruled by the Saulides, among other reasons because it does not correspond to any later reality in the history of ancient Israel. The location of Ephraim, Benjamin, and the Gilead is clear. The Ashurite district should probably be sought in the southwestern sector of the hill country of Ephraim (Edelman 1985). Jezreel must refer to the valley or its southern margins. Edelman noted that the verse uses two different Hebrew prepositions: Eshbaal was made king 'al (over) Benjamin and Ephraim and 'el (to) the Gilead, the Ashurites, and Jezreel. She proposed that the first term refers to direct rule, while the second represents outlying areas where Saul's (and thus Eshbaal's) sovereignty would have been respected but that were not directly administered by the Saulides.

The minimalist view on the extent of the kingdom of Saul speaks about Benjamin, Ephraim, and the Jabbok area (e.g., Miller and Hayes 1986, 141), while the maximalists add the Gilead and northern Samaria as far as the Jezreel Valley (e.g., Knauf 2001b, 16). Taking into account the strong memories that link Saul to Mount Gilboa and Beth-shean in the southern Jezreel Valley, I tend to join the latter. There is no logic in the account of the battle of Gilboa without the Saulide territory reaching the Jezreel Valley. The Saulide dynasty probably ruled the Israelite highlands up to the margin of the Jezreel Valley in the north, with an extension into the Gilead-Jabbok areas in the east. There is good reason to assume, then, that parallel to the situation in the Amarna period, a north highlands entity attempted to expand into the Jezreel Valley and by doing so menaced the renewed Egyptian interests there. In the previous chapter I raised the possibility that the late-Canaanite (New Canaan) cities of the Jezreel Valley were devastated by expanding Israelites from the highlands. Attack of the highlanders on the Jezreel Valley—the breadbasket of Canaan and the route of a strategic and commercially important road to the north—could have been one of the reasons for the Egyptian campaign against the hub of the early Israelite polity. The memory of a decisive battle at Mount Gilboa on the southern margin of the Jezreel Valley, near the age-old Egyptian stronghold of Beth-shean, should probably be understood against this backdrop. With the passage of time, and Egypt no longer on the scene, the enemy of Israel in this memory was replaced with the ever-present Philistines.

I should reiterate that the disparity in time between the Sheshonq I campaign and the possibly historical Saulides is not a real obstacle here, since: (1) as mentioned above, we have no way of knowing the actual number of rulers that reigned in the early north Israelite entity; (2) the vague memories that found their way into the biblical text after having been transmitted orally (and later in written form?) over the course of a long period of time could have muddled places, people, time, and the identity of the adversaries of the Israelites.

2.6.2.2. How Far South? Khirbet Qeiyafa

It remains to be seen how far south and southwest the Saulide entity expanded.

It is impossible to tell whether Saul also ruled in Jerusalem. But his presence, according to the book of Samuel, in the Valley of Elah (1 Sam 17:1–2) needs an explanation. In this case, too—another story that deals with marginally important sites—there is no logic without a germ of a genuine memory behind it.

This brings to the center stage the recently investigated site of Khirbet Qeiyafa, located on a commanding hill on the southern side of the Valley of Elah, between Socoh and Azekah, approximately 10 km east of the Philistine city of Gath. The settlement was established in the late Iron I and came to an end within this phase or somewhat later, in the transitional late Iron I/early Iron IIA. In absolute chronology terms and based on radio-carbon results, the settlement of Khirbet Qeiyafa could have been built in the second half of the eleventh century and destroyed/abandoned in the mid- to second half of the tenth century B.C.E. The 2.5 hectare settlement is surrounded by an elaborate, stone-built casemate wall. The excavators interpret it as a Judahite Davidic fortress on the border of Philistia (Gar-finkel and Ganor 2009), while others see it as a late-Canaanite stronghold in the Shephelah (Na'aman 2012b; Koch 2012). Three main points are debated in relation to Khirbet Qeiyafa: the identity of the inhabitants, their territorial-political association, and the identification of the site.

The identity of the inhabitants of Khirbet Qeiyafa. The people who lived at Khirbet Qeiyafa could have considered themselves affiliated with the population of the highlands to the east, and in this case they may be seen as Judahites/Israelites; with the local people of the Shephelah—late Canaanite of sorts (Naʾaman 2012b); or with the people of the lowlands in the west, that is, with the mix of late Canaanite and Philistine population characteristic of this region.

Assigning identity to the inhabitants of an early Iron Age site solely on the basis of the archaeological record is notoriously difficult, as most material culture traits can be interpreted in more than one way (Finkelstein 1997; Dever 2003; Faust 2006). Indeed, the finds at Khirbet Qeiyafa do not provide sufficient data for a clear-cut answer to this question. The pottery assemblage from the site is typical of a settlement in this location—the Shephelah between the coastal plain and the highlands (Singer-Avitz 2010)—and hence cannot disclose the identity of the inhabitants. The excavators called attention to the lack of pig bones as indicating an Israelite identity of the inhabitants. The absence of pig bones is reminisccent of the situation in Iron I highlands sites, to differ from what we know about the contemporaneous urban centers of Philistia, in which the ratio of pig bones is exceptionally high (Hesse 1990, 216). Several years ago this would indeed have been interpreted as indicating Israelite identity (Finkelstein 1997), yet recent archaeozoological research has proven the picture to be more complicated, as pig bones are also rare at non-Israelite inland Iron I sites in the lowlands and even at rural sites in the heartland of Philistia.

The language of a late proto-Canaanite ostracon found at Khirbet Qeiyafa was identified by some as Hebrew (Misgav, Garfinkel, and Ganor 2009; Galil 2009; Puech 2010), but other scholars argued against this interpretation (Rollston 2011; Millard 2011). Almost all known late proto-Canaanite and the slightly later "post proto-Canaanite" inscriptions found in excavations come from the Shephelah and the southern coastal plain, with a special concentration around the ancient city of Gath. The Egyptian hieratic inscriptions of the Late Bronze III are found in the same area, with a special intensity around Lachish. This region was the hub of the Egyptian administration in Canaan in the Late Bronze Age, and hence the concentration of late proto-Canaanite inscriptions there may reflect a long-term, continuous administrative and cultural tradition in the south (Finkelstein, Sass, and Singer-Avitz 2008). To sum up this point, the Khirbet Qeiyafa ostracon does not shed clear light on the identity of the inhabitants of the site.

The territorial affiliation of Khirbet Qeiyafa. In the late eleventh to late tenth century B.C.E., the area of Khirbet Qeiyafa could have been dominated by a Philistine city-state to its west, an emerging highlands territorial formation to its east, or a local Shephelah polity (for the latter, see Na'aman 2012b; Koch 2012). The only clues that hint at an answer come from its architectural tradition. I refer to the phenomenon of a hilly settlement surrounded by a casemate wall with houses (some pillared) using the casemates as their back broadrooms (fig. 14). Iron I–early Iron IIA casemate sites of this type are known only in the inland parts of the Levant, in Ammon, Moab (Routledge 2004; Finkelstein and Lipschits 2011), the Negev highlands (e.g., Meshel and Cohen 1980; Meshel 1994), and the highlands north of Jerusalem (discussed above, and see fig. 11). No site of this type has thus far been found in the lowlands. This should come as no surprise, since the site layout in question best fits hilly environments. Hence, from the architectural/layout perspective it is reasonable to affiliate the builders of Khirbet Qeiyafa with the highlands.

There are two alternatives for a highlands polity that could have ruled Khirbet Qeiyafa: Judah or the early north Israelite Gibeon/Gibeah polity dealt with in this chapter. From the strictly geographical proximity perspective, affiliating Khirbet Qeiyafa with Judah is the more logical possibility. However, in the late Iron I–early Iron IIA the Judahite highlands were sparsely settled and demographically depleted (Ofer 1994), which means that in terms of manpower, direct rule of Jerusalem as far west as Khirbet Qeiyafa and the organization of a complicated construction project there are questionable. Of no less importance, no contemporary significant building activity is known in the highlands of Judah, including Jerusalem, meaning that in this case Khirbet Qeiyafa would be the only elaborately constructed site thus far found in Judah.

The other possibility is to affiliate Khirbet Qeiyafa with the north Israelite territorial entity discussed here. At first glance, this proposal may sound somewhat far-fetched—mainly because the site is located quite far to the southwest and because of the natural tendency, influenced by late-monarchic realities, to link the Shephelah with Jerusalem. However, there are parallels to the involvement of north-highland forces in this region: (1) in the Amarna period, Shechem intervened in the affairs of Keilah in the southeastern Shephelah and possibly Rubutu in the northern Shephelah (EA 280:289); (2) two early north Israelite kings besieged Gibbethon of the Philistines (1 Kgs 15:27; 16:15, 17), located in the northern Shephelah.

Figure 14. Aerial view of Khirbet Qeiyafa in the Shephelah (courtesy of Prof. Yosef Garfinkel, the Khirbet Qeiyafa Expedition, the Hebrew University, and Sky View).

There are several arguments in favor of the proposal to affiliate Khirbet Qeiyafa with the Gibeon/Gibeah entity:

(1) Unlike Judah, this territorial formation was densely inhabited and hence had no manpower problem.

(2) As indicated above, the relatively small area of the Gibeon-Bethel plateau features a dense system of contemporaneous casemate walls, including, possibly, at Gibeon. They are the only casemate or casemate-like walls thus far unearthed west of the Jordan that are concurrent with the fortification at Khirbet Qeiyafa.

(3) Affiliating the northeastern Shephelah with the Gibeon/Gibeah polity would explain the origin of the biblical memory about King Saul's presence in the Valley of Elah. It would also shed light on the topographical setting of the epic battle that took place there:

> Now the Philistines gathered their armies for battle; and they were gathered at Socoh, which belongs to Judah, and encamped between Socoh and Azekah, in Ephes-dammim. And Saul and the men of Israel were gathered, and encamped in the valley of Elah, and drew up in line of battle against the Philistines. And the Philistines stood on the mountain

on the one side, and Israel stood on the mountain on the other side, with a valley between them. (1 Sam 17:1–3)

The most straightforward geographical logic is that the Philistines camped to the south of the valley, somewhere between Socoh and Azekah, while the Israelites camped to its north, with the valley between them. The description of the Philistine camp fits a place to the south and opposite Khirbet Qeiyafa. The story as read today is no doubt Deuteronomistic in language, but it may have been based on an earlier layer, for instance, on the tradition of the heroic stories in Samuel regarding the killing of Goliath by a hero named Elhanan rather than David (2 Sam 21:19). This layer may be the earliest in the book (Isser 2003, 28–34; Finkelstein and Silberman 2006a, 53–57). The fact that the story does not name the Israelite camp is telling. It seemingly shows that certain details were no longer remembered when the text was put in writing, mainly regarding places that were no longer inhabited.

(4) The affiliation of Khirbet Qeiyafa with the north Israelite polity may provide an explanation for its end in destruction and/or abandonment—as a result of the Sheshonq I campaign.

Identification of Khirbet Qeiyafa. The excavators identify Khirbet Qeiyafa with Shaaraim, a place mentioned twice in the Hebrew Bible: in the description of the battle in the Valley of Elah (1 Sam 17: 52) and in the list of towns of Judah (Josh 15:36) (Garfinkel and Ganor 2009, 8–10). The basis for this identification is their conviction that every biblical text reflects the time it ostensibly describes. Consequently, they read 1 Sam 17 and Josh 15 as representing the eleventh or early tenth century B.C.E. However, the two sources that mention Shaaraim portray late Iron II realities. Especially important is Josh 15, which, as indicated by both textual evidence and archaeology, portrays the administrative organization of Judah in the late seventh century B.C.E. (Alt 1925a; Na'aman 1991). While one can argue that 1 Sam 17:52 preserves an ancient place name, Josh 15:36 certainly cannot be read against the background of a tenth-century site that *does not* include continuous activity in late-monarchic times (to account for its mention in the seventh-century Josh 15 list). Moreover, from the strictly geographical perspective, it is clear that Shaaraim must be located between the Valley of Elah and the Philistine cities of Gath and Ekron, probably in the area of the lower Elah Brook (Dagan 2009), hence the meaning of the name (from the Hebrew for "gate[s]"), referring to the approaches of Judah (Na'aman 2008b).

Na'aman (2008a) proposed identifying Khirbet Qeiyafa with Gob, which is mentioned twice (2 Sam 21:18, 19; or three times—v. 16 there) in reference to heroic acts against the Philistines. Needless to say, this suggestion cannot be verified; still, it is appealing for two reasons: (1) The heroic stories seem to form an early layer in Samuel that may depict old traditions related to the time of the founder of the Davidic dynasty (Isser 2003; Finkelstein and Silberman 2006a, 53–57). Indeed, Gob is not mentioned in the detailed list of seventh-century b.c.e. towns of Judah in Josh 15. (2) It would provide the missing place name—the encampment of the Israelites—in the 1 Sam 17 account.

Back to the Sheshonq I campaign. Scholars have suggested applying the principle of *boustrophedon* to rows I–II in the Sheshonq I list (B. Mazar 1957; Helck 1971, 238–45). Doing so, one obtains the following sequence: numbers 11 → 12 → 13 (row I) → 26 → 25 → 24 → 23 (row II). Except for numbers 11–12, the identification of the place names is quite certain, creating a logical route from the Shephelah to the highlands: number 11 → number 12 → Rubutu → Aijalon → Kiriathaim = Kiriath-jearim → Beth-horon → Gibeon (fig. 12). Place-name number 11 is the first in this group and hence probably the southernmost. All one can say about it with certainty is that it is short and starts with a -*g*-. In other words, although the traditional identifications of this place name with Gaza or Gezer remain viable options, Gob, suggested by Na'aman (2008a) for Khirbet Qeiyafa, is equally plausible (Finkelstein and Fantalkin 2012).

To sum up this section of the discussion, I would suggest the possibility that Khirbet Qeiyafa served as the southwesternmost post of the Gibeon/Gibeah polity, facing Gath, the most important Philistine city of that period (Finkelstein and Fantalkin 2012). This would explain the centrality of Gath in the memories regarding the battle in the Valley of Elah. An expansion of the north Israelite polity to this area would have posed a threat to Egyptian interests in Canaan and may have accounted—in addition to what has been said above about the Jezreel Valley—for the campaign of Sheshonq I against this polity.

2.7. Philistines or Egyptians?

The biblical description of the rise and rule of King Saul fits well the long-term phenomenon of strongmen who established early territorial formations (larger than the typical city-states) in the highlands of the Levant. The expansion attempts of such highland entities took place in different regions and periods (ch. 3); they usually transpired in twilight periods, when no great empires ruled over the region, when a great empire was weak and unable to impose its rule, or in a friction zone between two neighboring powers.

Despite differences in the geopolitical situation, I see great similarity between the nature and mode of expansion of Shechem under Labayu and his sons in the fourteenth century and the Saulide territorial entity in the tenth century B.C.E. Both advanced from their highland hubs to the western slopes of the Gilead in Transjordan, threatened cities in the Jezreel Valley, intervened in the Shephelah in the south, and were halted because they endangered Egyptian interests in Canaan.

According to this reconstruction of events, the expanding late-Iron I/ early Iron IIA Gibeon/Gibeah (Saulide) polity to the north, into the Jezreel Valley or its margins, near the traditional old Egyptian stronghold of Beth-shean, and to the southwest, near the international road on the coastal plain, posed a threat to the revived Egyptian interest in Canaan in the early days of the Twenty-Second Dynasty. Sheshonq I decided to intervene, making the highlands entity a major target of his campaign. He assaulted the hub of this growing formation around Gibeon as well as the most important centers of its eastern flank in the area of the Jabbok River, and he took over the towns of the Jezreel Valley. The latter act could have been associated with the rise of a new north Israelite power around Shechem (ch. 3).[7]

This scenario may explain several peculiar elements in the biblical story of King Saul. First, it sheds light on the otherwise difficult-to-explain memory that Saul died in battle on Mount Gilboa—far from the hub of his territory around Gibeon/Gibeah in the highlands and that his corpse was displayed on the wall of Beth-shean, the ancient Egyptian stronghold in the valley. Second, it may clarify the otherwise strange mention of the Philistines in the battle of Gilboa. The notion of a Philistine league of cities capable of assembling a great army is influenced by Greek realities of late-monarchic times—close to the days of compilation of the story (Finkel-

---

7. It is possible that the first to profit from these events was Jerusalem. As vassals under a short-lived Egyptian domination or after the Egyptian withdrawal from the hill country, the Jerusalem chiefs could have taken over the ex-Saulide territories in the hill country (and the western Gilead?). This could have been the historical seed behind the memory in late-monarchic Judah of a great "united monarchy" in the time of the early Davidides.

stein 2002b). In the late Iron I no Philistine city could assemble a force strong enough to march as far north as Beth-shean. The book of Samuel may retain an ancient memory of an Egyptian army, possibly assisted by Philistine city-states. When the material was put in writing, Egypt was already long gone, yet the Philistines were a current reality; in other words, the Philistines "took over" the role of Egypt in the story.[8]

A Gibeon/Gibeah late Iron I–beginning of the early Iron IIA (tenth century B.C.E.) polity seems to be attested in archaeology, in the Shoshenq I list, and in vague, positive northern traditions regarding the house of Saul in the Hebrew Bible. This is the first recorded north Israelite territorial entity. It probably stretched over a large area—the entire northern part of the central hill country and the western Gilead—and attempted to push into the Jezreel Valley and the coastal plain. This expansion collided with the renewed interest of Egypt in Canaan. Shoshonq I assaulted the Gibeon/Gibeah polity and brought about its decline. Further, in order to assert his rule in the region, he may have promoted the rise of a competing north Israelite entity: the Tirzah polity.

---

8. This explanation also holds true for the biblical reference to Philistine garrisons in the highlands (1 Sam 13:3; 2 Sam 23:14). This, too, is highly unlikely. But for a while after the campaign, Egyptian troops may have been stationed in a few strategic places in the highlands. In this case, too, the late-monarchic historian, who had a vague memory of these events, substituted the Egyptians with their allies—the Philistines—who were better known to him.

3
THE EARLY DAYS OF THE NORTHERN KINGDOM:
THE TIRZAH POLITY

In the previous chapter I described the rise and fall of the first north Israelite territorial entity in the late Iron I and early years of the early Iron IIA (the tenth century B.C.E.), which seems to have had its hub in the Gibeon-Bethel plateau north of Jerusalem. I proposed that this polity can be identified both archaeologically, in a group of sites in this area, some protected by casemate walls that were abandoned in the early years of the Iron IIA, and textually, in the account of the Sheshonq campaign as well as in memories relayed in the books of Samuel regarding the house of Saul. In this chapter I wish to deal with the rise of the north Israelite territorial entity that replaced the Gibeon/Gibeah polity. I refer to the early days of the northern kingdom of Israel, which was ruled from the town of Tirzah in northern Samaria. I suggest labeling this territorial entity the "Tirzah polity."

3.1. RELATIVE DATES, ABSOLUTE DATES, AND HISTORICITY

Let me start with chronology. From the perspective of relative, ceramic typology, in this chapter I will deal with the period between the late Iron I and the first years of the early Iron IIA of the Gibeon/Gibeah polity and the late Iron IIA of the Samaria polity. In other words, the spotlight here is on the early Iron IIA. The chronological model based on hundreds of radiocarbon determinations from a large number of sites in Israel puts this phase of the Iron Age at circa 920–880 B.C.E. (Finkelstein and Piasetzky 2010). For reasons which have to do, *inter alia*, with the Sheshonq I campaign, the transition from the Iron I to the Iron IIA should probably be fixed somewhat earlier, in the beginning of the second half of the tenth century B.C.E.[1] Turning to archaeo-historical considerations, if one accepts the biblical testimony about the foundation of Samaria by Omri, the inner chronology of the Bible regarding the early north Israelite kings (below), and the data from the site of Samaria (Franklin 2004; ch. 4 here), it is reasonable to propose that major construction efforts in the north did not take place before the middle of Omri's reign. All in all, I would place the early Iron IIA between circa 940/930 and 870 B.C.E.

The Hebrew Bible names seven north Israelite kings who reigned during this time span. Once the biblical information on the length of their reigns is coordinated with extrabiblical sources from the mid-ninth century, their reigns can be fixed at:

Jeroboam I:	931–909 B.C.E.
Nadab:	909–908
Baasha:	908–885
Elah:	885–884
Zimri:	884
Tibni:	884–880 (rival rule with Omri)
Omri:	884–873 B.C.E.

Taking into account that the early version of the books of Kings was put in writing in the late seventh century B.C.E. (e.g., Cross 1973, 274–88; Na'aman 2002b; Römer 2007), 250–300 years after the supposed reign of these kings and when the northern kingdom no longer existed, one may ponder the reliability of these dates.

I see no reason to doubt the names, order, and dates of these kings. The order of the Israelite and Judahite monarchs with their length of reign and cross-information between the two kingdoms is supported by the mention of some of them (all but Omri later than the first kings listed above) in extrabiblical texts. Regarding the northern kingdom, one should note the mention of Omri in the Mesha Stela, Ahab in the Kurkh Inscription describing the Battle of Qarqar between a coalition of Levantine kingdoms and Shalmaneser III king of Assyria in 853 B.C.E., the killing of Joram king of Israel and Ahaziah king of Judah in the Tel Dan Stela (842 B.C.E.), and

---

1. The appearance of Megiddo in the Sheshonq I list and the fragment of his stela found at the site must be associated with the settlement of Stratum VB of the early Iron IIA. This is so because radiocarbon determinations indicate that the previous city was destroyed in the first half of the tenth century—too early for his reign.

Jehu as a vassal of Shalmaneser III in the Black Obelisk. Also, the exact length of reigns given for these and other kings seems reliable, inasmuch as they are different from the forty years each given to David and Solomon, the founders of the Davidic dynasty. The latter is a typological number meaning no more than "long time" or "many years." This means that the early Deuteronomistic Historian of the late seventh century B.C.E. (Dtr 1 of Cross 1973, 274–88) had access to a record of the Israelite and Judahite kings. Taking into consideration the accuracy of the information, this material must have been a written document. Regarding the Israelite kings, this could have been a record that was put in writing at Samaria (the capital) or Bethel (location of an important shrine) in the early eighth century B.C.E., just over a century after the days of the early Israelite kings. The information on the Israelite monarchs could have been brought to Judah by Israelites after the collapse of the northern kingdom in the late eighth century B.C.E. (Finkelstein and Silberman 2006b). Needless to say, there is a meaningful difference between keeping king lists and recording historical events. Hence the fact that the Hebrew Bible accurately records the order and length of reign of the northern kings does not mean that the descriptions of the events in their days are fully historical; each story should be studied on its own terms according to archaeological information and text exegesis. This is especially so in view of the strong ideology of the Judahite authors, that is, the tendency to blacken and delegitimize the northern kingdom and its kings.

3.2. Note on Material Culture

A few general words about the archaeology of the early Iron IIA in the territory of the northern kingdom are in place here. The material culture of this phase of the Iron Age is well-identified because of its difference from that of the late Iron I. It features, among other traits, a new ceramic tradition characterized mainly by red-slipped burnished vessels (Herzog and Singer-Avitz 2006), a new town layout at sites such as Megiddo, and the very beginning of an iron industry (Veldhuijzen and Rehren 2007; Eliyahu-Behar et al. forthcoming). It is also different from the material culture of the next phase, the late Iron IIA, in the sense that it features no evidence of public architecture—palaces or fortifications—even in central sites such as Megiddo and Tirzah. Most of the information on this phase comes from sites in the Jezreel Valley: Megiddo, Yokneam, Taanach and Rehov (A. Mazar et al. 2005; Arie 2013). There is no clear evidence of this phase in the mountainous Galilee and in the Jordan Valley north of the Sea of Galilee. In the latter area both Hazor and Dan experienced an occupational gap at that time (for Dan, see Arie 2008).

In the highlands, the evidence of the capital, Samaria, is not clear. A small rural settlement existed there in the Iron I (Stager 1990), and the great royal acropolis is probably a product of the late Iron IIA (Finkelstein 2011b); for the time being, the early Iron IIA is missing or not identified. In fact, this phase has not been clearly identified in any highlands site. The results of the surveys present a no-less-difficult problem: the Iron I is easy to isolate in the sherd collections, and so is the Iron II in general, but the distinction between the different phases of the Iron II is possible only in large sherd assemblages; it is undistinguishable in the many sites that yielded a small number of Iron Age sherds. In those sites in the northern highlands where the sherd collection was large enough to establish minute observations, there is evidence of continuity of occupation from the Iron I to the Iron IIB. Hence one can assume that the number of sites in the highlands in the early Iron IIA was at least as sizable as in the Iron I and possibly a bit larger.

The biblical text describes Tirzah as the capital of Israel in its early days. I will now deal with this site and will then turn to the territorial scope of the northern kingdom of that time.

3.3. TIRZAH

The biblical town of Tirzah is safely identified at Tell el- Far'ah in the highlands, northeast of Shechem (e.g., Albright 1931; de Vaux 1956, 135–40; Briend 1996; fig. 15). The mound is set in a fertile valley near two rich springs, at the head of Wadi Far'ah, which leads to the Jordan Valley.

The book of 1 Kings (12:25) says that Jeroboam I built Shechem, but it also hints (14:17) that he later moved to Tirzah; 1 Kings specifically mentions Tirzah as the capital of the northern kingdom in the days of Baasha (15:21, 33; 16:6), Elah (16:8–9), Zimri (16:15), and the first half of the reign of Omri (16:23). Assuming that Jeroboam ruled at least part of his reign from Tirzah, as did his son Nadab, as well as Tibni, Tirzah was the seat of the first six or seven northern kings, for a period of forty to fifty years. I see no reason to doubt the authenticity of the consistent and deeply rooted information on Tirzah as the capital of Israel. The authenticity of this memory is highlighted by the fact that Tirzah does not play an important role in the rest of the Deuteronomistic History. In other words,

Figure 15. Aerial view of Tell el-Far'ah (N), location of Tirzah, looking northeast.

one cannot argue that a situation in the later days of the northern kingdom was retrojected to the past, into the description of its early days. Another support for the Tirzah tradition comes from archaeology, which seems to support the biblical account that Samaria was built only in the days of the Omrides (ch. 4). The Tirzah memory, too, probably reached the author of Kings with northerners who settled in Judah after the fall of Israel in 720 B.C.E. All this makes Tell el-Far'ah, the site of Tirzah, a crucial place for the study of the early days of the northern kingdom.

3.3.1. THE SITE, ITS EXCAVATION, AND ITS STRATIGRAPHY

Tell el-Far'ah was explored by Roland de Vaux between 1946 and 1960. De Vaux excavated four fields, three of them (Chantiers [Field] II, III, and IV) on the western side of the mound and one (Chantier I) in the north. In addition, five soundings were carried out on the northeastern slope, between Chantier I and Ein el-Far'ah (fig. 16). Admittedly, much of the site—especially its heart and eastern sector—have not been investigated. Still, the information from Tell el-Far'ah is significant: the mound spreads across roughly 5 hectares, of which 0.5 hectare was dug in Chantier II alone. This means that the total area excavated in the three western fields

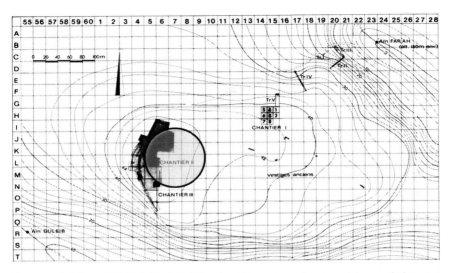

Figure 16. Map of Tell el-Farʿah (N), showing areas of excavations and the suggested location of the Period VIIa settlement in the western, higher sector of the mound.

seems to make up circa 15 percent of the site (Chambon 1984, 19, 151)—more than the relative proportion of the excavated fields in most biblical mounds.

De Vaux published a series of preliminary reports on the results of his dig (for the periods discussed here, see de Vaux and Steve 1947; 1948; de Vaux 1951; 1952; 1957; 1961). He described continuous occupation from the Late Bronze II through the Iron I to the Iron II, with Niveau (Level) 4 standing for the Late Bronze Age and Niveaux 3–1 covering the Iron Age (table in Chambon 1984, 11; table 2 below). The final report on the Iron Age finds was published by Chambon (1984) many years after the conclusion of the dig. Chambon introduced a new stratigraphic system, with Period VI standing for the Late Bronze Age and Period VII, divided into five phases, standing for the Iron Age (1984, 11–12; table 2 here; for a short evaluation of the stratigraphy and chronology of Tell el-Farʿah in the Iron Age, see Herzog and Singer-Avitz 2006).

Here I wish to put the spotlight on Period VIIa, which dates to the later days of the late Iron I and the early Iron IIA, the period discussed in this chapter. I have no interest at this point in details of architecture and specific finds. What I wish to establish is the settlement history of Tell el-Farʿah and to correlate it to the textual evidence about Tirzah.

Table 2: The stratigraphy of Tell el-Farʿah from de Vaux to this book

de Vaux		Chambon		Revisions on the date of the Tell el-Farʿah layers	
Niveau	Date	Period	Date	Herzog and Singer-Avitz 2006	Finkelstein
4	Late Bronze	VIIa	12th–11th century B.C.E.	Early Iron IIA, ca. 950–900 B.C.E.	Late Iron I-early Iron IIA, second half of 10th and early 9th centuries B.C.E.
3	Iron I	VIIb	(11th)–10th	Late Iron IIA, ca. 900–840/830	Late Iron IIA, ca. 870–second half of 9th century
Gap		Not detected		ca. 840/830–800	ca. 840/820–770/760
"unfinished building"		VIIc	Early 9th	Iron IIB, ca. 800–720	Iron IIB, ca. 770/760–720
2	Iron II	VIId	9th–8th		
1		VIIe	7th	Not discussed	Not discussed

3.3.2. EXCAVATION RESULTS

The Late Bronze settlement of Tell el-Farʿah is represented in the excavation of Chantier I and in tombs. The nature of the Late Bronze finds in Chantier II is not clear, but Chambon mentioned Late Bronze remains there, too. In any event, the remains are poor and not well preserved. This is also reflected in the number of scarabs—only three, dating to the Late Bronze, versus a large number of items that can be assigned to the Middle

Bronze (Keel 2010, 2–27). The settlement seems to have been destroyed by fire, but with the data at hand the exact date of this destruction is impossible to determine.

Contra both de Vaux and Chambon (table 2), there is no evidence of an Iron I layer at Tell el-Far'ah. Not a single sherd that can safely be attributed solely to this period has been found at the site. This evidence is especially weighty in view of the large number of Iron I pottery sherds collected at sites in the highlands, including the area around Tell el-Far'ah, even in surface surveys.

Regarding the Iron Age occupation, I basically agree with Herzog and Singer-Avitz's recent analysis (2006; table 2 here). Only a limited number of vessels from Period VIIa, the focus of the article, were published (fig. 17); most of them fit into the Iron IIA, but some are better suited to the late Iron I. However, even in the northern valleys the type-strata of the late Iron I exhibit large collared-rim storage jars, which do not appear in Period VIIa at Tell el-Far'ah. As mentioned above, this is even more significant for a site in the highlands, where these jars abound. The next layer at Tell el-Far'ah, Period VIIb, produced a rich assemblage of pottery that belongs to the late Iron IIA (Herzog and Singer-Avitz 2006, 175–76). If one weighs all these considerations, Period VIIa at Tell el-Far'ah should be dated to the very end of the Iron I and the early Iron IIA. In terms of absolute chronology, this means that Period VIIa was established sometime in the mid- or early second half of the tenth century and lasted until the early ninth century. In other words, Period VIIa covered several decades that parallel almost exactly the time when Tirzah functioned as the capital of the northern kingdom.

The remains of Period VIIa were found in a restricted area, in the northwest of Chantier II. The negative evidence is also significant:

(1) The rest of Chantier II north was excavated down to the Early Bronze layers; significant remains of Periods VIIb and VIId— the two more elaborate Iron Age layers at the site—were uncovered (Chambon 1984: plans III, V), but no remains of Period VIIa were found.

(2) No less noteworthy, Chantier II south was excavated down to the Middle Bronze layers with no Period VIIa remains encountered.

(3) In Chantier IV excavation reached the Middle Bronze, with no Period VIIa remains found (Mallet 1987–1988).

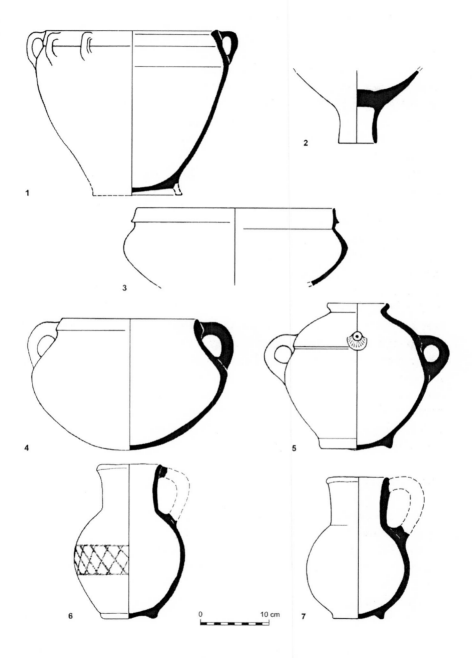

Figure 17. Pottery of the Period VIIa settlement at Tell el-Far'ah (N).

(4) In Chantier I, Period VIIb was found directly on top of Late Bronze remains.

Tell el-Far'ah features an elevated area of just over one hectare in the western sector, described by Albright as an acropolis "situated at the western end which is the highest and most easily defended part of the mound as well as the part which is nearest the spring" (1931, 246; see also de Vaux and Steve 1947, 395). It seems, therefore, that the Period VIIa settlement was restricted to this acropolis—in fact, to the northwestern part of it— an area of less than a hectare (fig. 16). Even if remains of this layer are uncovered in the future further to the east, we are apparently dealing with a relatively small, sparsely built settlement. This settlement was unfortified—buildings of this layer run over the ancient Bronze Age fortifications (Chambon 1984, plan I).

The Period VIIb settlement, dating to the late Iron IIA, is denser than that of Period VIIa and better planned. The development from one to the other was organic (Chambon 1993, 439), with no evidence of destruction. Continuity is evident in most places, though some changes can be observed here and there. An intermediate phase, labeled VIIa1, was detected in one location (Chambon 1984, 22), indicating again that the transition between the two settlements was peaceful and gradual. Period VIIb seems to have ended in crisis. The rich assemblage of complete vessels probably implies destruction (see picture in Chambon 1984, pl. 40:g, indicating devastation by fire). The possible abandonment of the site in the end phase of the Iron IIA (Herzog and Singer-Avitz 2006, 185) may provide another piece of evidence of this crisis.

3.3.3. Discussion

The gap in occupation at Tirzah for most of the Iron I is surprising, given the dense habitation in this part of the highlands and the fact that the mound is located on rich springs, in a fertile valley, in a strategic spot on the road leading east to the Jordan Valley and the Gilead. The abandonment of Tell el-Far'ah may have resulted from local (superstitious?) traditions following the destruction of the Late Bronze settlement. This cessation of activity may hint that the reality behind the genealogy of Manasseh, including the daughters of Zelophehad, with Tirzah among them (Num 26:29–33; Josh 17:2–3), cannot be sought before the days of Period VIIa. Further, since the geographical reality behind the list was already fully developed at the time of the Samaria ostraca in the first half of the eighth century B.C.E. (Niemann 2008), it stands to reason that this tradition reflects the organization of the northern kingdom in the Iron IIA.

With the data at hand it is impossible to decide whether Jeroboam I established a new settlement at Tirzah after a two-century gap or if the site was resettled a short while before his time. In any event, during Period VIIa—the early days of the northern kingdom in the late tenth and early ninth centuries B.C.E.—Tirzah was a relatively small, sparcely built, unfortified settlement. It was probably singled out as a "capital" in order to avoid the traditional center of Shechem with its old feuds and deeply rooted Late Bronze–Iron I institutions, aristocracy, and traditions. Tirzah must have been chosen because of the advantages of its immediate environment (arable land and a rich water source) and its location on the main road to the Jordan Valley and the Israelite territories on the western slopes of the Gilead (de Vaux 1956, 139).

There is no way to know if the unexcavated sector of the "acropolis" included a ruling compound with palace and temple, but the part of the acropolis that was investigated shows no sign of public architecture. Following the first seasons of excavations at Tell el-Farʿah, de Vaux (1951, 430) even questioned whether to identify the site with Tirzah because the ruins did not seem fit for the capital of Israel. Franklin (2004) proposed that the first Iron IIA phase at Samaria comprised no more than an agricultural estate. If one dates this phase to the days of Omri, then the nature of the capital of the northern kingdom changed only with the construction of the large ruling compound at Samaria somewhat later, in the main period of prosperity of the Omride dynasty (ch. 4).

The character of the capital of Israel in its first half-century probably speaks for the nature of the kingdom itself as a formative territorial entity. On the one hand, the "capital" exhibits no evidence of monumental architecture and was unfortified. On the other hand, there is the relatively large number of late Iron I–early Iron IIA seals that originated from the Period VIIa layer (Keel 2010, 2–6); this, which stands out especially against the background of paucity of such seals in the much richer and more vastly exposed Periods VIIb and VIId, may indicate the existence of a bureaucratic apparatus. It is noteworthy that this early territorial kingdom, which was ruled from a humble settlement, was strong enough to expand to the Jezreel Valley and its environs (below). In other words, there is no correlation between the modest nature of the seat of the kings and the ability of the kingdom to expand territorially. This is in line with what I presented for both Late Bronze Shechem and late Iron I Gibeon/Gibeah of the time of the house of Saul (chs. 1 and 2, respectively).

3.4. The Territory Ruled by the Tirzah Polity

Archaeological finds, ancient Near Eastern texts, and the biblical record testify that in the time of the Omride dynasty the northern kingdom ruled in the mountainous Galilee, at Hazor in the upper Jordan Valley, in large parts of Transjordan between the Arnon and the Yarmuk Rivers, and in the coastal plain of the Sharon (ch. 4). This raises the question of which territories had been ruled by Israel in its early days, in the time of the Tirzah polity.

The biblical text gives two possible indications of the territorial extent of the northern kingdom before the Omrides: (1) the reference to Jeroboam I as the founder of a cultic place at Dan in the northern Jordan Valley (1 Kgs 12:29); (2) the statement that, in the days of King Baasha, Ben-hadad king of Damascus "conquered Ijon, Dan, Abel-beth-maacah, and all Chinneroth, with all the land of Naphtali" (1 Kgs 15: 20).[2] These accounts need to be verified both archaeologically and according to critical biblical exegesis.

3.4.1. Dan

Scholars did not doubt the tradition of the Jeroboam I cult at Dan (even those with a more critical approach to the text, e.g., Miller and Hayes 2006, 275; Na'aman 2006, 352), yet Arie (2008) has now convincingly argued from the pottery evidence that Dan:

(1) was destroyed by the end of the late Iron I;
(2) was deserted during much of the Iron IIA, certainly in the early Iron IIA—the time of Jeroboam I;
(3) was rebuilt by Hazael in the late ninth century; and
(4) became Israelite for the first time ca. 800 B.C.E. or, preferably, somewhat later.

---

2. Two additional stories ostensibly describe events that took place in the far north in the tenth century B.C.E., before the rise of the northern kingdom: the flight of Sheba the son of Bichri to Abel-beth-Maacah (2 Sam 20) and the Joab census (2 Sam 24), yet they were probably written against a later, eighth-century background.

In other words, the evidence from Dan does not support the tradition about Jeroboam I at Dan.

Bethel is the other site mentioned in 1 Kgs 12:29 as a cult place that was erected by Jeroboam I. The mound at the village of Beitin east of Ramallah, the location of biblical Bethel, was thoroughly excavated in the 1930s and 1950s. A comprehensive investigation of the finds from this dig, stored in Jerusalem and Pittsburgh, also cast doubt on the historicity of this verse. This investigation revealed that most of the Iron IIA pottery types known from sites in the vicinity, for example, Stratum 14 in the City of David in Jerusalem, are rare or absent at Bethel and that there are no diagnostic early Iron IIA items at the site (Finkelstein and Singer-Avitz 2009). In other words, Bethel, too, produced no clear indication of activity in the time of Jeroboam I.[3]

Scrutinizing the biblical material, Berlejung (2009, 1) has now reached a similar conclusion: "1 Kings 12:26–33* is a polemic dtr fiction that has no reliable historical information about the time of Jeroboam I, but reflects historical facts … of the time of Jeroboam II" (see also Hoffman 1980, 59–73, who raised the possibility that 1 Kings 12:29 is a nonhistorical construct representing Deuteronomistic religious concerns).[4]

This means that the tradition about the erection of the *bamah* at Dan is a retrojection into the past of a reality from the days of Jeroboam II, in the first half of the eighth century B.C.E.

3.4.2. BEN-HADAD

Scholars took the report about the campaign of Ben-hadad king of Damascus in the northern part of Israel in 1 Kgs 15:20 as a description of a historical event that took place around 885 B.C.E. (e.g., Dion 1997, 182–83; Lipiński 2000, 372). Yadin (1972, 143; also Ben-Tor 2000, 12) proposed that the destruction of Stratum IX at Hazor was inflicted by Ben-hadad in the course of this campaign. However, radiocarbon results put the destruction of this stratum significantly further along, in the late ninth

---

3. The idea that the Bethel sanctuary was located outside of the town, to the east (recently Blenkinsopp 2003), is baseless in view of the intensive archaeological surveys that did not reveal the slightest clue for an Iron II site, let alone cult site, in this area.

4. For the possible late nature of the story about the bull cult at Dan and Bethel, see Pakkala 2008. But note that Bethel was uninhabited or sparsely inhabited in the sixth and fifth centuries B.C.E. as well.

century B.C.E. (Sharon et al. 2007; Finkelstein and Piasetzky 2009) and leave no destruction layer at Hazor for such a campaign. In fact, from the radiocarbon perspective the only destruction layer in the north that may fit a campaign in the early ninth century is that of Rehov V, a site not mentioned in 1 Kgs 15:20, which is located to the south of the campaign route as described in 1 Kings. Moreover, the similarity between the 1 Kgs 15:20 account and the description of the campaign of Tiglath-pileser III king of Assyria against Israel in 732 B.C.E. (2 Kgs 15:29) raises the possibility that the idea of a Ben-hadad campaign was adopted by the author of 1 Kings from the latter. The two texts are written in the same genre and describe the same campaign route; they also mention several similar locations. Two more pieces of information are relevant here: first, the main Damascene attack on the northern kingdom was carried out in the days of Hazael, not earlier than 842 B.C.E.; second, the only Ben-hadad king of Damascus known from extrabiblical texts ruled circa 800 B.C.E.; he, too, applied pressure on the northern kingdom, at least in his early days. Therefore, the story about a Damascene campaign against the northern kingdom in the early ninth century is constructed according to later historical realities, and there is good reason to doubt its historicity.

3.4.3. What Does Archaeology Say?

Archaeology testifies to significant activity in the Jezreel Valley in the early phase of the Iron IIA (see, e.g., Herzog and Singer-Avitz 2006). Settlements represented by strata such as Megiddo VB and Taanach IIA are the first to exhibit the material culture of the later phases of the Iron Age—the late-Iron IIA and Iron IIB—and hence can be seen as Israelite. In contrast, no clear evidence of Israelite presence in the early Iron IIA exists in the upper Jordan Valley sites. At Hazor, Stratum X follows an occupational gap; it dates to the late Iron IIA, probably to the time of the Omride dynasty (Finkelstein 1999a, 2000). Dan was deserted after having been destroyed in the late Iron I (Arie 2008). Kinneret on the northern tip of the Sea of Galilee was deserted or declined after peaking in the late Iron I (Münger, Zangenberg, and Pakkala 2011).

3.4.4. Sheshonq I and the Jezreel Valley

The list of cities vanquished (rather than destroyed; Ussishkin 1990) in the course of the Sheshonq I campaign in the second half of the tenth century

B.C.E. is in line with this evidence. In the previous chapter I dealt with places mentioned in the list that are located in the highlands north of Jerusalem and in the area of the Jabbok River in Transjordan. In the north, the campaign reached the Jezreel Valley. The list refers to Megiddo, Taanach, Rehob, Beth-shean, and Shunem (Kitchen 1986). Indeed, the excavations at Megiddo in the 1920s yielded a fragment of a Sheshonq I stela, unfortunately not found *in situ*. The pharaoh did not proceed further to the north, into the mountainous Galilee or the upper Jordan Valley.

As I indicated in chapter 1, Sheshonq I could not have been responsible for the destructions in the Jezreel Valley in the late Iron I because:

(1) at least some of these destructions are radiocarbon dated before the highest possible date of his reign;

(2) the radiocarbon evidence indicates a gradual demise of these cities, not a single event (Finkelstein and Piasetzky 2009);

(3) there was no reason for a pharaoh who was probably interested in reestablishing Egyptian rule in the area to devastate the fertile valley, the breadbasket of the entire country (Ussishkin 1990); and

(4) it is illogical that Sheshonq I would set up a stela in a deserted Megiddo.

Combining these arguments, it is now clear that the Egyptian monarch directed his campaign in the Jezreel Valley in the early Iron IIA. The circumstances of the destruction of the late Iron I system (ch. 1) and the drastic change in material culture in the valley's sites between the late Iron I and the early Iron IIA indicate that in the latter period the valley had already been dominated by the north Israelites. In fact, it seems that the Israelite towns of the Jezreel Valley were a major target of the campaign. Therefore, the fact that Sheshonq I did not continue further north is telling. It seems to hint that at this time the lowland territory ruled by the highland Israelites was limited to the Jezreel Valley.

3.4.5. West and East

In the west there is no indication that the Tirzah polity managed to expand to the coast. Tel Dor is a test case; excavations at the site have yielded no hints of north Israelite rule before the late Iron IIA. In Transjordan, the western Gilead had already been included in the territory of the Gibeon/

Gibeah polity (ch. 2). This territory must have been inherited by the Tirzah polity.

The Israelite area in the Gilead can be delineated according to the location of the most important towns mentioned in the biblical text, in Samuel as well as in the core text of the Jacob cycle in Genesis, the written form of which should probably be dated before 720 B.C.E. Mahanaim, Penuel, Jabesh-gilead, and a few other less-important sites are all located on the western slopes of the Gilead, 5–15 km from the Jordan Valley (Finkelstein, Koch, and Lipschits 2012). There is no evidence of Israelite rule in the plateau of the northeastern Gilead (the town of Ramoth-gilead) before the days of the Omride dynasty (ch. 4).

All this seems to indicate that the Tirzah polity ruled over the highlands north of Jerusalem, the Jezreel Valley, and the western Gilead but that the mountainous Galilee and the upper Jordan Valley north of the Sea of Galilee were not included in its territory and were ruled by Damascus and the Phoenician cities (fig. 18; Liverani 2005, 105, reconstructs an even smaller area, limited to the territory of the house of Joseph and the Gilead).

3.5. HIGHLANDS-BASED EXPANDING EARLY TERRITORIAL POLITY

The Tirzah polity was ruled from a modest, unfortified settlement. The kings of the north dominated a mainly rural landscape both in the highlands and the Jezreel Valley, with no evidence of monumental architecture, fortifications, or developed administrative centers. There is no trace of writing in the centers of the northern kingdom in its early days. Tirzah lost its importance in the early ninth century, when Omri (884–873 B.C.E.) moved the capital of the northern kingdom to Samaria, possibly in his desire to establish a link with the coastal plain and the port of Dor (de Vaux 1967, 382). Indeed, the beginning of the transformation of Israel into a more complex kingdom came with the construction of the first palace at Samaria, probably by Omri. A full-scale urban transformation of the capital and the kingdom characterizes the more advanced phase of the Omride dynasty, probably in the days of Ahab (873–852 B.C.E.).

Several years ago Nadav Na'aman and I compared the territorial expansion of the northern kingdom during the reign of the Omride kings to that of Shechem of the Amarna period (Finkelstein and Na'aman 2005). In fact, Shechem of the Amarna period better fits my current reconstruction of the territorial extent and nature of the northern kingdom *before*

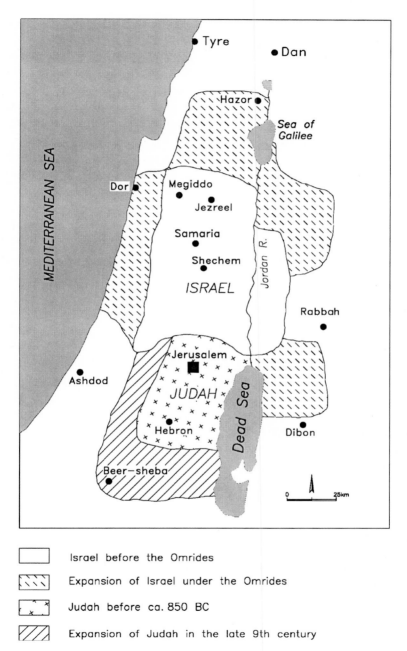

Israel before the Omrides

Expansion of Israel under the Omrides

Judah before ca. 850 BC

Expansion of Judah in the late 9th century

Figure 18. The territory of the northern kingdom in its early days and in the time of the Omride Dynasty.

the Omrides. Both were ruled from a modest settlement with no evidence of monumental buildings. Shechem of the Amarna period ruled over the northern part of the central highlands, part of the Jordan Valley, and possibly areas in the highlands to the east of the Jordan; its maneuvers, as recorded in the tablets, were aimed at expanding into the Jezreel Valley (Finkelstein and Na'aman 2005). Israel before the Omrides ruled over similar areas in the highlands and east of the Jordan and successfully expanded into the Jezreel Valley.

As I have already noted (ch. 2), the phenomenon of an expanding early territorial polity ruled from a rural, unfortified settlement in the highlands is known from different periods in the history of the Levant. To mention only the sedentary parts of the region, and to start with recent centuries, it resembles the eighteenth century C.E. "capital" of Dahr el-Umar in the village of Deir Hana in the Lower Galilee (Rafiq 1966; Cohen 1973, 7–18) and the circa 1600 C.E. hub of Fakhr ed-Din in the village of Deir el-Qamar in the Chouf mountains of Lebanon (Abu Husayn 1985; Marfoe 1979, 25–30). Much earlier examples come from the Late Bronze and Iron Ages. For the former—and apart from the example of Shechem—one should note the case of the kingdom of Amurru of the Amarna period, which started expanding from a modest settlement in Mount Lebanon (Goren, Finkelstein, and Na'aman 2003). For the early days of the Iron Age, one should recall the Gibeon/Gibeah polity described in chapter 2. The Hellenistic period provides at least two examples of this phenomenon: the Ituraean kingdom that emerged in Mount Lebanon (see, e.g., Marfoe 1979, 23–25; Myers 2010) and the Hasmonean kingdom that began its expansion from a modest settlement in Jerusalem.

3.6. The Rise of Jeroboam I

The relationship between the very late Iron I–early Iron IIA Tirzah formative territorial polity and the somewhat contemporary, or just a bit earlier, Gibeon/Gibeah polity that was described in chapter 2 is not clear. The latter probably ruled over vast territories in the northern part of the central hill country and the western Gilead (Na'aman 1990; Edelman 1992, 997; Knauf 2001b, 16; Finkelstein 2006a) and possibly reached the margin of the Jezreel Valley—in fact, much of the same area that was ruled by the Tirzah polity. So what was the sequence of events in the northern part of the central highlands in the tenth century B.C.E.?

It seems that the first territorial entity that ruled over the entire area up to the Jezreel Valley was that of Gibeon/Gibeah. The destruction of at least some of the late Iron I city-states in the Jezreel Valley took place in the early tenth century and should possibly be associated with the expansion of this entity (chs. 1–2; Finkelstein and Piasetzky 2009). In parallel, Egypt started showing renewed interest in the Levant. The expansion of the Gibeon/Gibeah polity to the lowlands raised the concern of Egypt and instigated the campaign of Sheshonq I in the second half of the tenth century. The pharaoh assaulted the plateau of Gibeon-Bethel and the area of the Jabbok River and brought about the (gradual?) decline of the early north Israelite polity. It is possible that Tirzah is mentioned in the Sheshonq I list (no. 59; Kitchen 1986, 438), yet no other place in the northern sector of the hill country appears in it.

The decline of the Gibeon/Gibeah polity could have opened the way for the rise of Jeroboam I and the northern kingdom with its center in the Shechem-Tirzah region. Jeroboam, who seems to have come from Zeredah, probably a small stronghold in the rugged, isolated area to the northwest of present-day Ramallah (Kochavi 1989), emerged as a typical highlands strongman. The connection between Jeroboam I and Shishak king of Egypt is recounted in 1 Kings 11:40. This story is more elaborate in the Septuagint version, which may have been based on an old, pre-Deuteronomistic source "resembling the books of Judges and Samuel" (Schenker 2000, 256 with reference to past studies; 2008).[5] One can propose that, similar to positive Saulide traditions in 1 Samuel and the Book of Saviors in Judges, for instance, the memory of Jeroboam I's Egyptian connection originated from old northern traditions that reached Judah after 720 B.C.E. (Galpaz 1991). If this is the case, this material may hint that the emerging northern kingdom, with its founder Jeroboam I, replaced the Gibeon/Gibeah polity as a result of Egyptian intervention, if not initiative. Whether Sheshonq I campaigned in the Jezreel Valley when it was already ruled by the Tirzah polity or whether Sheshonq I handed over the valley (which was ruled by the Giboen/Gibeah polity) to the Tirzah polity following the campaign[6] is impossible to say.

---

5. See also Galpaz 1991; for a different view on the LXX version, emphasizing its midrashic nature and thus proposing a late date for its compilation, see Talshir 1993; Sweeney 2007.

6. As suggested to me by my student Ido Koch.

3.7. TIRZAH AND JERUSALEM

Since our knowledge of the archaeology of Tell el-Far'ah, the location of Tirzah, is much more comprehensive than that of contemporary capital sites such as Damascus, Jerusalem, and Amman, the Tirzah case may shed light on the formative phase of other territorial kingdoms in the Levant and their capitals.

The character of late Iron I–early Iron IIA Tirzah is especially instructive for the case of Jerusalem and Judah. In its formative days, the northern kingdom ruled over a larger, richer, and much more densely settled territory than Judah; still, it was ruled from an unassuming, unfortified settlement with seemingly no monuments. The idea that Jerusalem of the tenth century featured monumental buildings (recently E. Mazar 2009; A. Mazar 2006, 2010; Faust 2010) contradicts the archaeological evidence (Finkelstein et al. 2007; Finkelstein 2011a) and, as demonstrated above, goes against what we know about formative kingdoms in the Levant in the Bronze and Iron Ages. The desperate attempts to prove the existence of monumental buildings, including fortifications, in Jerusalem in the early days of Judah stems solely from an uncritical reading of the biblical text.

As far as one can judge from the archaeological data and meager textual evidence, in the Late Bronze, Iron I, and early Iron IIA, that is, until the first half of the ninth century B.C.E., the northern sector of the central highlands suffered from instability and the rule of a series of strongmen who tried to establish large territorial entities by attempts to expand to the nearby lowlands in the north and west. These strongmen ruled from modest, unfortified highland towns. This situation changed dramatically in the next phase of the history of the region, with the rise to power of the Omride dynasty.

4

THE NORTHERN KINGDOM
UNDER THE OMRIDE DYNASTY

Fully developed territorial kingdoms, with evidence of monumental architecture and great armies, emerged in the southern Levant starting around 900 B.C.E. Royal inscriptions appear in the second half of the ninth century B.C.E. (Sass 2005). This marks the end of centuries in which the mountainous areas featured formative territorial polity with no signs of advanced bureaucracy and major public works, which were ruled by strongmen from modest "capitals." The strongest and most prosperous territorial kingdoms were Israel and Damascus. In the ninth and eighth centuries B.C.E. they struggled for hegemony in the region under the influence of a third player: the Assyrian Empire.

This chapter deals with the northern kingdom of Israel under the Omride dynasty. My intention here is neither to write a full history of this period nor to discuss the biblical material on the Omride kings (see, e.g., Timm 1982; various articles in Grabbe 2007). Rather, I wish to deal with several archaeological phenomena as well as historical issues that have recently been illuminated by archaeological research.

The four Omride kings—Omri, Ahab, Ahaziah, and Joram—ruled for approximately forty years, between 884–842 B.C.E. In terms of relative chronology, that is, the ceramic-based phases of the Iron Age, this period falls in the late Iron IIA. A Bayesian model based on the large number of radiocarbon results from many sites in Israel puts the late Iron IIA at circa 880–760 B.C.E. (Finkelstein and Piasetzky 2010). This means that the days of the Omride dynasty cover the *beginning* of the late Iron IIA. Indeed, it is possible to identify a post-Omride, terminal Iron IIA phase in northern Israel (Herzog and Singer-Avitz 2006; for Megiddo, see already Finkelstein 1999a) and possibly also in the south (ch. 5).

In the time of the Omrides, the northern kingdom featured the first monumental building operations and reached its first period of economic prosperity and territorial power. Its military achievements are recorded in three extrabiblical texts. In the Kurkh Inscription Shalmaneser III describes "Ahab the Israelite" as a prominent player in the anti-Assyrian coalition that faced him in the Battle of Qarqar in 853 B.C.E.; Ahab pitched the largest force of chariots in the coalition force. In the first preserved lines of the Tel Dan Stela, which was erected in the late ninth century, Hazael king of Aram Damascus says that "the king of Israel entered previously in my father's land," probably hinting at Israelite territorial expansion before his rise to power circa 842 B.C.E. (on Hazael, see Lemaire 1991; Dion 1997; Lipiński 2000); Hazael must refer to the time of the Omrides. Whether the territory taken by Israel was located near Dan or elsewhere, for instance, in the northeastern Gilead (today's northern Jordan), is impossible to say. The Mesha Inscription, which was erected by the king of Moab in the late ninth century in Dibon, describes the Israelite expansion in Transjordan east of the Dead Sea several decades earlier: "Omri king of Israel humbled Moab many days.... Omri had occupied the whole land of Medeba and he dwelt in it" (on the Mesha Stela, see different articles in Dearman 1989b).

Detailed information on the period of the Omrides appears in the books of Kings. These accounts must be carefully scrutinized before employing them for historical reconstruction.

(1) Many of the descriptions belong to the cycles of prophetic stories (of Elijah and Elisha); they should be read as such and not necessarily as straight-forward historical descriptions (e.g., Na'aman 2007).

(2) The date of compilation of these prophetic cycles is debated (e.g., Schmid 2012b, 60).

(3) The books of Kings were put in writing two and half centuries after the time of the Omride dynasty, so the question arises: How did the author(s) know about this period? Information about this period may have first been kept as a written north Israelite document, but then again, when could such texts have been put in writing? As I have already noted earlier in this book (see also below), what we know about the spread of writing and literacy in Israel makes it highly unlikely that this took place before the first half of the eighth century B.C.E. The time that passed and the transmission from oral testimony to north Israelite written record and then to Judahite text could have distorted the original account.

(4) The Judahite author of Kings takes a negative approach to the northern kingdom in general and to the Omride kings and specifically Ahab in particular. This is a result of the Judahite pan-Israelite ideology, which developed in the late eighth and more so in the late seventh century B.C.E. (in any event, after the fall of Israel), according to which all *Bene Israel* must acknowledge the dominant role of Judah, be ruled by a Davidic king, and worship in the Jerusalem temple. Strong positive memories about the prosperity and power of Israel in the time of the Omride dynasty, including supremacy over Judah, which could have been carried to Judah by Israelites after the fall of the northern kingdom (Finkelstein and Silberman 2006b), may have stimulated much animosity in Judahite circles.

A good demonstration of the tension between the information on this period in biblical versus extrabiblical sources is provided by the description of the killing of King Joram of Israel and King Ahaziah of Judah in one momentous event. In 2 Kgs 9 we read that the two kings were killed in the course of the Jehu revolt, while in the Tel Dan Stela it is Hazael who takes credit for this event. One can argue that Jehu acted as a vassal of Hazael (Schniedewind 1996) or that the conflicting descriptions originate from the different distance between the compilation of the text and the event—longer in the case of the biblical text (Na'aman 2007; for a different explanation, see Lemaire 2007).

Archaeology is free of these difficulties, and the days of the Omrides are easy to identify stratigraphically and ceramically and are well-documented. They are easy to identify because of the many Iron IIA destruction layers in the north that are well-dated by radiocarbon results (Finkelstein and Piasetzky 2009) and that can be historically affiliated with the assault of Hazael of Damascus on the northern kingdom (Na'aman 1997a) in the end days of Omride rule; they are well-documented because of the grand-scale building operations that characterize this period.

4.1. OMRIDE ARCHITECTURE

The most prominent archaeological feature of this period is monumental building activities. In what follows I wish first to describe the main characteristics of Omride architecture, starting with a detailed account of a case study—the capital Samaria—and then, in a briefer account, describe other sites west and east of the Jordan River (fig. 19).

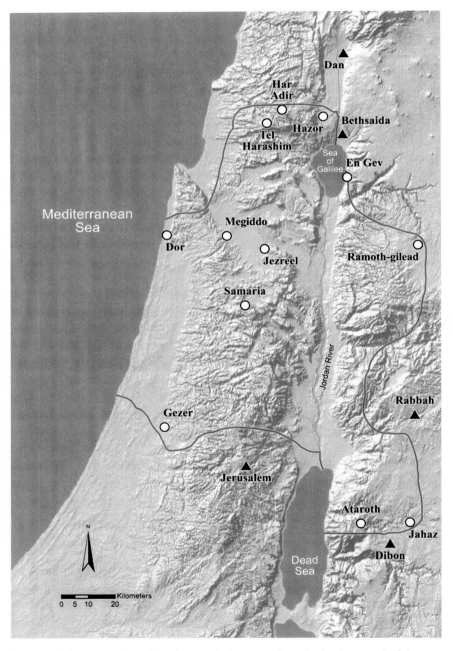

Figure 19. Sites mentioned in chapter 4 shown against the background of the territory of the northern kingdom in the days of the Omrides.

4.1.1. SAMARIA

Samaria was the capital of the northern kingdom and is therefore a highly important site for the study of the archaeology of Israel in the Iron II in general and the days of the Omride dynasty in particular. However, dating the Samaria strata according to pottery typology is unfortunately impossible because of the nature of the hilly site and the character of past excavations, in the early twentieth century and in the 1940s. Still, based on what seems to be reliable biblical material (e.g., Williamson 1996), one can accept the notion that the first major construction efforts at the site—Building Periods I and II—should be dated to the days of the Omrides (Reisner, Fisher, and Lyon 1924; Crowfoot, Kenyon, and Sukenik 1942; Kenyon 1971). This notion is supported by: (1) the allusion in Assyrian texts to the northern kingdom as *Bit Humri*, in reference to Omri as the founder of the dominant dynasty or the capital; and (2) the architectural similarity between the royal acropolis at Samaria and Jezreel, on the one hand, and Jezreel and two sites in Moab, on the other; the Moabite sites are specifically mentioned in the late ninth-century B.C.E. Mesha Inscription as having been built by the Omrides.

The study of Iron Age Samaria focused on the royal casemate compound with the remains of the palace on the summit of the hill. Sporadic Iron Age remains unearthed below the royal compound led the excavators to propose that the Iron Age city spread across an area almost as large as the later Roman city. However, according to the conventional interpretation, ninth-century B.C.E. Samaria encompassed only the royal compound; scholars attributed the maximal expansion of the site beyond the summit to the first half of the eighth century B.C.E.

In what follows I present several new observations regarding the topography, extent, and layout of Iron Age Samaria based on recent visits to the site, the study of aerial photographs, and comparisons with other Omride sites that was not possible until recent years. In the main, I propose that the sector of the site that shows characteristics of Omride architecture was three times larger than the circa 2.5 hectare royal casemate compound. I argue that Omride Samaria comprised two parts: the royal compound on the upper platform, and a large lower town described here as the "lower platform" (fig. 20, contra Niemann 2007, 2012, who understands Omride Samaria as a royal residence on the upper platform). In both parts the hill was artificially shaped. Needless to say, without renewed investigation in the field, the observations below remain hypothetical.

4.1.1.1. The Acropolis (the Upper Platform)

There was a small settlement at Samaria in the Iron I (eleventh and first half of the tenth centuries B.C.E.), which is represented by rock-cut installations, several flimsy walls, and typical pottery forms (Stager 1990; Tappy 1992, 96–97, 213–14). These are probably the remains of what the biblical text (1 Kgs 16:24) refers to as the estate of Shemer (Stager 1990). In the next phase an intensive building operation took place, obliterating the remains of the earlier settlement. It involved the construction of a casemate wall and a palace. Franklin (2004) suggested that the palace was built first and that the casemate wall was added in a second stage. This is possible, although both could have taken place during the forty years of Omride rule. I would therefore see the first phase, in which a palace was constructed on a scarp and surrounded by agricultural installations, as dating to the time of Omri, and the second phase, featuring the extension of the palace and the construction of the royal compound on a podium, as dating to the time of Ahab.

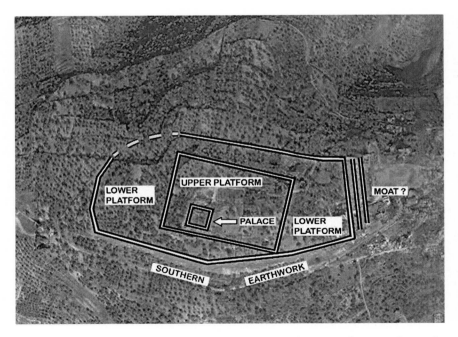

Figure 20. Google Earth view of Samaria, indicating the main elements that make up the site.

The excavation results failed to provide enough data to clarify the chronological relationship between the different buildings on the acropolis. According to the excavators (Crowfoot, Kenyon, and Sukenik 1942, 9–11; Kenyon 1942, 94–97), Building Period I is characterized by the construction of an ashlar-block wall that created a rectangular, elevated open area around the palace. The large casemate wall that surrounded the summit was attributed by them to Building Period II (Crowfoot, Kenyon, and Sukenik 1942, 11–13; Kenyon 1942, 97–100; fig. 21). Kenyon

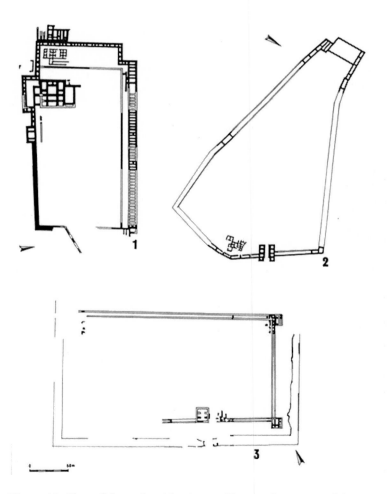

Figure 21. Plan of three Omride sites: 1. The royal compound (upper platform) at Samaria; 2. Hazor; 3. Jezreel.

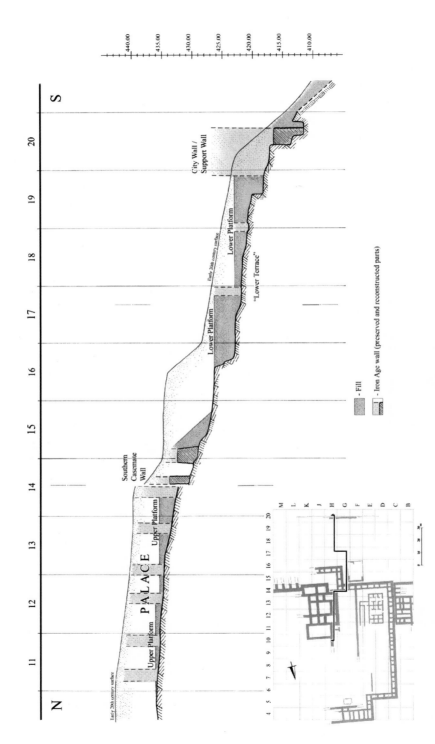

Figure 22. An architectural section through the southern side of the Acropolis and lower platform at Samaria.

Figure 23. All that can be seen today of the walls of the palace at Samaria. Note the rock scarp and the headers and stretchers building method (wall on upper left side belongs to the temple of Augustus).

described its construction as indicating a change of concept, from a royal quarter to a fortified acropolis. The casemate wall was more a support system than a real fortification. It was built in order to extend the summit and hence served as a sort of a terrace that supported a huge earth podium. A significant difference in levels, of several meters, was thus created between the inner and outer sides of the casemate wall, that is, between the slope and the platform (fig. 22). The casemates, built typically of ashlars in the headers-and-stretchers technique, were filled with earth to a considerable depth. It is not clear whether there was a superstructure on top of the casemate wall; in any event, the casemate wall did not function as a fortification, as in some places it is not built on the edge of the upper platform (see below).

The palace was built of massive, roughly dressed blocks on a solid core of rock with perpendicular scarp made by quarrying away the rock around it (Reisner, Fisher, and Lyon 1924, 61, 93–94; Franklin 2004; fig. 23). The part of the palace that was exposed (foundations of walls only) is circa 55 x 40 m in size. The Samaria palace is one of the largest Iron Age buildings known in the Levant; in scale and grandeur it matches the Iron II palaces of northern Syria (fig. 23). The palace was surrounded by several auxiliary buildings of an administrative nature on the west and northeast.

The gate of the royal enclosure was located on its eastern side, where the slope is the most moderate. Six of the seven proto-Ionic capitals uncovered at Samaria, three of them almost identical, were found in secondary use in this area. Originally they may have decorated a monumental entrance (Crowfoot, Kenyon, and Sukenik 1942, 14) similar to the (somewhat later) gate of Khirbet Mudeibi in southern Jordan (Mattingly and Pace 2007).

4.1.1.2. The Lower Platform

The southern side of the lower platform supplies the most detailed information. Towering over the Roman colonnaded street is a major earthen slope up to 20–30 m high and circa 400 m long (fig. 24). The slope is too steep and too straight in line to be considered a natural phenomenon, and it therefore should be interpreted as a man-made earthwork. The southern earthwork was probably laid along a rock scarp that can be seen popping out of the earth debris here and there. It dominates—in fact, shapes—the entire site and can be seen from afar. It is reasonable to assume that in the Iron Age the level of floors in the royal compound was roughly 10 m higher than those in the lower platform. Crowfoot, Kenyon, and Sukenik described "a sort of a gully" (1942, 50) under the colonnaded street below and to the south of the southern earthwork. This depression may have been a moat, the cutting of which could have supplied much of the material for the southern earthwork and the fills inside the lower platform.

A strong stone wall that served as part of the construction of the southern earthwork was unearthed by the Harvard Expedition team on the (top) southern edge of the lower platform (Reisner, Fisher, and Lyon 1924, 86, 121–22). Its bossed stones were set in headers and stretchers, and its foundations were sunk in a trench cut in the rock—characteristics of the method of Iron Age construction in the royal compound on the summit. Hence it is safe to attribute this element to the Iron Age building activity and identify it as part of the fortification system of the city.

In the west the elevation difference between the upper and lower platforms was circa 20 m. Here, too, the slope must have been formed by laying earth over the natural rock scarp. The distance between the casemate wall and the slope seems to indicate that the wall did not serve as an outer fortification system. The lower platform extends from the royal compound for about 70 m and ends in another prominent terrace line (fig. 24).

Figure 24. Aerial view of Samaria, looking east, indicating the extent of the lower platform (courtesy of Dubi Tal, Albatross).

In the north the extent of the lower platform is not clear because of massive construction in Roman times. The eastern side of Samaria is the most vulnerable, as the natural ridge connects here to the mound. Judging from the layout of other Omride sites (below), one can speculate that the ridge was cut in its flat, narrowest point by a moat. In the Iron Age this saddle in the ridge was much narrower than it is today; it was reshaped— leveled and filled—in Roman times.

There are two options for the date of construction of the lower platform. According to the first, in the time of the Omrides the site was limited to the royal compound; Samaria was extended to the lines of the outer, lower platform in the first half of the eighth century B.C.E., the second period of great prosperity in the northern kingdom. According to the second option, both the upper and lower platforms were constructed in the ninth century B.C.E.; in the eighth century the site would probably have extended farther down the slopes.

The first option may be supported by the fact that key Omride sites were no more than fortified administrative strongholds. Even so, as the capital of the northern kingdom, Samaria, must have presented a different case. Indeed, several circumstantial considerations lead me to prefer the second option, that the lower platform, too, was constructed in the ninth century B.C.E.

(1) The eighth-century B.C.E. city must have been larger than the circa 8 hectares of the upper and lower platforms combined, for instance compared to Jerusalem of the late eighth century, which stretched across an area of over 60 hectares, or even to Hazor, which covered roughly 12 hectares.

(2) It is logical to assume that Omride Samaria was at least as big as Omride Jezreel, which covered an area of circa 4 hectares (compared to 2.5 hectares of the royal compound at Samaria).

(3) Podium construction, with terracing, filling, and leveling, is typical of Omride architectural concepts (more below).

(4) The fact that the casemate wall of the summit was not built on the edge of the upper platform hints that it did not serve as an outer city wall. In other words, the upper platform was not protected by a fortification, and hence the city must have been defended by the wall on the edge of the lower platform.

I would suggest that the two platforms served different purposes: the upper one was the royal compound and included the palace, probably a royal shrine, official administrative buildings, and open spaces, while the lower platform functioned as the town proper, with habitation quarters for the officials who served the bureaucratic apparatus of the kingdom.

The construction of the two platforms involved the building of support walls as well as major filling operations. The result was an awe-inspiring artificial hill that could be seen from afar.

4.1.2. JEZREEL

Excavations at this site, located in the southeast of the Jezreel Valley (Ussishkin and Woodhead 1992, 1994, 1997), revealed a casemate enclosure of a grand scale and uniform plan bearing certain similarities to the Samaria enclosure. The rectangular casemate compound, with uniform towers in the corners, measures 270 x 140 m (ca. 3.8 hectares; fig. 21). Ashlars were used in only a few places. The construction aimed at creating a flat platform. A large amount of soil was dumped as a fill between the casemate wall and the center core of the hill, where the rock was quite high. The casemates were also filled with earth. The gate, located slightly to the east of the center of the southern wall, is probably of the six-chambered type (see Hazor below).

Figure 25. The moat in Jezreel (courtesy of Professor David Ussishkin, Tel Aviv University).

Two additional elements—an earthen glacis and a moat—were uncovered outside the casemate wall. The glacis sloped from the casemate wall to the edge of the moat. In the south it was 17 m long and 2.5 m thick. The lower part was stabilized by a revetment wall. Apparently it had both constructional (supportive) and defensive functions. A rock-cut moat disconnected the compound from the surrounding areas. Its total length along the eastern, southern, and western sides reaches 670 m. It was at least 8 m wide and 5 m deep (fig. 25). There was no moat in the north, where the site is naturally protected by the slope to the valley.

It is difficult to establish whether the inside of the enclosure was fully built-up. First, much of the area was badly eroded or destroyed by later occupation, especially in the west, where a medieval and Ottoman village was located. Second, the inside of the enclosure has not been sufficiently excavated. In any event, it seems reasonable to assume that it was not densely settled. Ussishkin and Woodhead suggested that a royal residence was built somewhere along the northern periphery of the enclosure, taking advantage of the pleasant view and the cool breeze. Comparing Jezreel to other ninth-century B.C.E. sites, I would suggest that the residency was located in the northwestern sector of the compound, which is also the optimum spot from the perspective of climate and view.

The Jezreel compound could have served as a breeding and training facility for horses for the strong Israelite chariot force mentioned by Shalmaneser III king of Assyria in relation to the Battle of Qarqar (Cantrell 2011). It was destroyed by Hazael king of Damascus around 840 B.C.E. and never fully recovered. Hence in the first half of the eighth century B.C.E. the horse facility of the northern kingdom was moved to Megiddo (ch. 5).

4.1.3. HAZOR

The city of Stratum X, which dates to the late Iron IIA in the ninth century, covered the western half of the upper mound. A casemate wall creates a triangular compound (fig. 21) that covers an area of approximately 2.5 hectares. Its layout was dictated by the topography of the Bronze Age mound. A six-chambered gate is located in the east, slightly to the north of the east-west axis of the compound. Its construction involved "enormous leveling operations" and filling (Yadin 1972, 137–38), which raised the gate in relation to the area to its east. Remains of two other features typical of Omride architecture—a moat and a glacis—were seemingly unearthed outside the casemate wall, but their affiliation with the Iron Age is not certain.

A citadel was built on the western tip of the mound in a later phase of the Iron Age (Stratum VIII) and continued to function until the destruction of the city in the late eighth century B.C.E. Although the citadel was not removed by the excavators, enough evidence was found to indicate that a major building stood here in Stratum X, too (Yadin 1972, 140). The space available for the supposed building is circa 20 x 30 m. The size of the building and its location on the edge of the mound, enjoying the western breeze, may indicate that it was a palace. The two beautiful proto-Ionic capitals found reused in a later stratum in this area probably decorated the Stratum VIII building, but they could have originated from the previous edifice.

Theoretically, one could suggest that Hazor X was built by King Hazael of Aram Damascus, who also built Dan (Arie 2008) and conquered large parts of the northern territories of Israel in the second half of the ninth century (Na'aman 1997a). However, the pottery assemblage of Hazor X belongs to an early phase of the late Iron IIA (Herzog and Singer-Avitz 2006) and hence should be dated to the first half of the ninth century—the time of the Omride dynasty.

4.1.4. Jahaz and Ataroth in Moab

The Mesha Inscription refers to two strongholds that were built by the Omrides in Moab east of the Dead Sea—Jahaz and Ataroth:

> and the king of Israel built Ataroth for himself. I fought against the city and took it, and I killed all the warriors. ... Now the king of Israel had built Jahaz, and he dwelt therein while he was fighting against me. But Chemosh drove him out before me. I took from Moab two hundred men, all its divisions/heads of family, and I led them against Jahaz, and captured it to annex (it) to Dibon. (lines 10–11, 18–21; translation by Na'aman 2007)

Based on the references to Jahaz in the Hebrew Bible, it should be sought to the south of Madaba, on the desert fringe, not far from Dibon (present day Dhiban). Dearman (1984, 122–25) suggested identifying it with the fortified site of Khirbet el-Mudeyine eth-Themed in Wadi el-Walla, northeast of Dibon, an identification that is now broadly accepted. Ataroth should be located close to Dibon and the Arnon River. Its name is preserved at Khirbet Atarus to the northwest of Dibon. Jahaz and Ataroth were built as the southeastern and southwestern pivots of the Omride border with Moab, facing the territory of Dibon (Dearman 1989a, 181–82; Na'aman 1997b, 89–92). Both places portray many of the characteristics known from Omride sites west of the Jordan that have been described above.

4.1.4.1. Khirbet el-Mudeyine eth-Themed = Jahaz

The site was visited by early explorers who noticed its main features, including a wide moat that encircles the mound halfway down the slope. Glueck (1934, 13) published an aerial photograph in which the site looks flat and rectangular, hinting that the top of the hill was shaped by a large podium-fill. The site has been excavated since 1996 (e.g., Daviau 2006a; Daviau and Steiner 2000; Daviau and Dion 2002). Little attention has thus far been given to the shape of the hill, the layout of the site, and the main features of its fortification. The description here is based mainly on observations made during several visits to the site.

The fortress was built on an elongated hill located inside the valley of Wadi eth-Themed. Its form, a perfect rectangle (fig. 26), indicates that the natural hill was shaped by a filling-and-leveling operation. A casemate wall "boxed" the natural hill and created the rectangle that encloses

Figure 26. Aerial view of Khirbet el-Mudeyine eth-Themed (= Jahaz). Note the rectangular shape of the compound and moat surrounding it (© David L. Kennedy, Aerial Photographic Archive for Archaeology in the Middle East [APAAME_19980520_DLK-0008], http://www.humanities.uwa.edu.au/research/cah/aerial-archaeology).

an area of 140 × 80 m (including the moat; ca. 120 × 50 m for the top of the elevated podium). The fills deposited between the slopes of the natural hill and the casemate wall must have put pressure on the wall, and thus the latter required the support of an earthen glacis, which was revealed in a section cut on the southern side of the site. The moat was dug halfway down the hill. It surrounds the site from all sides except, seemingly, the northeastern, at the approach to the gate. The outer side of the moat was lined with a stone wall, which was, in turn, supported by the continuation of the glacis. A six-chambered gate (smaller than the Hazor and Gezer gates) protrudes from the rectangle on its northeastern end. A depression to the west of the gate may indicate the location of a water-supply system.

Most structures unearthed inside the compound thus far are of a public nature, mainly a shrine near the gate and pillared houses to its south. The finds retrieved from the floors of these buildings date to the late Iron II, probably circa 600 B.C.E. (e.g., Daviau and Steiner 2000). They represent the end phase in the history of the site, on the eve of the Babylonian occupation of Moab. But when was the site founded? The fact that it was built several centuries earlier is evident from radiocarbon dates of beams from the gate, which gave a 2 SD (standard deviation) result of 810–755 B.C.E. (Daviau 2006a, 17); the beams may represent a renovation of an earlier gate. Iron IIA sherds present at the site (Daviau 2006a, 28 n. 21; 2006b, 566) indicate that it was established in the ninth century B.C.E. This isolated place did not experience destruction, apparently not even at the end of the Omride rule; Mesha makes a clear distinction between his conquests of Ataroth and of Jahaz, the latter seemingly taken without force. In other words, buildings constructed in the ninth century continued to be in use for a long period of time, until the Babylonian conquest, or structures were added in open spaces during the lifetime of the site. In short, the shaping of the hill of Khirbet Mudeyine eth-Themed and the construction of its fortification must have taken place in the Iron IIA, in the ninth century B.C.E.

4.1.4.2. Khirbet Atarus = Ataroth

The site is located on a ridge that commands a broad view to the east over the plain of Madaba, to the south, and to the west (including a stretch of the Dead Sea). A limited excavation carried out at the site in 2000 and 2001 by Ji (2002) uncovered an Iron IIA cult place that was destroyed by fire (for objects found here, see, e.g., http://www.arabnews.com/node/354248; I refer to the pictures only; the text accompanying them is inadequate). A visit to the site in January 2010 revealed that in the north it is probably covered by a post–Iron Age ruin, while in the south Iron Age remains seem to be exposed close to the surface.

The site is shaped as a flat, elevated rectangle. This is best seen in an aerial photograph (fig. 27). The size of the rectangle is circa 155 × 90 m (as measured on Google Earth) and is approximately 5 m higher than the area around it. The shape is similar to that of Khirbet el-Mudeyine eth-Themed, but the latter seems to be somewhat smaller in size (as probably dictated by the natural hill). In the south, a well-preserved wall marks the edge of the podium. Remains of a similar wall can be seen on the western side. Without excavation, it is impossible to verify the nature of the wall (and whether it was supported by a glacis on the outside). In the north and east, the edge of the podium is more difficult to discern.

As already observed by the early explorer Musil (1907, 395–96), the most striking feature of the site is a rock-cut moat that is clearly seen on two or three sides of the rectangle. In the south (fig. 28) and west the moat is circa 4 m wide. In one place the exposed vertical cut is circa 3 m deep (the rest is filled with earth). It seems that there was no moat in the east, probably because on this side the podium ends in a relatively steep slope.

The layout of Khirbet Atarus—a rectangular, elevated compound surrounded by a rock-cut moat on three sides and protected by a steep slope on the fourth—is identical to the Omride compound in Jezreel.

4.1.5. TELL ER-RUMEITH IN THE GILEAD

Tell er-Rumeith is located in the northeastern Gilead, in the plateau to the east of the modern Jordanian city of Irbid. Based on their name, this site and the town of Ramtha, located 7 km to its north, were suggested as alternative locations to biblical Ramoth-gilead, the place of a major battle between Israel and Aram Damascus in the ninth century B.C.E. (for the biblical references, see ch. 5; for identification, see Glueck 1943; Knauf 2001a). Both sites are strategically located near the junction of the King's Highway, which runs along the Transjordanian plateau to Damascus, and the west-east road from the Jordan Valley to the desert.

Tell er-Rumeith was excavated in the 1960s by Paul Lapp (1963; N. L. Lapp 1993), who uncovered a small square fort roughly 40 x 40 m. Lapp identified several phases of construction, one of which "involved the creation of a platform ... leveling off the area with debris"; he also recorded several destruction layers. His description, translated to what we know

Figure 27. Google Earth view of Khirbet Atarus in Moab.

Figure 28. The rock-cut moat in Khirbet Atarus.

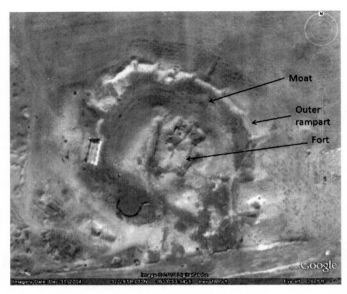

Figure 29. Google Earth view of Tell er-Rumeith in northwestern
Jordan, indicating a square elevated podium surrounded by a moat.

today about Iron Age pottery and the absolute dating of the different
ceramic phases of the Iron Age, makes it clear that the site was active in the
ninth century B.C.E. and that it suffered destructions at that time. The finds
of Lapp's excavations have not been published, and hence it is difficult to
evaluate their archaeological and historical significance.

Lapp did not notice two important features of the site: (1) that the fort
was constructed on an elevated podium; and (2) that it is surrounded by a
broad moat (fig. 29), which was surrounded in turn, on its outer side, by
an earthen rampart (Finkelstein, Lipschits, and Sergi 2013). The moat and
the rampart resemble similar elements at Khirbet Mudeyine eth-Themed
in Moab (glacis in the latter).

Whether this is the location of Ramoth-gilead or not, the site must
have played an important role in the struggle between Israel and Aram
Damascus in northern Transjordan in the days of the Omride dynasty.

4.1.6. OTHER SITES

Several additional sites in the territory of the northern kingdom display
architectural features similar to ones described above.

At Gezer a six-chambered gate and a section of a casemate wall belong to Stratum VIII, which dates to the early ninth century B.C.E. The gate (Dever et al. 1971, 112–20; Ortiz and Wolf 2012) was built of fine masonry, with ashlars at the jambs. The casemate wall was uncovered on both sides of the gate, to a total length of approximately 70 m. The construction of the gate and the casemate wall involved the levelling of a terrace on the hillside and the import of a massive fill. Away from the area of the gate, the contour of the Stratum VIII casemate wall is not clear.

At En Gev on the eastern shore of the Sea of Galilee, a casemate fortress was erected on a podium. It was apparently protected by a glacis. The fort, estimated to be approximately 60 x 60 m in size, was dated to 950–790 (B. Mazar et al. 1964) or 945–886 (B. Mazar 1993). In the radiocarbon-dictated absolute chronology used here, this means that the fort was built in the ninth century B.C.E. (for recent excavations and date of the casemate fortress in the ninth century B.C.E., see Hasegawa and Paz 2009).

At Har Adir in the mountainous Upper Galilee, an 80 x 80 m casemate fortress protected by a strong glacis was uncovered in the 1970s and never published. According to Ilan (1999), the pottery from the fort is contemporary with that retrieved in Stratum X at Hazor; if so, it dates to the late Iron IIA in the ninth century B.C.E. It is possible that meager remains of a somewhat similar fort were uncovered in the 1950s at Tel Harashim, also located in the Upper Galilee, 8 km to the southwest of Har Adir (Ben Ami 2004).

4.1.7. SUMMARY: CHARACTERISTICS OF OMRIDE ARCHITECTURE

It seems that the Omrides used similar architectural methods on both sides of the Jordan River. It is impossible to identify the Israelite king who built Jahaz and Ataroth, but the most probable guess is Ahab, in whose days the northern kingdom seems to have reached its peak military power, economic prosperity, and territorial expansion.

The sites described above show clear similarities in the following architectural concepts (for details, see Finkelstein 2000; Finkelstein and Lipschits 2010):

- *Construction of a podium*: artificially shaping a hill by leveling and filling operations aimed at the construction of an elevated platform. Elevated podia are best known from Samaria, Jezreel, and the two sites in Moab.

- *Casemate compound*: the best examples are known from Samaria, Jezreel, Hazor, and Khirbet el-Mudeyine eth-Themed. The area surrounded by the casemates measures between circa 0.5 hectare (Khirbet el-Mudeyine eth-Themed) and 3.8 hectares (Jezreel). The Omride compounds were either rectangular (Samaria, Jezreel, Khirbet el-Mudeyine eth-Themed) or irregular, adapted to the shape of the hill (Hazor).
- *Gate*: The similarity of the Hazor and Gezer gates in both plan and size was noted by Yadin long ago (1958). The Jezreel gate should be added to the list of ninth-century six-chambered gates (Ussishkin and Woodhead 1997, 12–23). These gates are almost identical in size. A smaller six-chambered gate was uncovered at Khirbet el-Mudeyine eth-Themed in Moab.
- *Moat and glacis*: elaborate rock-cut moats surrounded the compounds of Jezreel and Khirbet Atarus in Moab on three sides. A glacis supported the casemate walls at Jezreel, Khirbet el-Mudeyine eth-Themed, and probably Samaria.

In each case these elements, or some of them, were adjusted to the special characteristics of the site. Most of these sites served as royal and administrative centers or border fortresses rather than standard towns. They were devoted to public buildings and had large open spaces. Very little was found that attests to domestic quarters.

Most features characteristic of Omride architecture were known in the Levant before the Iron II. The casemate wall and rock-cut moat are interesting cases, because they are known in Transjordan in the Iron I.[1] The earliest prototype of a casemate wall in the Iron Age Levant was uncovered at middle Iron I Tell el-Umeiri (Herr and Clark 2009; for the date, see Finkelstein 2011e). More developed casemate walls are known in the late Iron I sites in southern Moab; some of the latter also feature short rock-cut moats (Routledge 2008, 146, 151; Finkelstein and Lipschits 2011). A developed casemate wall is known in late Iron I/very early Iron IIA Khirbet Qeiyafa in the Judahite Shephelah (Garfinkel and Ganor 2009).

Two comments are in place before closing this discussion. (1) The appearance of these architectural features is not completely unique to

---

1. An elaborate Late Bronze casemate wall has recently been uncovered at Tell ez-Zira' in Jordan (Vieweger and Häser 2007). This find is beyond the scope of the current discussion.

Omride sites. They are also known, for example, at Arair (biblical Aroer), probably a late ninth- or eighth-century B.C.E. Moabite fort guarding the King's Highway where it crosses the canyon of Wadi Mujib (the biblical Arnon; Finkelstein and Lipschits 2010). However, the architectural concept that includes the entire complex described above has not been found thus far in any early ninth-century (or earlier) site outside the borders of the northern kingdom.

(2) The layout of the late Iron IIA town at Megiddo (Stratum VA–IVB) shows both similarities to—and differences from—the sites discussed here. On the one hand, a detailed analysis of the two Megiddo palaces (for their publication, see Lamon and Shipton 1939, 11–24; Yadin 1970; Cline 2006) reveals certain similarities to the ninth-century architectural features described above, especially the use of ashlar masonry. On the other hand, unlike Samaria, Jezreel, and Hazor, the site lacks the typical layout of a raised podium with casemate compound. Other ninth-century B.C.E. towns in the territory of the northern kingdom, such as Jokneam and Tirzah, do not display the characteristics of monumental Omride architecture either. These features appear mainly at administrative sites (or fortresses) newly built by the Omrides or at sites that had been small villages or lay abandoned before their time.

4.2. The Territory Ruled by the Omrides

The Elijah-Elisha cycle in Kings contains genuine material about the northern kingdom at the time of the Omride dynasty, for instance, regarding Jezreel, the end of the dynasty, and the assault of Hazael king of Damascus on Israel (Schniedewind 1996; Na'aman 1997a, 2000). The stories are told against the background of a relatively detailed geography. They are focused on the Jezreel Valley and its vicinity, with no mention of Israelite sites further to the north. Sites mentioned are Jezreel, Shunem, Mount Carmel, Megiddo, Beth-haggan (Jenin?), and Ibleam (located on the road connecting the Jezreel and Dothan Valleys). Places such as Hazor, Dan, Ijon, and Abel-beth-maacah—or sites in the hilly Galilee referred to in the (much later) list of towns of Naphtali in Josh 19—are not mentioned (see also Kuan 2001, 143–44). Regardless of the chronological order of the ninth-century B.C.E. clashes between Israel and Aram Damascus referred to in the Bible (e.g., Miller 1966; Lipiński 2000, 375, 378, 397–99), none of them took place north of the Sea of Galilee and the Gilead. Therefore, from the perspective of the biblical text, there is no reason to assume that the Omrides expanded to areas north of the Jezreel Valley and the Gilead.

The Tel Dan Stela may reveal a different reality. In lines 3–4, the author of the inscription, King Hazael of Damascus, states that "the king of Israel entered previously in my father's land," probably meaning that before his days an Israelite king had conquered territories that he (Hazael) conceived as legitimately belonging to Damascus. Who could that king of Israel have been, and what were these territories? A review of the geopolitical situation before Hazael reveals that the expansion of an Israelite king into Damascene territories could not have occurred when Israel and Damascus collaborated against Assyria, that is, prior to the Battle of Qarqar in 853 B.C.E. Hence, the most logical time would be in post-Ahab days, possibly during the reign of Joram, a short while before the accession of Hazael to power. The territories to which Hazael refers could have been the Jordan Valley north of the Sea of Galilee around Hazor, and even further to the north if one reconstructs the opening lines of the Dan Inscription (line 2) as evidence that the king of Israel fought Hazael's predecessor at Abel-beth-maacah (e.g., Biran and Naveh 1995, 13; Schniedewind 1996, 79; Na'aman 2000; needless to say, the name Abel-beth-maacah refers to an Aramean town). Another possibility that cannot be ruled out is that Hazael points to Omride expansion into what he considered Damascene territories in the northeast Gilead. This may explain the location of the decisive battle between Aram and Israel at Ramoth-gilead, probably in the days of Joram (842 B.C.E.; ch. 5).

Archaeology tells the story in clearer terms (fig. 18). As shown above, Stratum X at Hazor, which dates to the early days of the late Iron IIA in the first half of the ninth century (Sharon et al. 2007; Finkelstein and Piasetzky 2009, 2010), features Omride architectural characteristics. Of course, one can argue that similar architectural elements were deployed by Israel's neighbors, including Damascus. Aramean affiliation of the inhabitants of Hazor X may be indicated by the fact that Hebrew replaced Aramaic in the (few) Hazor inscriptions only in the eighth century B.C.E. (Sass 2005, 85–86). Still, the Hazor evidence is based on five fragmentary inscriptions, and the language of the Hazor inhabitants does not necessarily indicate the identity of the ruling power there. More important, Dan and Bethsaida, which present Aramean characteristics in the later (terminal) phase of the Iron IIA (the late ninth century B.C.E.), do not show the typical Omride features (more below). I therefore see no alternative to the Omride identity of Hazor X.

Archaeology seems to provide a similar clue for the mountainous Upper Galilee. I refer to the fortress of Har Adir, possibly to another fortress at Tel Harashim, which display Omride architectural features. Who could have built a strong casemate fortress supported by a glacis at isolated and remote Har Adir in the ninth century B.C.E.? The only possibility except for the Omrides is Tyre. However, taking a long-term perspective on the territorial history of the region, there can be no doubt that the Upper Galilee always belonged to territorial entities/administrative divisions to its south and southeast, while Tyre ruled only over the lower hilly areas to its east and southeast (there is a clear topographic border between the two units). This was so in Roman-Byzantine times as well as in the Crusader, Mamluk, and Ottoman periods (details in Finkelstein 1981). In short, Tyre never ruled in the Upper Galilee, and hence the only possibility for the construction of the Har Adir fortress is the Omride kingdom. The fort of Har Adir must have been built by the kings of the northern kingdom as a center of control over the wooded, sparsely inhabited Upper Galilee, facing the territory of Tyre in the west. The coastal plain and low hills north of Acco were probably in Phoenician hands. The ninth-century farmhouse of Horvat Rosh Zayit (Gal and Alexandre 2000) was seemingly located in Phoenician territory. The legendary narrative of Solomon's transfer of the district of Cabul to Hiram king of Tyre (1 Kgs 9:10–13) should probably be interpreted as an etiological story that explains why, in late monarchic times, areas in the western Galilee were held by the kingdom of Tyre.

Regarding the north, we are left with the question of the boundary between Israel and Damascus in the area of the Sea of Galilee. The casemate fortress of En Gev is pivotal for the answer to this question: Who built the fortress—a northern kingdom king or an Aramean ruler? A possible answer comes from the comparison between En Gev and nearby Bethsaida, the latter located at the northern tip of the Sea of Galilee. The fortifications of Bethsaida are similar to those of Tel Dan. Both are surrounded by a solid (rather than casemate) city wall with offsets and insets, and both are equipped with similar, exceptionally broad, four-chambered city gates. Aramean elements were found at both sites near the gate: two basalt column bases (and possibly the Dan Stela) at Tel Dan and a stela with a representation of the moon-god at Bethsaida (Biran 1994; Bernett and Keel 1998, respectively). The casemate on a fill at En Gev, on the other hand, resembles the architecture of Hazor X and Har Adir. It is reasonable, therefore, to affiliate En Gev with the northern kingdom. This is possibly the place of Aphek mentioned in 1 Kgs 20:26–30 as the location of the battle between Israel and Aram. This description seems to depict post-Omride events that took place in the days of Joash king of Israel (e.g., Lipiński 2000, 397; ch. 5).

The biblical account of the battle of Ramoth-gilead (1 Kgs 22; 2 Kgs 8:28–29; 9:1, 4, 14), which took place in the days of Joram (ch. 5), seems to record a genuine memory of a devastating clash during the end days of the Omride dynasty, in 842 B.C.E. (e.g., Dion 1997, 191–200; Lipiński 2000, 377–83). This memory provides a clue for Omride rule in the plateau of the northeastern Gilead. The question is: Who ruled in Ramoth-gilead? Locating a stronghold there, on the road from southern Transjordan to Damascus, is in line with the Omride construction of two fortresses in Moab, north of the Arnon River. The control of the King's Highway could have served economic goals, such as domination over the flow of copper from Khirbet en-Nahas far to the south of the Dead Sea (see below).

The question of the western boundary of the Omrides must focus on Dor. In this case archaeology has not provided conclusive data, so one needs to rely on the documentary evidence. Dor is mentioned in the list of Solomonic districts (1 Kgs 4:11), a document that must represent eighth-century B.C.E. realities under Assyrian or (earlier) north Israelite rule (Na'aman 2001; Finkelstein and Silberman 2006a, respectively). In the first half of the eighth century Dor was an Israelite city, and it is only logical to assume that Israelite rule there had been established in the ninth century. Dor was strongly connected by maritime trade to Phoenicia (Stern 2000; Gilboa 2005) and must have served as the main maritime gate of the northern kingdom. The fact that Ahab married a Phoenician princess (1 Kgs 16:31) testifies to the close commercial interests of the northern kingdom on the coast and in Phoenicia.

Turning to the southwest, Gezer is located on what was the boundary between Israel and Philisita. It must have been the Israelite logistical center for the two sieges of nearby Gibbethon in the early days of the kingdom (1 Kgs 15:27; 16:15–17). The mention of Gibbethon of all places—not one of the major cities on the coastal plain—lends historical credibility to these accounts. The appearance of Omride architectural features in Stratum VIII at Gezer, which dates to the ninth century B.C.E., may provide the archaeological reality behind this geopolitical situation.

The southern border of the northern kingdom ran south of the important Israelite cult center of Bethel. In fact, the Israel-Judah border probably passed farther south, nearer to Jerusalem, as Mizpah seems to have changed hands from Israel to Judah only in the second half of the ninth century B.C.E. (ch. 2). Israel dominated Judah, and the Omrides probably attempted to take over the southern kingdom from within by marrying an Omride princess (Athaliah) to an heir of the Davidic family (2 Kgs 8:18, 26). In the southeast, Jericho was in the hands of the north, as indicated by the reference to its construction in the time of Ahab (1 Kgs 16:34) and some prophetic stories (2 Kgs 2:4–5, 18–22). It served to protect the important road that connected Bethel with northern Moab. In other words, there was hardly a means of ruling in Moab without having an anchor at Jericho.

To sum up, the most important point regarding territory is to fix the boundary of Omride rule in the north. At that time the northern kingdom expanded its territory far beyond the Jezreel Valley, into the Lower Galilee and the southern part of the Upper Galilee, into the area of the Sea of Galilee, and into the Jordan Valley as far north as Hazor. It did not rule farther to the north at Dan and its surroundings (Arie 2008); in the first half of the ninth century, Dan was deserted.

The architectural program of the Omrides seems to have been conceived in order to serve their territorial ambitions: casemate forts or administrative centers were built on the borders of the kingdom (figs. 18, 19): Har Adir (and possibly Tel Harashim) facing Tyre; Hazor and En Gev facing the territory of Aram Damascus; Ramoth-gilead opposite Aram Damascus in the Bashan; Jahaz and Ataroth facing Moabite Dibon; and Gezer facing the Philistine city-states. Except for the capital Samaria, only Jezreel seems to have been located in the heartland of Israel. The Omride compound there could have been erected as a center of command in the demographically Canaanite valley and as a military post related to the chariot force of the kingdom (Cantrell 2011).

4.3. Demographic Composition of the Omride Kingdom

What were the resources of the northern kingdom that facilitated such large-scale public works? The first is population: Israel was densely populated, which enabled the deployment of large working forces without jeopardizing agricultural output. Estimation of population is based on the results of surface surveys; if done properly, the collection of pottery sherds at a given site can shed light on the size of the site in every period of habitation. Accordingly, one can draw a settlement map for a given period with all sites, classified according to size, and compute the total built-up area. Deploying a density coefficient (number of people living on one built-up hectare in premodern, traditional towns and villages), it is possible to reach the total number of inhabitants. The population of Israel on both sides of the Jordan River in its peak prosperity in the middle of the eighth century can accordingly be estimated at 350,000—three times larger than the population of Judah of that time (Broshi and Finkelstein 1992).

But who were these people? The special demographic structure of the northern kingdom, especially the relationship between "Israelites" in the highlands and "Canaanites" in the lowlands, has been discussed by a considerable number of scholars. Northern Israel was a multifaceted kingdom made up of several different ecosystems and a heterogeneous population, though all groups were indigenous to Canaan. The highlands of Samaria—the core territory of the kingdom and the seat of the capital—featured a settlement system that had its roots in the sedentarization of pastoral groups in the Iron I. In the northern lowlands—the Jezreel and the Jordan Valleys—the population was made up of a mix of the local descendants of late second-millennium groups and ex-highlanders; as demonstrated in chapter 1, there was an impressive settlement and cultural continuity in the Late Bronze/Iron I transition in the northern valleys, and although the late Iron I cities came to a brutal end in devastating conflagrations, the rural sector—or at least part of it—seems to have survived. In the northeast, Israel bordered on another emerging power: Aram Damascus. Throughout the Iron II the population in this region was at least partially Aramean. This seems to be demonstrated by the meager though significant epigraphic material, that is, the Aramaic inscriptions found in central sites in this region: Hazor, Dan, Bethsaida, Tel Hadar, and En Gev (e.g., Yadin et al. 1960, 70–75). The strong Aramean presence in the Beth-shean Valley is seen in the material culture, especially inscriptions, of Tel Rehov (A. Mazar and Ahituv 2011). Another area where the distinction between Arameans and Israelites was not very clear is the northeastern Gilead, and this is reflected in the Gen 31:45–48 tradition about the establishment of the boundary stone between Israel and Aram in this region. As for southern Transjordan, the reference in the Mesha Stela to Gad as apparently belonging to the local Moabite population (Na'aman 2000; a different interpretation in Lemaire 2007) seems to demonstrate that at least at that time the ethnic line between "Israelites" and "Moabites" in the area of Madaba was fluid. Finally, the highlands of the Galilee and the territory bordering on the northern coastal plain must have been at least partially inhabited by groups related to the Phoenician coastal cities.

This demographic and cultural diversity of the northern kingdom may indicate that, in addition to the administrative and military roles of the monumental architecture activities of the Omrides, there was another, less-functional need. State-establishing dynasties that engage in territorial expansion into neighboring lands do so seeking legitimacy. They also seek to pacify the population and secure its loyalty. In the case of the Omrides, this was especially important, since at the same time competing kingdoms emerged in neighboring Damascus and Moab. This was therefore the moment when territorial boundaries had to be defined. The peripheral territories could have been won by military power, but this would have been insufficient to maintain long-term stability. The ongoing territorial disputes in the northeast, in the vicinity of Hazor and Dan, which are manifested both textually (the Tel Dan Stela) and archaeologically (destruction layers in these and other sites), demonstrate this point. Controlling the population of the "Canaanite" valley and the border areas in the north and east must have been the most important task of the Omrides. Israel's need to secure its grip over the northern valleys also had a practical dimension, as these regions became the backbone of the economy of northern Israel. Whoever controlled the valleys could profit from their agricultural output, could utilize their manpower for further military exploits, and could dominate some of the most important trade routes in the Levant.

The construction of strongholds in the Jezreel Valley, on the border with Aram Damascus, in Moab, and in the mountainous Galilee should therefore be seen against the backdrop of several objectives. First, these strongholds functioned as administrative centers and fortresses close to the borders of the Omride kingdom. Second, they aimed at dominating the "non-Israelite" (that is, in fact, non-highlands) populations of the kingdom. Third, they must have served the propaganda and legitimacy needs of a dynasty ruling from the highlands. According to Williamson (1996), the building of Jezreel in the valley should be seen in terms of the Omrides' need for social control and their search for legitimacy. The idea was to overawe, even intimidate, the local population. The building activities in Moab carried with them a message of power and domination that was probably aimed at impressing both the populations of the Plain of Madaba and the Dibon territory further to the south. They demonstrated the great administrative, engineering, and human resources capabilities of the Omrides.

Monumental building activities for both actual needs and propaganda were not enough, however, for stability and prosperity. They must have been complemented by clever policies vis-à-vis the rural, "Canaanite" population. The settlement stability in the rural sector of the Jezreel Valley is an indication that the Israelite monarchs did not attempt to revolutionize the rural system in the northern lowlands.

It is noteworthy that Judah never established similar standard monumental architecture, not even in the late eighth century B.C.E., when it became a fully developed kingdom, or in the seventh century B.C.E., when it reached its cultural zenith. Judah was never in need of such a show of monarchic power, as its highlands (and Shephelah) population was homogeneous. But even if it had wanted to, it did not have the economic or demographic resources to engage in such monumental construction endeavors. The same holds true for the fringe kingdoms of the Transjordanian plateau. They, too, lacked the preconditions extant in northern Israel: sufficient economic and demographic resources and the need to establish effective rule over territories inhabited by diverse population groups. The only parallel to the Omrides seems to be contemporary Aram Damascus, which must have competed with Israel for the loyalty of the population of the border areas between the two kingdoms and over hegemony in the region. Indeed, at least two northern sites that can be identified as Aramean—Dan and Bethsaida—feature monumental, unified architecture in the late Iron IIA, probably in the second half of the ninth century following the Hazael conquests (ch. 5).

4.4. Economic Resources of the Omrides

The northern kingdom enjoyed several specific economic advantages that must have boosted its economy. Its strong olive-oil and wine output is reflected in the somewhat later Samaria ostraca, which date to the first half of the eighth century B.C.E. (Niemann 2008 and bibliography). Indeed, sites in the highlands provide evidence of an intense olive-oil industry. Olive-oil presses dating to the Iron Age have been recorded in surveys and excavations (Eitam 1979). Those found in surveys are difficult to date to a specific phase of the Iron Age, but it is logical to assume that this industry, which had probably flourished as early as the Iron I, expanded in the Iron IIA–B.[2] Israel could have been a major supplier of olive oil to both Egypt

---

2. Note that at least in the urban centers of the northern valleys, elaborately built olive-oil presses are known as early as the Late Bronze Age (Frankel 2006).

and the Assyrian Empire, which lacked the environmental conditions for developed, large-scale olive-orchards.

Khirbet en-Nahas south of the Dead Sea was the largest and most important copper source in the Levant (Levy et al. 2004, 867; Hauptmann 2007, 127; fig. 30). Production there reached a peak in the late tenth and early ninth centuries B.C.E., which includes the days of the Omride dynasty (fig. 31). At that time demand for copper was high—for the military build-up (weaponry and devices for chariots) in Assyria and the kingdoms of the Levant. The mention of thousands of chariots in relation to the Battle of Qarqar in 853 B.C.E. provides good testimony for this development. Khirbet en-Nahas must have supplied much of this copper; trade relations with Cyprus—the most important source of copper in the eastern Mediterranean—had almost ceased in the late twelfth century and seemingly resumed only in the second half of the ninth century B.C.E. The Khirbet en-Nahas copper must have flowed to the north, along the King's Highway in Transjordan, and to the west, to Egypt and the coastal plain. The King's Highway was dominated by the Omride fortresses in Moab and the Gilead, and the coastal plain was ruled by Gezer and the port of Dor. This means that Israel must have been the most significant beneficiary of the copper industry and trade in the Levant.

Chariot forces needed large, strong Egyptian horses. Therefore, horses for the significant chariot contingents of both Assyria and the kingdoms of the Levant—mentioned by Shalmaneser III king of Assyria regarding the Battle of Qarqar—must have originated from Egypt. In the early eighth century B.C.E., before the Assyrian expansion to the south, Israel was the main supplier of Egyptian horses to the north. This is testified by the large-scale horse facility at Megiddo and hinted at by ancient Near Eastern texts and by the Hebrew Bible (Cantrell 2006, 2011; Cantrell and Finkelstein 2006; ch. 5). The dedication of Megiddo, a prime real-estate location of the northern kingdom, to the breeding and training of horses hints at the high economic value of this industry. The mention of a large Israelite chariot contingent in the Battle of Qarqar testifies that this must have been the situation already in the ninth century B.C.E. The training facility of that time could have been located at Jezreel (Cantrell 2011, 112–13).

4.5. WRITING

One can expect large-scale building activities such as the ones carried out at Samaria, Jezreel, and the other Omride sites and a prosperous economy to be accompanied by an advanced bureaucratic apparatus, including writing, yet evidence of writing in the entire region in the early ninth century is sparse. In fact, not a single early ninth-century B.C.E. inscription has thus far been found in the heartland of Israel—at Samaria, Jez-

Figure 30. General view of the copper production site of Khirbet en-Nahas in Jordan, south of the Dead Sea.

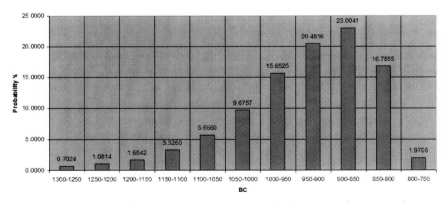

Figure 31. Intensity of copper production at Khirbet en-Nahas according to number of radiocarbon determinations.

reel, Megiddo, Yokneam, and Taanach (Finkelstein and Sass forthcoming). Daily administration related to the recording of agricultural output is evident in Israel only in the first half of the eighth century B.C.E., first and foremost in the Samaria ostraca. One may argue that in the ninth century, before the burgeoning of writing, most scribal activity was carried out on papyrus and parchment. However, the lack of significant testimony for writing is also evident in royal inscriptions. Monumental inscriptions, including those commemorating building activities, appeared only in the second half of the ninth century, for example, the Mesha and Tel Dan inscriptions (Sass 2005). Future research can, of course, change this picture, but with the material at hand it seems that literacy and scribal activity during the time of the Omrides was weak at most. Archaeology supplies examples for strong kingdoms that engaged in significant building projects with no widespread literacy. Speaking about Canaan, one may note the immense construction undertaken at Megiddo at the end of the Early Bronze I, close to 3000 B.C.E., or the erection of huge earthen ramparts in the Middle Bronze Age (Adams, Finkelstein, and Ussishkin forthcoming; Burke 2008, respectively).

4.6. CULT

One more piece of evidence hints at the still somewhat formative nature of the northern kingdom even in the period of the Omride dynasty. I refer to cult. Regardless of the identity of the deities that were worshiped in northern shrines (see, e.g., Köckert 2010), in the ninth century cult had not yet been centralized, seemingly not even at a given site. Archaeological evidence of cult at Samaria is lacking, and the same holds true for Jezreel. A cult place was unearthed at Khirbet Atarus in Moab, but the finds have not yet been published. Pictures in a press release (http://www.arabnews.com/node/354248; I refer to the pictures only; the text accompanying them is inadequate) and a visit to the Madaba Museum, where the finds are stored, reveal that they probably date to the Iron IIA. Whether they come from the Omride layer or from a late ninth-century Moabite activity at the site after the withdrawal of the Omrides, and whether this is the cult place of Atarot referred to in the Mesha Inscription, is impossible to say at this stage. Local, rural cult places were discovered at Taanach and Tel Amal near Beth-shean. The two elaborate Taanach cult stands—one unearthed at the beginning of the twentieth century and the other in the late 1960s—

Figure 32 (right). Ninth-century B.C.E. cult stand from Taanach depicting strong second-millennium traditions (courtesy of the Staff Archaeological Officer in the Civil Administration of Judea and Samaria; Photo © The Israel Museum, Jerusalem).

Figure 33 (below). Cult room with two standing stones uncovered at Megiddo in the 1920s in an early ninth-century context near the gate (Loud 1948, 46).

demonstrate strong connections to second-millennium art and cult practices (Beck 1994; fig. 32).

Megiddo provides the best testimony for the cult practices in the northern kingdom during the time of the Omride dynasty. The central temple that served the population of Megiddo during the second millennium—from the Middle Bronze through the Late Bronze and until the late Iron I—was destroyed with the entire city in the early tenth century B.C.E. The Israelite town of the late Iron IIA features several small, local cult places in different quarters of the town. The Oriental Institute team unearthed a small shrine in a domestic complex near the gate (fig. 33); a cache of cult items, including stone altars, was uncovered in the southeastern sector of the mound; Schumacher uncovered a cult room in the eastern sector of the site; and the current expedition discovered what seems to be evidence of the existence of a cult place in the southern part of the settlement. It is noteworthy that cult corners of this type do not exist at Megiddo in the Iron IIB. Indeed, a certain process of cult centralization apparently took place in Israel in the eighth century B.C.E. (ch. 5).

The economic prosperity and military might of the northern kingdom was short-lived. The rise of Hazael to the throne of Damascus in 842 B.C.E. and the temporary weakening of Assyria brought about a change in the pendulum of power in the Levant—the decline of the northern kingdom and the rise of Damascus to prominence.

5

THE FINAL CENTURY OF THE NORTHERN KINGDOM

The international scene changed dramatically in the second half of the ninth century. Hazael ascended the throne in Damascus around 842 B.C.E. (Lemaire 1991) and immediately thereafter began expanding his power in the Levant. It became possible to fulfill his ambitions as a result of the decline in Assyrian interest in the west. Shalmaneser III carried out campaigns against Damascus and may have reached the Mediterranean in 841 B.C.E. (for details, see, e.g., Younger 2007). But these were the last acts of the empire in this region for several decades to come.

5.1. HAZAEL'S ASSAULTS ON THE NORTHERN KINGDOM

Immediately after his accession to the throne, Hazael assaulted the northern kingdom. The clashes between Israel and Aram in the ninth century are documented both archaeologically and textually (Na'aman 1997a). Archaeologically, there is evidence of destruction in practically all major late Iron IIA layers of the northern kingdom in the valleys. I refer to the end of Hazor IX, Megiddo VA–IVB, Yokneam XIV, Jezreel, and Taanach IIB. Before proceeding, we need to look at the dates of these destructions and identify those that can be affiliated with Hazael's attacks. This can be done with the help of a large number of radiocarbon determinations from these and other sites.

5.1.1. FOUR LATE IRON IIA DESTRUCTION HORIZONS IN THE NORTH

Destruction layers provide an excellent opportunity for radiocarbon dating. This is so because of the large amount of organic material found in them and also because it can be assumed that all short-lived samples, such as carbonized grain and olive pits, come from a single event in the history of the site—the moment of destruction or the last months/a few years before this event. Six sites in the north provide samples from late Iron IIA destruction layers; three of them produce samples from superimposed strata, a fact that helps reaching nuanced results. The date for the latest destruction layer at Tel Rehov in the Beth-shean Valley (Stratum IV) is 92 uncalibrated years earlier than the early (lower) of two conflagration layers at nearby Tell el-Hammah. Since this difference is more than four standard deviations apart, the two can hardly be contemporaneous. A minimum of four late Iron IIA destruction horizons can accordingly be detected in the northern valleys: the early and late Tel Rehov and the early and late Tell el-Hammah destruction layers (Finkelstein and Piasetzky 2009). Other conflagrations in the north can then be associated with one of the four Tel Rehov–Tel Hammah sequenced destructions (table 3). Of course, devastations in a given horizon could have occurred together or within an interval of a few years.

Table 3: Four radiocarbon-dated Late Iron IIA destruction horizons in the north

Stratum	Rounded dates B.C.E. (68 percent probability)*
Rehov V	895–870
Rehov IV	875–850
Hammah lower, Hazor IX (Megiddo VA-IVB?) + Tell es-Safi IV in the south	830–800
Hammah upper	800–780

* Finkelstein and Piasetzky 2007; for a Bayesian model with slightly different dates, see Finkelstein and Piasetzky 2009.

The destruction layers in question cover about one hundred years, broadly speaking, in the ninth century B.C.E. The earliest in the sequence, Rehov V, can be affiliated with the conflicts between Israel and the Arameans at the time of the Omride dynasty or can be sought even somewhat earlier. The destruction of Rehov IV probably took place earlier than the accession of Hazael in 842 B.C.E. The devastation of this settlement can also be interpreted against the background of possible early conflicts between Israel and Aram Damascus. These conflicts are hinted at in the text of the

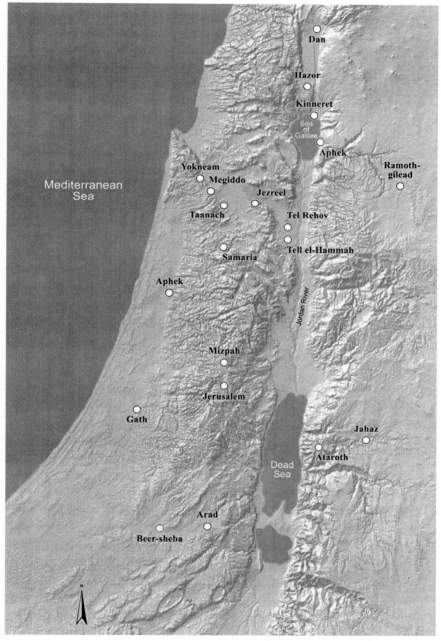

Figure 34. Sites mentioned in chapter 5 in relation to the days of Hazael in the second half of the ninth century B.C.E.

Tel Dan Stela, in which Hazael complains that "the king of Israel entered previously in my father's land" (Biran and Naveh 1995; see below).

The third destruction horizon—that of the lower stratum at Tell el-Hammah and Hazor IX further north—is radiocarbon dated to circa 830–800 B.C.E.; this is the only conflagration horizon among the four that fits Hazael's reign (ca. 842–800 B.C.E.). New radiocarbon dates from Megiddo (Toffolo et al. forthcoming) seem to show that it was put to the torch at the same time. It is reasonable to assume that nearby Jokneam and Taanach were also destroyed at the same time. In the south, the destruction of late Iron IIA Tell es-Safi (biblical Gath) should also be affiliated with the campaigns of Hazael; his conquest of Gath is reported in 2 Kgs 12:18 and hinted at by the prophet Amos (6:2), references that are considered historically reliable (Maeir 2004).

The upper destruction at Tell el-Hammah is radiocarbon dated to approximately 800–780 B.C.E. This conflagration layer seems to represent events related to the counterattack of Israel against Aram Damascus, which commenced in the days of King Joash circa 800 B.C.E. (2 Kgs 13:25; more below) following the weakening of Damascus by Adad-nirari III king of Assyria (e.g., Miller and Hayes 1986, 289–302; Lemaire 1993; Lipiński 2000, 395) and continued in the days of Jeroboam II (Briend 1981; 2 Kgs 14:25–28).

5.1.2. The Textual Evidence

Hazael's attack is referred to in several texts in the Hebrew Bible (e.g., 2 Kgs 10:32–33; 13:3, 22) and in the Tel Dan Inscription (Na'aman 1997a; Lipiński 2000, 377–83). The momentous affair of the killing of Joram king of Israel and Ahaziah king of Judah in one event is mentioned by both sources. The Hebrew Bible says that they were killed in the course of the Jehu revolt (2 Kgs 9), while the Tel Dan Stela recounts that this had been done by Hazael: "[I killed Jeho]ram son of [Ahab] king of Israel, and [I] killed [Ahaz]iahu son of [Jehoram kin]g of the House of David" (Biran and Naveh 1995; for possible explanation for this discrepancy, see, e.g., Schniedewind 1996; Na'aman 2007; Lemaire 2007).

No less interesting are the detailed descriptions in the books of Kings of the battles between Israel and Aram Damascus (tables 4–5). These verses cannot be read as precise historical accounts. First, the biblical account comes from prophetic stories that were put in writing in later periods, some close to the events and others a long time after they took place.

Second, the final shape of the stories was projected through the prism of southern, Judahite authors. Table 4 gives the war accounts in the order in which they appear in the Hebrew Bible.

Table 4: The Israel-Aram battles according to the books of Kings

Reference	Aramean King	Israelite King	Location of Battle	Result of Battle from Israel's Perspective
1 Kgs 20:1	Ben-hadad	Ahab	Samaria	defeat and victory
1 Kgs 20:32–33	Ben-hadad	"king of Israel"	Aphek	victory
1 Kgs 22	——	Ahab	Ramoth-gilead	Ahab dies (but see 1 Kgs 22:40)
2 Kgs 6:24	Ben-hadad	"king of Israel"	Samaria	hunger at Samaria
2 Kgs 8:28–29	Hazael	Joram	Ramoth-gilead	Joram dies
2 Kgs 9:1, 4, 14	Hazael	Joram/ Jehu	Ramoth-gilead	coup
2 Kgs 13:3, 7, 22	Hazael and Ben-hadad	Johoahaz	——	pressure and defeat
2 Kgs 13:17	——	Joash	Aphek	victory
2 Kgs 13:25	Ben-hadad	Joash	——	victory three times

When one reads these accounts critically, taking into consideration the geopolitical situation, extrabiblical texts, and the results of archaeological excavations, a different order emerges (table 5). It seems that the Hebrew Bible speaks about three events: the battle of Ramoth-gilead in northern Transjordan in 842 B.C.E., where Israel was defeated and King Joram killed; the resulting dwindling of the territory of Israel, which included a siege of Samaria in the days of Jehoahaz (817–800 B.C.E.); and the recovery of Israel following the victory of King Joash (800–784 B.C.E.) over Ben-hadad king of Damascus at Aphek, probably to be identified as

En Gev on the eastern shore of the Sea of Galilee (for a critical treatment of these events, see Miller 1966; Miller and Hayes 1986, 297–302; Bordreuil and Briquel-Chatonnet 2000, 283–88; Lipiński 2000).

Table 5: The Israel-Aram battles: a historical reconstruction

Reference	Aramean King in Reality	Israelite King in Reality	Location of Battle	Result of battle from Israel's Perspective
1 Kings 22	Hazael	Joram	Ramoth-gilead	Joram dies
2 Kings 8:28–29	Hazael	Joram	Ramoth-gilead	Joram dies
2 Kings 9:1, 4, 14	Hazael	Joram	Ramoth-gilead	coup against Joram
1 Kings 20:1	Hazael/Ben-hadad	Jehoahaz	Samaria	siege of Samaria
2 Kings 6:24	Hazael/Ben-hadad	Jehoahaz	Samaria	hunger at Samaria
2 Kings 13:3, 7, 22	Hazael/Ben-hadad	Johoahaz	——	pressure and defeat
1 Kings 20:32–33	Ben-hadad	Joash	Aphek	victory
2 Kings 13:17	Ben-hadad	Joash	Aphek	victory
2 Kings 13:25	Ben-hadad	Joash	——	victory three times

5.2. HAZAEL'S NEW ORDER

A short description of Hazael's maneuvers—including his actions in the southern coastal plain and farther to the south—is essential for understanding the fate of the northern kingdom in the second half of the ninth century B.C.E. Hazael established the strongest kingdom in the history of the the Iron Age in the Levant. What concerns us here is the situation in the southwest of his territory. Following the defeat of the northern kingdom in the battle of Ramoth-gilead, Hazael seems to have taken over from Israel the Galilee, the Gilead, and the northern valleys. Farther south he conquered and destroyed Gath, the strongest and largest Philistine city in the late Iron I and Iron IIA (Maeir 2004; Uziel and Maeir 2005). Excavations at Tell es-Safi revealed that the city was brutally destroyed in the late Iron IIA; it never recovered from this event to its former status. This destruction can be affiliated with the biblical account in 2 Kgs 18 (Maeir 2004). The conquest of Gath seems to have given Hazael control over the entire southern coastal plain. This may be hinted at by two other sources (although both are disputed). The first is the Lucianic version of 2 Kgs 13:22, which refers to the takeover by Hazael of the territory between the sea and Aphek, usually taken as the area between the Mediterranean and Aphek of the coastal plain, located at the source of the Yarkon River. The second is a reference to somewhat later events: following four decades of Damascene hegemony, at the end of the ninth century, Adad-nirari III king of Assyria managed to reestablish Assyrian domination in the west, pressed Damascus, and actually inherited its territories. His possible mention of Philistia is telling, because it may indicate that this part of the southern coastal plain was taken over from Hazael.

Two small kingdoms in the southern Levant that were pressed by Israel in the days of the Omrides—Moab and Judah—profited from Hazael's victory. In fact, the new order set by him brought about a change in the borders of these kingdoms, a change that shaped the territorial landscape of the region until the end of the Iron Age.

As mentioned in the Hebrew Bible (2 Kgs 3:5) and the Mesha Inscription, Moab threw off the yoke of the Omrides. The Moabites took over Jahaz and Ataroth—the Israelite forts that faced Dibon—and expanded their rule to the Plain of Madaba. These events fixed the northern border of Moab for the remainder of the Iron Age: even with the recovery of Israel in the early eighth century B.C.E. and Jeroboam II's renewed expansion, the Israel-Moab border continued to be stable north of Madaba.

Judah also grew stronger as a result of the Omride defeat. Archaeologically, Judah expanded in the late Iron IIA to establish fortified settlements in the north, west, and south. The late Iron IIA persisted for about a century, and it is not easy to make a distinction between the early (time of the Omrides) and the late (hegemony of Hazael) in its pottery assemblages. Historical considerations seem to indicate that the rise of Judah took place in the later phase of the late Iron IIA, in the second half of the ninth century B.C.E., and 2 Kgs 12:19 hints that, as a result of the expansion of Hazael, the southern kingdom turned from the sphere of Omride hegemony to Damascene vassaldom, but the two situations were different. While the Omrides pressed and dominated Judah, Damascus used the southern kingdom in order to advance its interests in the region.

In the west, the defeat of Gath opened the way for the territorial expansion of Judah to the Shephelah (Fantalkin and Finkelstein 2006; Fantalkin 2008). The earliest Judahite public building activities at Lachish and Bethshemesh should be dated to this phase of the Iron Age. These towns became the main administrative centers in the west and continued to function as such until the campaign of Sennacherib king of Assyria against Judah in 701 B.C.E. In the north, the decline of Israel opened the way for Judah to take over the area of what is now Ramallah and fortify Mizpah as its main center in the highlands north of Jerusalem (Finkelstein 2012). This was a pivotal moment in the history of this region, when it shifted hands from north Israelite to Judahite hands (ch. 2). Judahite control here lasted until the end of the Iron Age.

Two consecutive systems can be observed in the south: in the Beersheba Valley, the Negev highlands, and the copper production area of Wadi Faynan. (1) The early Iron IIA and the beginning of the late Iron IIA (ca. 950–850 B.C.E.) is characterized by two main phenomena: the peak of copper production at Khirbet en-Nahas south of the Dead Sea (fig. 31) and the rise of a desert polity in the Negev, with its center at Tel Masos in the Beer-sheba Valley. The Khirbet en-Nahas copper was probably transported to the north, along the King's Highway in the Transjordanian plateau, and to the west, through the Beer-sheba Valley to the coast. The Omride forts in Moab controlled the former, while Gath was the dominant power in the southern coastal plain and could have dominated the latter.

(2) Copper production began to diminish in the terminal phase of the Iron IIA (late ninth century B.C.E.) and ceased around 800 B.C.E. (fig. 31). The sites of the southern desert polity in the Negev highlands and the Beer-sheba Valley disappeared during the ninth century B.C.E. (for their date, see Boaretto, Finkelstein, and Shahack-Gross 2010). In the Beer-sheba Valley the previous system was replaced by two Judahite centers: the fortress of Arad in the east and the fortified town at Tel Beer-sheba in the west.

What caused the change from one system to the other? The most important copper production center in the eastern Mediterranean was Cyprus. Cypriot copper was traded in large amounts in the entire region in the Late Bronze Age and again in the late Iron IIA and later. Khirbet en-Nahas was secondary because of its location in an arid zone, devoid of large resources of wood needed for smelting and far from the coast and the international roads of the ancient Near East. It replaced Cyprus for a period of about three centuries following the collapse of the Bronze Age system and cessation of strong trade contacts in the eastern Mediterranean in the late twelfth century B.C.E., until the resumption of significant trade between Cyprus and the Levant in the late Iron IIA, during the ninth century (Knauf 1995). These oscillations are also evident in the import of Cypriot pottery to the Levant: strong contacts in the Late Bronze Age, decline in the Iron I and early Iron IIA, and resumption of trade in the late Iron IIA.

The renewed import of Cypriot copper to the Levant was probably the reason for the decline of Khirbet en-Nahas. Since trade relations with the Levant in the second half of the ninth century were dominated by Damascus and its ally/vassal towns on the Phoenician coast, the suppression of copper production at Khirbet en-Nahas could have served the interests of Hazael. One can therefore speculate that the Damascene campaign against Gath and the south aimed, among other reasons, at stopping the desert copper production in order to monopolize copper trade in the Levant. The construction of the two Judahite fortresses in the Beer-sheba Valley—the main route between Khirbet en-Nahas and the coast—could have served these goals. According to this scenario, Judah expanded for the first time to the Beer-sheba Valley as a vassal of Damascus in the days of King Jehoash, in the late ninth century. Judahite control in this region continued until the fall of the southern kingdom over two centuries later.

5.3. DAN AND BETHSAIDA

While, as evident from the discussion above, we know much about the late ninth century B.C.E. in Judah, the situation in the north is more obscure. The reason is simple: the main Israelite centers in the northern valleys were destroyed as a result of the Hazael assault. Jezreel never recovered: the evidence of activity there in the eighth century B.C.E. is insignificant. The late ninth-century finds at Yokneam and Taanach are also less significant than those of the first half of the ninth century. Other places, such as Megiddo, Tel Rehov, and possibly Tirzah, seem to have been deserted in the late ninth century and recovered only in the early phase of the Iron IIB (Herzog and Singer-Avitz 2006; for Megiddo, Finkelstein 1999a). Hazor, too, may have experienced a short occupational gap. Samaria, the only major excavated site where life probably continued uninterrupted, was explored in such a way that does not allow distinction between phases in the late Iron IIA; in fact, it hardly allows distinction between phases in the entire Iron II. In the north we are therefore left with only those sites that were built by Hazael following his territorial expansion: Dan and Bethsaida.

Dan had prospered in the Iron I and was probably deserted in the early Iron IIA and in most of the late Iron IIA; it was resettled in an advanced phase of the late Iron IIA (Arie 2008). This was the moment when the Tel Dan Stela was erected. It commemorated Hazael's victories and probably also recorded his building activities. The renewed town was surrounded by a solid wall and equipped with a strong four-chambered gate displaying unique, broad proportions.[1] An installation in front of the gate features two carved basalt stones typical of sites in Syria (Biran 1994, 238–40). This spot could have been the original location of the Tel Dan Stela. Late Iron IIA Bethsaida features somewhat similar elements: a solid stone city wall and an exceptionally broad four-chambered gate similar in dimensions to the one at Dan. A stela depicting the moon-god in relief found at the site probably stood in front of the gate (Bernett and Keel 1998).

The two Damascene fortified towns are located on the boundaries of the Aramean heartland. No city in the northern valleys or coastal plain displays evidence of Damascene building activity. Either the Aramean king was not interested in establishing strongholds away from his core territory, or the period of Hazael's domination was simply too short and ended before such building activities could have been deployed: the geopolitical pendulum changed again in the closing years of the ninth century. Assyria was back on the scene, and Adad-nirari III's renewed pressure on Damascus enabled the recovery of the northern kingdom (Lemaire 1993; Lipiński 2000, 395; Miller and Hayes 2006, 331–47).

---

1. The front wall is the long one and the axis short, contrary to the Omride gates, in which the front wall is shorter than the axis of the structure.

5.4. Israel's Swan Song

5.4.1. Territorial Expansion

Israel's recovery probably took place under Assyrian hegemony, since Joash is mentioned as paying tribute to Adad-nirari in the Tell el-Rimah stela. It is attested to in both the Hebrew Bible and archaeology (fig. 35). The book of Kings says that King Joash "took again from Ben-hadad the son of Hazael the cities that he had taken from Jehoahaz his father in war. Three times Joash defeated him and recovered the cities of Israel" (2 Kgs 13:25). It is not clear where these cities were located, but one could imagine that the author's reference is to the Jezreel Valley and/or the Gilead. According to the interpretation of the biblical materials on the battles between Israel and Aram offered above, Joash was the king who defeated Ben-hadad at Aphek on the eastern shore of the Sea of Galilee, and if one accepts the story in 2 Kgs 14:8–14, Joash subjugated Judah and made it his vassal.

Jeroboam II, Joash's son, ruled over Israel for forty years (788–747 B.C.E.). During his reign Israel continued to expand and reached a second and last period of territorial prosperity. The Bible says that Jeroboam "restored the border of Israel from the entrance of Hamath [Heb. Lebo-hamath] as far as the Sea of the Arabah" (2 Kgs 14:25). Though an Israelite expansion as far as Lebo-hamath (Lab'u of ancient Near Eastern sources, located in the Valley of Lebanon; Na'aman 2006, 262–67) and the continuing reference that Jeroboam "recovered for Israel Damascus and Hamath" (verse 28) cannot be taken as fully historical (Na'aman 2006, 231), Israelite territorial gains in the northern Jordan Valley are evident from other sources.

(1) As I have shown in chapter 3, the description in 1 Kgs 12:29 of the establishment of an Israelite cult place at Tel Dan probably depicts eighth-century realities (Arie 2008; Berlejung 2009).

(2) The recurring biblical expression "from Dan to Beer-sheba" (e.g., 2 Sam 3:10; 1 Kgs 5:5) probably reflects late-monarchic ideas (after the fall of Israel) about the two extreme Hebrew towns: Israelite Dan in the north and Judahite Beer-sheba in the south. This notion, too, must represent eighth-century realities.

(3) Domination of the northern kingdom in the upper Jordan Valley is confirmed by the biblical description of Tiglath-pileser's campaign in this territory (732 B.C.E.): the Assyrian king

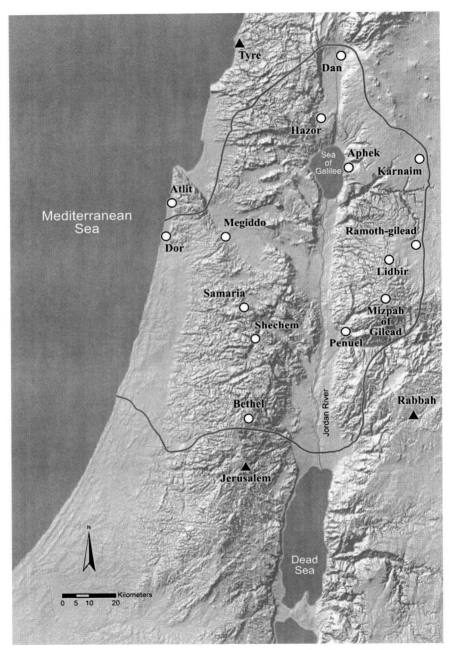

Figure 35. Sites mentioned in chapter 5 in relation to the first half of the eighth century B.C.E.

is said to have conquered "Ijon, Abel-beth-maacah, Janoah, Kedesh, Hazor, Gilead, and Galilee, all the land of Naphtali" (2 Kgs 15:29).

(4) The Joab census may also depict early eighth-century realities, in which Israel ruled as far north as "Dan-jaan" (2 Sam 24:6, probably meaning Dan and Ijon).

Jeroboam II seems to have taken back the ex-Omride territories in northern Transjordan—not only the areas inhabited by Israelites on the western slopes of the Gilead but also the plateau of Ramoth-gilead farther to the northeast. This is attested by several sources. Jeroboam II's expansion here may be referred to by Amos (6:11–14), who hints that Israel conquered Lidbir and Karnaim. Lidbir should be sought in the area of Irbid in northern Jordan, probably at the large mound of el-Husn, and Karnaim is identified by most scholars at Sheikh Sa'ad in the Bashan. Lidbir here represents the northern Gilead, while Karnaim stands for the area of the Bashan immediately north of the Yarmuk River. The inclusion of the Ramoth-gilead–Havvoth-ja'ir–Argob area in the list of Solomonic districts in 1 Kgs 4:13 may also represent a memory of an Iron II reality in the time of Jeroboam II (Finkelstein and Silberman 2006a, 161–62; for a somewhat later-date reality, see Na'aman 2001). Regardless of the date of compilation, the strong biblical tradition on the conquest of the land of Og and the settlement of the Israelites in Havvoth-ja'ir and the land called Argob (e.g., Num 32:33, 41; Deut 3:3–4, 13–14; 4:47; Josh 12:4; 13:12, 30–31) may also reflect an old memory.

Archaeology has not yet given us data for the area of northern Jordan, but it certainly supports Jeroboam II's expansion in the Jordan Valley. Hazor VI–V features Israelite material culture, including Hebrew inscriptions, and the same holds true for Dan III–II. Indeed, Dan became Israelite for the first time in the first half of the eighth century (Arie 2008). This is attested by the dismantling of the Tel Dan Stela that was erected there by Hazael. The smashing of the moon-god stela at Bethsaida may also be interpreted against the background of a takeover of the town by the northern kingdom in the days of Jeroboam II.

5.4.2. Economic Prosperity

In the eighth century B.C.E., with the decline of Khirbet en-Nahas, the northern kingdom could no longer profit from transporting desert copper.

All the other foundations of its previous prosperity in the days of the Omrides were still in place: olive-oil and wine production in the highlands, strong trade relations with Phoenicia, and the trade of trained war horses. In addition, Israel seems to have dominated the desert trade route along the Darb el-Ghazza in northeastern Sinai, which led from the head of the Gulf of Aqaba to the Mediterranean ports. Archaeology sheds new light on all of these points.

5.4.2.1. Oil and Wine

The importance of olive-oil and wine production in the highlands of Israel is attested by the Samaria ostraca. The sixty-three inscriptions were not found in a clean stratigraphic context. They are dated according to paleographical considerations to the early eighth century B.C.E., probably to the time of Jeroboam II (Lemaire 1977; recently Niemann 2008). They mention years of reign of an Israelite king (or kings), the latest being year 17; Jeroboam II was the only king of that time who ruled for seventeen years and more. The ostraca refer to types of oil and wine, names of places and regions around the capital, and names of officials. Regardless of whether they represent shipments of olive oil and wine to the capital or another kind of interaction between the capital and countryside estates/towns, they certainly attest to a large-scale oil and wine "industry" at that time. This is supported by the results of the archaeological excavations of a few sites in the highlands south of Samaria, where a large number of Iron IIB olive-oil installations were unearthed (e.g., Eitam 1979; Riklin 1997). Other such sites were found in surveys. The surveys also indicate that the eighth century B.C.E. saw the densest settlement system in the highlands, including those in rugged areas that are amenable to nothing but terraced orchard agriculture.

5.4.2.2. Eastern Mediterranean Trade

The eighth century B.C.E. was a period of strong commercial activity in the eastern Mediterranean that involved the Assyrian Empire, Phoenician maritime city-states, and Egypt (Frankenstein 1979; Briquel-Chatonnet 1992, 2010; Diakonoff 1992; Lipiński 2006, 180–90). Dor was the main port of the northern kingdom, the gate to the maritime routes. Atlit, located about 10 km north of Dor, features an elaborate port with Phoenician characteristics. Radiocarbon results from timber used underwater to strengthen the mole of this port provided dates around the ninth century B.C.E. (Haggi 2006). It seems that Atlit was a Phoenician trading post on the Israelite coast.

The nature of eastern Mediterannean trade in the eighth century B.C.E. is demonstrated by the most common trade container of the Iron IIB: the "torpedo" storage jar (so named because of its shape). It was found in large numbers in dozens of excavated sites in Lebanon and Israel, mainly along the coast but also at inland sites located along trade routes such as Hazor and Megiddo. Their unique morphology and homogeneity raised the possibility of a single place of production. A systematic petrographic examination of torpedo storage jars proved that the Phoenician coast was their main place of origin (Aznar 2005).

The shape of these jars made it easy to stock them on ships. Indeed, their best representation is found in two Phoenician shipwrecks discovered in deep waters off the coast of Ashkelon (Ballard et al. 2002). The two ships had minimum cargoes of 385 and 396 intact torpedo jars (which were visible to the underwater archaeologists; fig. 36), compared to a total of less than 300 complete torpedo storage jars found in all excavated land sites. The two ships had probably sailed from a Phoenician port in the direction of Egypt. Twenty-two torpedo storage jars were retrieved from the sea. Petrographic investigation indicated that they were produced, as predicted, on the Phoenician coast. Analysis of their content showed that they had been lined with resin and probably filled with wine (Ballard et al. 2002). A study of their measurement indicated standardization in their shape and volume (Finkelstein et al. 2011), attesting to the existence of sophisticated trade networks.

5.4.2.3. Israelite Horse Industry

The strength of the Israelite horse industry is attested already in the mid-ninth century, in Shalmaneser III's account of the chariot forces of the anti-Assyrian coalition in the Battle of Qarqar; Ahab is mentioned by the Assyrian king as arriving with the largest number of chariots. As I have shown in chapter 4, no ninth-century Israelite horse facility has thus far been found, although it is possible that Jezreel was the hub of Israelite horse training at that time (Cantrell 2011, 112–13). The eighth century B.C.E. is a different case, as it reveals the secrets of Israelite horse business.

The single most impressive revolution in a north Israelite site during the Iron Age is the transformation in the layout of Megiddo. The ninth-

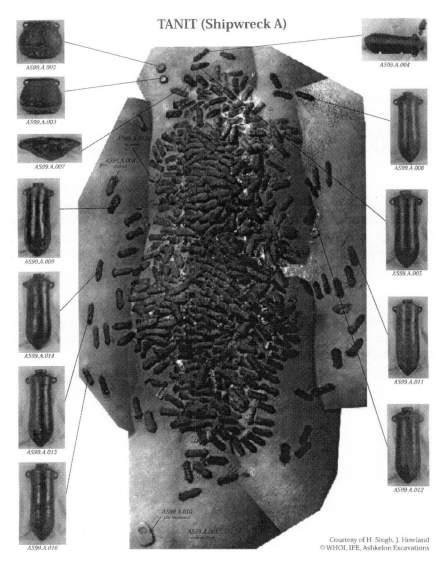

Figure 36. Shipwreck with eighth-century B.C.E. "torpedo" jars found in deep water in the Mediterranean off the coast of Ashkelon (courtesy of Professor Lawrence E. Stager, the Leon Levy Expedition to Ashkelon).

century settlement features domestic quarters and two or three palaces beautifully built in ashlar blocks and probably decorated with "proto-Ionic" capitals. This settlement had come to an end in the second half of the ninth century as a result of the Israel-Aram conflict. When the city recovered (seemingly after a short occupational gap) in the first half of the eighth century, it had a completely different function: much of its area was now devoted to pillared buildings of a unified plan. Renewed investigation of these buildings in the 1990s resolved the decades-long dispute over their utilization, showing that they were indeed stables, as suggested by the University of Chicago excavators in the 1920s (Cantrell 2006). But why should Megiddo, located in the most fertile part of the kingdom, be set aside for breeding and training horses?

The renewed study of these buildings assembled data that demonstrate their economic importance. Large Egyptian (Nubian) horses were essential for the chariot force of the Assyrian army. Before Assyria established direct contacts with Egypt in the late eighth century, Israel was the source of these horses, which were brought from Egypt, bred and trained at Megiddo, and then sold to Assyria and other kingdoms in the north. The great skill of Israel in chariotry is attested in Assyrian records (Cantrell 2011; Cantrell and Finkelstein 2006), and the memory of an eighth-century B.C.E. chariot city—brought to Jerusalem by Israelite refugees—may have given the reality background to the biblical tales that associated King Solomon with horses and chariots (Finkelstein and Silberman 2006a, 163–67). One way or another, the horse industry was probably one of Israel's most important economic ventures in the eighth century B.C.E.

5.4.2.4. Arabian Trade

Various pieces of information seem to indicate the existence of overland Arabian trade no later than the ninth century B.C.E. (e.g., Liverani 1992; Jasmin 2005; Sass 2005, 118). In the northwest there are two alternatives for how this early Arabian trade could have been transported to the Mediterranean coast: along the Edomite plateau in southern Transjordan (before the emergence of a territorial kingdom in Edom) or via the Darb el-Ghazza in northeastern Sinai (fig. 37). The latter route was shorter, so, despite the paucity of water sources, it served as the main road until the Assyrian takeover in the late eighth century B.C.E.

As in later periods, whoever controlled the outlets of the desert trade routes made the best profit from them. I have already noted that until the

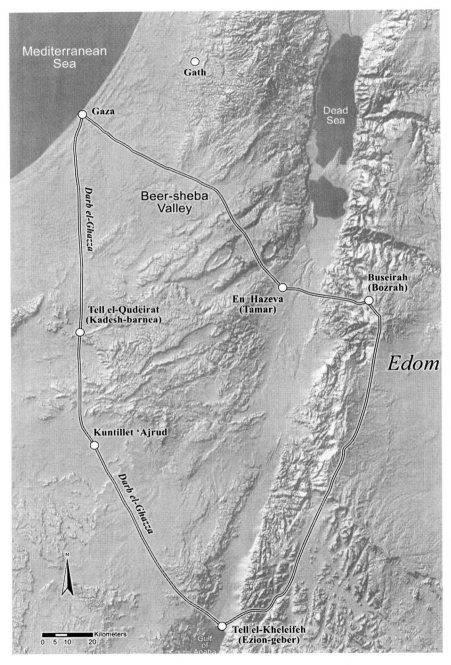

Figure 37. Sites and ancient roads in Edom, the Negev, and northeastern Sinai.

second half of the ninth century B.C.E. Gath was the most important city in the southern lowlands; it ruled the entire Shephelah, including the territory that had belonged to Late Bronze Lachish. This is expressed in the biblical memory (1 Sam 27:6) that Ziklag was a village in the southwestern corner of the Gath territory; in its size—Gath was the largest city in the south (Uziel and Maeir 2011; Maeir 2012); and in the extraordinary concentration of early alphabetic inscriptions in its territory (Finkelstein and Sass forthcoming). Gath was therefore the center that profited most from the southern trade in the Iron I and in much of the Iron IIA. This came to an end with its destruction by Hazael; following this event, in the final decades of the ninth century, the outlets of the desert trade routes were dominated by Damascus.

This situation was short-lived and changed again with the expansion of Adad-nirari III and the decline of Damascus in the closing years of the ninth century. The text of Adad-nirari mentioning Edom seems to indicate that he inherited the hegemony in the south from Damascus. However, with no policy of annexation of territories and direct rule, Assyria achieved its interests by promoting the power of the northern kingdom as an ally/vassal. Starting probably in the days of Joash, the northern kingdom controlled territories that had previously been ruled by Gath and then Hazael. This included domination of the Arabian trade route that passed along the Darb el-Ghazza.

Evidence for this scenario comes from Kuntillet 'Ajrud—a single-period site made up of two structures located on an isolated hill (fig. 38) on one of the branches of the Darb el-Ghazza, approximately 50 km south of Ein el-Qudeirat (Kadesh-barnea; fig. 37). This extraordinary site (final report of the finds in Meshel 2012) yielded a unique assemblage of inscriptions (Ahituv, Eshel, and Meshel 2012) and drawings on pottery vessels and plaster (Beck 1982; Ornan forthcoming). The site dates to the first half of the eighth century B.C.E. (Lemaire 1984 for paleography; Finkelstein and Piasetzky 2008 for radiocarbon results, now supported by new, as-yet-unpublished measurements provided by Boaretto in a lecture at Tel Aviv University, January 2013).

The finds retrieved at Kuntillet 'Ajrud point to a strong connection with the northern kingdom (overview in Mastin 2011; Ahituv, Eshel, and Meshel 2012, 95, 126–29; Na'aman 2012a). This is expressed in the inscriptions in the Israelite orthographic system and in the mention of "YHWH of Samaria," probably alluding to a temple of YHWH in the capital of the northern kingdom (e.g., Keel and Uehlinger 1998, 228; Schmid 2012b, 53).

Figure 38. The hill of Kuntillet 'Ajrud in northeastern Sinai.

Thus Na'aman (2012a, 4–5, 8–9) identified the monarch hinted at in the inscriptions as the king of Israel, and Beck (2000, 180–81) alluded to the possible appearance of the king of Israel sitting on a throne on a plaster drawing on the entrance wall to the site. Ornan (forthcoming) has recently deciphered more of the Kuntillet 'Ajrud paintings as representing royal scenes and accordingly interpreted the site as a royal Israelite trade station. The Kuntillet 'Ajrud finds indicate, therefore, that in the first half of the eighth century, probably in the days of Jeroboam II, Israel controlled the desert trade route along the Darb el-Ghazza and hence its northern outlet.[2]

5.4.3. Reorganization of Cult

Na'aman (2002a) suggested that the northern kingdom centralized its cult activity in the transition from the ninth to the eighth century B.C.E. This is indeed evident at Megiddo. As I have shown in chapter 4, in the late Iron IIA Megiddo had at least two, if not three or four, domestic shrines connected to different quarters of the town. Other modest countryside shrines are known at Tel Amal near Beth-shean and at Taanach in the

---

2. For more on the site and its finds, see chapter 6.

Jezreel Valley south of Megiddo. These local cult places disappeared in the early eighth century. At Megiddo no shrine survived this transition. Archaeologically speaking, no site in the entire territory of the northern kingdom has thus far shown continuity of cultic activity from the late Iron IIA to the early Iron IIB.

To the contrary, it seems that in the first half of the eighth century the cult of the northern kingdom was reorganized. Samaria must have had a royal shrine as early as the ninth century, although we know nothing about it on the ground. The Bible portrays it negatively as a temple of Baal (1 Kgs 16:32), but judging from the reference in an inscription from Kuntillet 'Ajrud to "YHWH of Samaria," it could have been dedicated to YHWH (Schmid 2012b, 53; see also Köckert 2010, 365–66). As I have already shown, the biblical tradition about the northern kingdom's border cult places at Dan and Bethel (1 Kgs 12:28–29; both probably dedicated to YHWH, Köckert 2010) depicts realities of the early eighth century B.C.E. (Berlejung 2009). At that time Dan became an Israelite city for the first time, and Bethel seems to have prospered as never before. The *bamah* (high place) that was uncovered at Dan is well built, far better than what we know in any late Iron IIA cult site. Judging from the biblical text (ch. 6), Penuel must also have served as a principal northern shrine—probably the most important in the Israelite territory in the Gilead. The reason for the reorganization (though not full centralization) of the cult could have been the advance of a more organized kingdom and the desire of the king to dominate the cult economically and ideologically.

This reorganization of cult in Israel predates the more thorough process of centralization that took place in Judah, also for political-economic reasons, in the late eighth century. Judah shows evidence of the existence of countryside shrines—at Arad, Beer-sheba, and probably Lachish—as late as the second half of the eighth century B.C.E. These shrines were abolished in the closing years of that century (Finkelstein and Silberman 2006b, with references to the dispute over this issue). Judah's centralization of cult was also strongly connected to the rise of a more organized and sophisticated society. Centralization was more effective in Judah, where the Jerusalem temple became the sole official focus of the kingdom's cult. Still, changes in cult practice in Israel several decades earlier could have given the model to Judah. In this case, too, the idea could have reached Jerusalem with Israelite refugees. Further, in Israel, as in Judah, reorganization of cult seems to have been connected to the beginning of compilation of sacred texts, probably in central, king-dominated shrines such as Bethel.

5.4.4. ADVANCE OF WRITING AND COMPILATION OF NORTHERN TEXTS

The intense economic activity described above called for the development of advanced administration and hence writing. Hebrew inscriptions appear for the first time, in small quantity and in a limited number of places—mostly at Tel Rehov and its vicinity on the periphery of Israelite domination—in the late Iron IIA. They quickly spread throughout the territory of the kingdom in the Iron IIB (Finkelstein and Sass forthcoming). This is manifested by the Samaria ostraca as well as finds at sites such as Hazor and Beth-shean. How fast this happened is demonstrated by the expansion of writing even to remote places such as Kuntillet ʿAjrud in northeastern Sinai (above and ch. 6). Scribal activity in Judah started spreading at about the same time or a few decades later.

The spread of writing facilitated the earliest compilation of northern texts, which later found their way to Judah and into the Hebrew Bible. These early northern texts are of a local nature. The core of the Jacob cycle, dating to the Iron Age, deals with the border between Israelites and Arameans in the Gilead and with the establishment of temples in Penuel on the Jabbok River, Bethel, and possibly Shechem and Mizpah of the Gilead (ch. 6). In other words, this cycle deals with the Gilead and the area between Shechem and Bethel. The positive Saul cycle in 1 Samuel takes place mainly in the area of Gibeon-Gibeah and the territory immediately to the north, as well as the area of the Jabbok River and the town of Jabesh in the Gilead. The stories about savior leaders in the book of Judges are set against the background of the central highlands between Bethel and Shechem, the Jezreel Valley, and the Gilead. The Elijah-Elisha prophetic stories are connected to the Jezreel Valley, the northern Gilead, and Samaria. It seems that these materials could have been written in parallel in the different shrines—at Samaria, Bethel, and Penuel—each representing local traditions. Since the eighth century B.C.E. reorganization of cult was not limited to a single temple in the capital, Israel had not developed an overarching story about its past, as Judah had in the late seventh century B.C.E.

But how did these written Israelite texts find their way into the Hebrew Bible? And now that we are approaching the fall of the northern kingdom, the time has come to ask: How was the term *Israel* transformed from the name of the northern kingdom to describe the entire Hebrew population—Israel and Judah—collectively? Before I answer these questions, let me elaborate on the two "charter myths" of the northern kingdom: the Jacob cycle and exodus.

6

Comments on the Two "Charter Myths"
of the Northern Kingdom

The northern kingdom seems to have had two foundation or "charter myths" (term of van der Toorn 1996, 301): the Jacob story and the exodus-desert tradition. Both appear in Israelite prophetic texts of the eighth century B.C.E. They were brought to Judah by Israelites after the collapse of the northern kingdom and were later "adopted" into Judahite ideology and identity narratives, elaborated on, incorporated into biblical texts, and redacted. In their current forms they therefore include several layers that represent realities and concerns of late-monarchic Judah and postexilic Yehud. In what follows I wish to comment on two issues related to their *early*, north-Israelite layer: the historical reality behind the core of the Jacob cycle in Genesis and the roots of the exodus-wandering tradition in Exodus, Numbers, and Deuteronomy. Both must have begun as oral traditions, were transmitted as such in the north for many decades, and were put in writing in the first half of the eighth century B.C.E. Whether at this early stage there was already a "connection" between them is impossible to say.

6.1. The Reality behind the Core of the Jacob Cycle

The core of the Jacob cycle in Genesis (de Pury 1975, 1991, 2001; Blum 2012b and bibliography; fig. 39) is probably the earliest material in the patriarchal stories, representing a time before the collapse of the northern kingdom. This is so because the outline of the story is hinted at in an eighth-century northern prophecy in Hos 12 (de Pury 2006; Blum 2009). Later layers in the narrative include the Laban story, the Esau tale, and Priestly materials. The configuration that puts Abraham (the hero of the southern highlands) first in the patriarchal order and Jacob last is also a

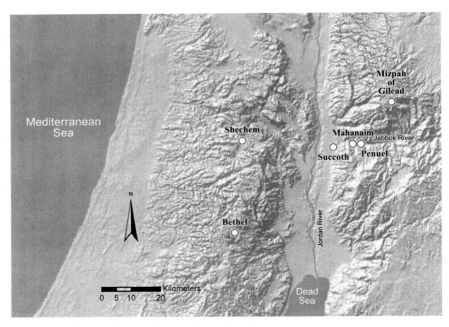

Figure 39. Places related to the Jacob cycle in Genesis.

late construct that aims at subordinating the Jacob stories to the Abraham ones, in essence, subordinating Israel to Judah.

The original Iron Age Jacob myth includes two main, well-integrated themes:

(1) It delineates the northeastern border of Israelite settlement in the Gilead (Gen 31:44–49). This theme includes Jacob's sojourn to the house of Laban in "the land of the people of the east" (*Eretz benei Qedem*). The only connection of Laban with Haran (Gen 29:4) is probably a later insertion; the original text deals with the Arameans' settled pastureland to the east of the Israelite territories in the Gilead.

(2) It deals with the foundation (and the etymology of the name) of the northern kingdom's shrines at Bethel (Gen 28:11–22), Penuel, located in the deep valley of the Jabbok River in Transjordan (32:23–32), and probably Shechem (33:20; I do not wish to deal here with the complex question of the identification of the deity worshiped in these shrines).

What is the settlement and historical reality behind this original Jacob cycle? Several clues in the text may help answer this intriguing question.

(1) *A fundamental myth of the northern kingdom.* As mentioned above, there is no logic in affiliating the development of the core of the Jacob cycle with a time later than the fall of the northern kingdom, especially since its main outline is already referred to in an eighth-century B.C.E. prophecy in Hos 12 (de Pury 2006; Blum 2009, 2012b).

(2) *Bethel.* The emergence of the Bethel myth in Genesis should be sought in one of the two periods of prosperity at the site: the Iron I and the Iron IIB (Finkelstein and Singer-Avitz 2009). Evidence of activity at Bethel in the early Iron IIA and in the Neo-Babylonian–Persian periods is lacking (contra Blenkinsopp 2003; Knauf 2006 regarding the latter), and activity in the late Iron IIA was weak at best.

(3) *The settlement boundary in the Gilead.* I refer to the erection of the cairn (Hebrew *galed*) on the border between the Israelites and the Arameans (Gen 31:45–49). This etiological story (that is probably based on a prominent feature in the landscape) is associated with a place called Mizpah: "And the Mizpah, for he said, 'The LORD watch between me and you, when we are absent one from another'" (Gen 31:49). Mizpah of the Gilead should be sought near the village of Suf, northwest of Jerash (e.g., Lemaire 1981, 44; details in Finkelstein, Koch, and Lipschits 2012). If so, it is located in a spot not far from the border between the hilly, western slopes of the Israelite Gilead and the plateau of Ramoth-gilead. In the two periods of its territorial expansion—in the days of the Omrides in the first half of the ninth century and during the reign of Jeroboam II in the first half of the eighth century B.C.E.—the northern kingdom expanded from the area of Mizpah of Gilead to the plateau in the northeast (chs. 4–5). The story of the erection of a boundary cairn between the Israelites and Arameans in Transjordan does not fit these two periods; it is only logical to assume that starting in the time of the Omrides Israel would claim the territory of the plateau.

(4) *No mention of Shiloh.* The Jacob stories are not related in any way to Shiloh and its shrine. As I have already indicated, the memory of an important cult place at Shiloh is a genuine one. According to the radio-carbon evidence, Shiloh was destroyed in the second half of the eleventh century B.C.E., probably around the transition from the early to late Iron I. It is logical, then, to understand the growth of the Jacob cycle, with Bethel at its core, against the background of a later phase in the history of Israel, after the destruction of Shiloh.

(5) *No mention of the northern territories of Israel.* The Jacob cycle deals with the central highlands between Bethel and Shechem and with

Transjordan along the Jabbok River.[1] There is no reference to the Jezreel Valley, the upper Jordan Valley, and the mountainous Galilee—territories that gradually constituted part of the northern kingdom starting in the late tenth century.

Admittedly, most of the above-mentioned considerations are inconclusive; still, it seems that, when seeking the reality behind the original Jacob story, one needs to look for a period before 720 B.C.E., preferably in days of prosperity at Bethel, preferably not in periods when Israel expanded into Aramean lands beyond Mizpah of Gilead, after the destruction of Shiloh, and preferably before the expansion of Israel into the northern valleys and the Galilee.

Going from late to early, these considerations seem to eliminate the first half of the eighth century (Israelite expansion in the northwestern Gilead), the second half of the ninth century (weak activity at Bethel), the days of the Omrides (Israelite expansion to the plateau northwest of Mizpah and weak activity at Bethel), the early days of the northern kingdom (probably no activity at Bethel), and probably the early Iron I (no mention of Shiloh). Also, starting with the beginning of expansion to the northern valleys in the early Iron IIA, such a text may have been expected to include a signal of affiliation of these territories with the Jacob story. The most probable (but far from certain) origin of the core of the Jacob cycle is therefore in the late Iron I (the tenth century B.C.E.), when identities in the future core territory of the northern kingdom were shaped, settlement boundaries formed, and shrines erected. Whether this assumption is correct depends very much on the finds at the site of Penuel (Tell edh-Dhahab esh-Sharqi in the ravine of the Jabbok River; Finkelstein, Koch, and Lipschits 2012, with bibliography). At this time reliable information for this site is not available.

Similar to other northern traditions, the original Jacob cycle must have been transmitted orally until it was put in writing, probably at Bethel, in the first half of the eighth century (Blum 2012b). Before that time, there is no evidence of sufficiently significant scribal activity in Israel (Finkelstein and Sass forthcoming; see chs. 4–5). Both archaeology and text exegesis testify to the prosperity of the Bethel temple at that time.

---

1. It is especially noteworthy that the Jacob cycle does not refer to the shrine of Dan, which, as I have noted above, was erected in the days of Jeroboam II.

6.2. The Origin and Development of the Exodus and Wandering Tradition

Scholars who have attempted to deal with the question of the historical reality of the exodus and desert wandering narrative (for the two being connected, see, e.g., Dozeman 2000, 64) are divided into two camps. Members of one adhere to the traditional research notion that the biblical material portrays the situation in the Late Bronze Age in the thirteenth century B.C.E., the time calculated according to the inner logic of biblical chronology (e.g., Halpern 1993; Kitchen 1998; Hoffmeier 2005). These scholars face two major problems. First, since there was no significant scribal activity in ancient Israel until close to 800 B.C.E. (Finkelstein and Sass forthcoming), they need to assume an oral transmission of the story with all its details over a period of four centuries with no infiltration of realities during the time passed. Second, there is no single piece of evidence to support an exclusive Late Bronze Age origin of the tradition; in other words, each item in the story can be understood against the background of later periods (e.g., Na'aman 2011a, 56–60). Members of the second camp propose that the story describes realities that fit the time of compilation of the text: in the late-monarchic to postexilic period (Redford 1987; Van Seters 2001; Finkelstein and Silberman 2001, 48–71; Liverani 2005, 277–82). The main difficulty that these researchers face is in explaining the strong tradition of both the exodus and the desert experience in the writings of the eighth-century B.C.E. northern prophets.[2]

Recent research on the Pentateuch sheds light on the nature and date of the exodus-wandering materials. It indicates that: (1) this narrative had an important status in northern Israel as early as the eighth century B.C.E. (e.g., Hoffman 1989; van der Toorn 1996, 287–315; Dozeman 2000); (2) it contains an "inner" literary history (e.g., Dozeman 1989; Römer 2002, 2003; Carr 2012 for Moses); (3) it was originally independent from, and earlier than, the patriarchal stories; (4) the two blocks—patriarchs and exodus—were connected by a Priestly author at a relatively late date; (5) in the present form the narrative represents a Priestly (or even late Priestly and/or post-Priestly) compilation (for points 3–5, see, e.g., Kratz 2005, 248–308; Schmid 2012a; various articles in Doze-

---

2. For a somewhat different version, emphasizing an earlier reality in the Iron Age, in the days of Jeroboam I, see van der Toorn 1996, 287–315; Albertz 2001.

man and Schmid 2006; Römer and Schmid 2007; Dozeman, Schmid, and Schwartz 2011). This means that the exodus-wandering tradition as we know it today is the final product of a long process of development and growth, first oral and then written, and a complex history of redactions in the light of changing political and historical realities (for a full account of this subject, see Finkelstein forthcoming).

From the prophecies of Hosea (2:14–15; 9:10; 11:1, 5; 12:9, 13; 13:4–5) and Amos (2:10; 3:1; 9:7), and possibly also from a Kuntillet 'Ajrud inscription that may refer to the theme of the exodus (Na'aman 2012a), it is clear that the exodus-desert tradition was well known in the northern kingdom in its later days. But what was the source of this tradition? How far back before the eighth century could one trace it? Further, what can be said about the nature of this tradition in Israel in the time of Hosea and Amos? Regarding the first question, as noted above, attempts to isolate a "moment in Egypt" in the thirteenth century B.C.E. that fits the exodus narrative are doomed to failure (Finkelstein and Silberman 2001, 48–71). With no clear evidence in the biblical text, in Egyptian sources, or in archaeology, there is nowhere else to turn but to historical speculation.

Redford (1987, 150–51; 1992, 412) suggested that the exodus tradition may have originated from the memory of the expulsion of Canaanites from the Delta of the Nile in the sixteenth century B.C.E. Na'aman (2011a, following Hendel 2001) proposed that the biblical story preserves the memory of oppression of the people of Canaan by the Egyptian administration in the Late Bronze II–III, in the thirteenth and twelfth centuries B.C.E. Bietak (1987) and Römer (2002, 54–67) also looked for the roots of the exodus-Moses tradition in the Late Bronze Age. The problem with these theories is that they do not explain why the memory was preserved and promoted in the northern kingdom. The southern lowlands—the Shephelah and southern coastal plain—make a more reasonable place for the perpetuation of such a story. The reminiscence of an expulsion from the Delta at the end of the Middle Bronze should have been maintained in the southern coastal plain and the area of Nahal Besor; hieratic inscriptions and other archaeological finds hint that economic oppression in the twelfth century B.C.E. was probably the severest in the southern lowlands. Even in the north, Egyptian rule should have been strongly felt mainly in the valleys, around Megiddo and Beth-shean, the latter having served as the main Egyptian stronghold in the area. Regarding the highlands, the weak control of Egypt of the Late Bronze Age there is demonstrated by the maneuvers of Shechem of Labayu and his sons in the Amarna period (ch. 1). There is no hint of Egyptian economic pressure in the hill country, and, in fact, this area, including the north Samaria hills, was sparsely settled at that time. Finally, it is noteworthy that the Hebrew Bible expresses no other knowledge of the situation in Canaan in the Late Bronze Age. In other words, one needs to look for a memory that can be connected to the northern part of the central highlands rather than the southern lowlands and that is preferably closer in time to the days of Hosea and Amos.

In chapter 2 I discussed the role of Egypt of the Twenty-Second Dynasty, more specifically the role of Pharaoh Sheshonq I's campaign in the decline of the first north Israelite territorial entity of the late Iron I, which was centered in the area of Gibeon-Gibeah north of Jerusalem. This polity was then replaced by the early northern kingdom, which was centered in the area of Shechem-Tirzah. The rise of the latter (ch. 3) may also have been an outcome of the Sheshonq I campaign and ensuing territorial arrangements. Possible involvement of Egypt in the history of Jeroboam I, founder of the northern kingdom, is hinted at in the LXX version of 1 Kgs 12: the "alternative story" on the division of the united monarchy. Van der Toorn (1996, 287–315) and Albertz (2001) pointed to the possible function of the exodus narrative as a charter myth or thanksgiving story in the days of Jeroboam I. Memories of these events could have been preserved in the areas of both Bethel and Shechem, and they could have been embedded into earlier salvation-from-Egypt traditions that were "imported" from the lowlands to the hill country when Israel expanded into the northern valleys. If indeed the alternative story is based on a pre-Deuteronomistic source (Schenker 2000, 2008), and assuming that there was a Moses story at this early stage (Smend 1995; Blum 2012a), another motivation for the adoption of this tradition could have been the thematic similarities between the biographies of Moses and Jeroboam I, the founder of the northern kingdom (see Albertz 2001; Schmid 2012b, 83 and bibliography).

This puts us in the late tenth–early ninth centuries B.C.E. There is no clear clue for the status of the exodus-wandering tradition in the later part of the ninth century B.C.E. A possible hint comes from the 1 Kgs 19 story about the prophet Elijah's journey to Horeb. Although the current text may represent late redactions (Schmid 2012b, 60 and bibliography) and Horeb is a Deuteronomistic expression (Dozeman 1989, 67–68), the origin of the tradition may go back to the ninth century B.C.E. (White 1997), especially if an (oral) desert wandering tradition already existed at that stage.

The key site for understanding the exodus-wandering tradition in the days of Hosea and Amos in the eighth century B.C.E. is Kuntillet 'Ajrud.

This fascinating single-period site is located on an isolated hill in the middle of the flat, arid zone of northeastern Sinai (figs. 38–39), approximately 50 km south of Ein el-Qudeirat (Kadesh-barnea). It is situated on one of the branches of the Darb el-Ghazza, the ancient road that led from the head of the Gulf of Aqaba to the Mediterranean. The site was interpreted as a trade way-station associated with cult, a shrine devoted to YHWH and Asherah, a cult place of Asherah associated with a sacred tree, and/or a station along a pilgrimage route to Mount Sinai (summaries in Meshel 2012; Na'aman 2012a). Kuntillet 'Ajrud yielded extraordinary assemblages of Hebrew inscriptions (Ahituv, Eshel, and Meshel 2012) and drawings on pottery vessels and plaster (Beck 1982; Ornan forthcoming; for a final report on the excavations, see Meshel 2012). Some of these finds are relevant to the history of the exodus and wandering tradition.

Kuntillet 'Ajrud dates to the first half of the eighth century B.C.E. This is attested by the pottery assemblage (Ayalon 1995), the inscriptions (Lemaire 1984), and evaluation of ^{14}C results (Finkelstein and Piasetzky 2008). New, as-yet-unpublished short-lived radiocarbon determinations support this date (Boaretto in a lecture at Tel Aviv University, January 2013). Historically, this means the site was active in the days of Jeroboam II (788–747 B.C.E.).

Regarding the inscriptions, for the issue discussed here the most important references are to: YHWH of Samaria, which appears once, in inscription 3.1 (see also inscription 3.8; numbering according to Ahituv, Eshel, and Meshel 2012); YHWH of Teman or YHWH of the Teman (inscriptions 3.6, 3.9 once in each, twice in 4.1.1 [three times according to Na'aman 2012a, 10]); and a king of Israel in inscriptions 3.1, 3.6, 3.9, and an inscription that was omitted from the final publication (Na'aman 2012a, 4–5, 8–9). To these I should add Na'aman's reading of plaster inscription 4.3 as a possible early allusion to the exodus story (2012a, 12–14).

Among the drawings, the most significant for this discussion is the possible appearance of the king of Israel sitting on a throne on the plaster on the entrance wall to the main building (Beck 2000, 180–81; Na'aman 2012a, 2–3). Ornan (forthcoming) has recently interpreted more of the 'Ajrud drawings as representing royal scenes; accordingly, she sees the site as a royal Israelite trade station.

The Kuntillet 'Ajrud finds point to a strong connection with the northern kingdom (overview in Mastin 2011; for the pottery and its provenance, Ayalon 1995; for the inscriptions, Lemaire 1984; Ahituv, Eshel, and Meshel 2012, 95, 126–29; Na'aman 2012a). They indicate that in the first half of the eighth century, in the days of Jeroboam II, Israel dominated the Darb el-Ghazza route (for the broader historical circumstances, see ch. 5).

Cult at Kuntillet 'Ajrud seems to have been devoted to YHWH of Teman, that is, YHWH of the southern arid zones, and Asherah. Teman is mentioned in the Hebrew Bible in relation to Edom, but also to Dedan in northwest Arbaia (Jer 49:7–8). Noteworthy are Habakkuk's words, "God came from Teman, and the Holy One from Mount Paran" (3:3; for this and other references that connect Teman, Paran, and Sinai, see Ahituv, Eshel, and Meshel 2012, 96, 130). YHWH of Samaria should probably be understood as the protection deity of the capital of Israel, comparable to the somewhat later YHWH of Jerusalem in the inscription from Beit Lei in the Judahite Shephelah (e.g., Lemaire 1984; contra Na'aman 2012a, who sees both as referring to the entire kingdom). The inscription may, in fact, refer to a temple of YHWH at Samaria (Keel and Uehlinger 1998, 228; Schmid 2012b, 53), which may have been a focal place in the preservation and promotion of the exodus and wandering tradition (for this temple having cultic literature of its own, see Schmid 2012b, 53). The strong connection of Kuntillet 'Ajrud to the king of Israel and the possible exodus-related inscription unearthed at the site may support this possibility.

Against this background, it is clear that people from the northern kingdom, including Samaria officials and merchants, frequented the site of Kuntillet 'Ajrud in particular and the Darb el-Ghazza in general. There they met local nomads who were involved in the southern trade. From their own experience and from these encounters they must have learned about places and routes in the "deep" desert, mainly those located between the head of the Gulf of Aqaba and the Mediterranean coast.

This is the place to turn attention to the biblical desert-wandering itineraries, especially the comprehensive summary in Num 33:1–49. Some of the toponyms in this list (mainly the group of twelve places in 33:18–30) do not appear in the narrative in the books of Exodus and Numbers and in the desert itineraries in Deuteronomy; in fact, they are not mentioned in any other biblical text. None (except one: Punon = Khirbet Faynan) can be identified. These place names probably come from an independent source (Noth 1968, 243). Whether they originally belonged to a pilgrimage itinerary (Noth 1940; 1968, 245–46), whether such an itinerary was connected to the story of the journey of Elijah to Horeb in 1 Kgs 19 (see above), and whether such a pilgrimage route was related to Kuntillet 'Ajrud is impossible to say. One thing is clear: these place names were no longer relevant to Judahite scribes in the seventh century, and hence they may have originated from the northern kingdom traditions of the eighth century B.C.E.

The details of the later layers in the exodus-wandering tradition, which came from the hands of Judahite scribes, are beyond the scope of this book, hence for the sake of this discussion it is sufficient to summarize them (for more, see Finkelstein forthcoming). This northern founding tradition probably "migrated" to Judah after 720 B.C.E. (Hoffman 1989, 181–82) with Israelite refugees. Between the late eighth and late seventh centuries B.C.E., the period when Judah served the interests of Assyria in the south as a vassal, Judahites who lived in the Beer-sheba Valley, and more so those who were stationed in places farther away such as the fort of Kadesh-barnea and possibly the fort of Tamar (En Hazeva; fig. 38) became intimately acquainted with the desert. This is expressed by the strong presence of Ezion-geber, Tamar, Kadesh-barnea, and Edom in biblical texts and more specifically the latter two in the wandering tradition.[3] Assyrian influence on the Moses story and anti-imperial strands in the narrative also belong to this period (Otto 2000, 51–67; Römer 2002, 24–29; 2003; Schmid 2012b, 81). Strong Judahite activity in the south, including in the fort of Kadesh-barnea, continued after the withdrawal of Assyria, under the hegemony of the Egyptian Twenty-Sixth Dynasty. The exodus tradition, with its message of victory over a mighty pharaoh, could have gained momentum as a result of the looming confrontation with Egypt in the time of King Josiah in the late seventh century (Finkelstein and Silberman 2001, 68–71) and in the sixth century B.C.E., when Judahites were present in the Nile Delta. Priestly scribes, who gave the exodus-wandering tradition its final shape and place in the Hebrew Bible, could not have been aware of the geography of the southern desert. Their work was strictly literary, aiming to serve the theology and circumstances of their time, such as the new exodus from exile in Babylonia (e.g., Hofmann 1998).

The exodus-wandering tradition is therefore a multilayered narrative. It was first transmitted orally and later put in writing in the north. It was then brought to the southern kingdom, accumulated levels, grew in volume and detail, and was transformed and redacted time and again in Judah and Yehud over a period of many centuries in the light of changing political and historical realities.

---

3. Information about the south was also probably brought to Judah by Arabs who took part in the Arabian trade of the time (see, e.g., Shiloh 1987; Thareani 2011, 223–28; Lemaire 2012).

6.3. SUMMARY

The original Jacob and exodus tales seem to have functioned in the northern kingdom as narratives of origins (Blum 2012b) or charter myths (van der Toorn 1996). Their sources can be traced to the early days of the kingdom (if not previously), and both are connected to historical realities: the formation of a settlement boundary between Israelites and Arameans in the Gilead in the Jacob story, and Egyptian intervention in the highlands in the tenth century B.C.E. in the exodus story. These original tales then developed gradually to form long-term cultural memory (Assmann 1998; Hendel 2001), rather than descriptions of specific events. They seem to have been related to the central shrines of the north: the Jacob story to Bethel and Penuel, and exodus to Samaria. As such, they may have originated from different areas of the central hill country: Ephraim and the Gilead versus northern Samaria, respectively. Van der Toorn (1996, 300) suggested that the Jacob tale was connected to El/Elohim, while the exodus story was associated with YHWH. The connection between the two narratives of origin—whether supplementary or conflicting—is still to be studied, as is the question whether in the later days of the kingdom they were both revered by all people of the north.

7
The End and Beyond: A New Meaning for "Israel"

The decline of Israel commenced after the days of Jeroboam II. This was a result of another change in the geopolitical scene that brought about the renewed strengthening of Damascus, combined somewhat later with a dramatic transformation in the Assyrian policies in the west—from remote influence to conquest and annexation. In 732 B.C.E. Tiglath-pileser III king of Assyria took over the Galilee and northern valleys of the northern kingdom and annexed them to the Assyrian empire. According to 2 Kgs 15:29, the Gilead was conquered at the same time. It seems, however, that Israel had already lost its Transjordanian territories to Damascus a few years earlier, as Tiglath-pileser III recounts that he took this territory from Damascus rather than Israel (Na'aman 1995). Samaria was captured by Assyria in 722–720 B.C.E. (for details, see Becking 1992). The northern kingdom disappeared forever, groups of its elite population were deported to Mesopotamia, and foreign groups were settled by the Assyrians in the territories of the fallen kingdom.

This was the end. Or was it? In a surprising twist of history, a short while later Israel was back, not as a kingdom but as a concept.[1] In fact, the fall of one Israel opened the way for the rise of another Israel—the children of Israel—composed of twelve tribes, encompassing the territory ruled by the two Hebrew kingdoms. In the course of this transformation, texts that originated in the northern kingdom were incorporated into the Bible, to form part of the great Hebrew epic.

---

1. On the development of the concept of early Israel, see details in Davies 2007b and bibliography.

7.1. Israelites in Judah after the Fall of the Northern Kingdom

Archaeology indicates a dramatic growth of Jerusalem in the Iron IIB, from a traditional highlands town to a large city of up to 60 hectares (e.g., Broshi 1974; Avigad 1983, 54–60; Reich and Shukron 2003; Geva 2003). The Iron IIA settlement was probably located in the mound (tell) on the Temple Mount, with limited additional activity near the Gihon Spring (Finkelstein, Koch, and Lipschits 2011), while the fortified Iron IIB city, probably the largest in the land of Israel at that time, expanded to the entire southeastern hill (the "City of David") and to the southwestern hill, the Jewish and Armenian Quarters of the Old City of Jerusalem and Mount Zion. Archaeology also shows that the number of settlements in Judah grew equally dramatically in the Iron IIB compared to the Iron IIA in both the hill country (from ca. 35 to ca. 120; Ofer 1994, 104–5) and the Shephelah (from ca. 20 to 275 [!]; Dagan 1992). It is true that, due to strong occupation in the Iron IIB–C, the Iron IIA may be somewhat underrepresented in archaeological surveys of multiperiod sites (for reasons, see Faust and Katz 2012), but from the point of view of total built-up area (which means population) this is compensated by the fact that the Iron IIB settlements were usually much larger than those of the Iron IIA.

Recent radiocarbon studies show that the transition from the Iron IIA to the Iron IIB pottery traditions took place sometime in the first half of the eighth century (Finkelstein and Piasetzky 2010), and it is reasonable to assume that Jerusalem had already reached its full size before the Sennacherib attack in 701 B.C.E. This means that the extraordinary increase in the population of Jerusalem and Judah took place in a matter of a few decades. Since the Iron IIB pottery traditions could have continued into the early seventh century, the population growth described above could have occurred over a slightly longer period of time, between the 730s and the early decades of the seventh century B.C.E. But even in this case we are dealing with exceptionally dramatic growth. The population of Judah at least doubled, if not tripled, in a very short period of time.

Such dramatic increase in population in antiquity could not be the result of natural growth, and Jerusalem and Judah had no economic appeal that could explain such escalation in the population over so relatively short a period of time.

An evaluation of the settlement patterns in the area between Shechem and Ramallah—the southern part of the territory of the northern kingdom in the highlands—shows a major decrease in population between the late eighth century and the Persian period, contrasted with stability in northern Samaria. Archaeology also testifies to the appearance in Judah, starting in the Iron IIB, of northern traits of material culture, such as olive-oil installations, burial traditions, and certain pottery types. Northern blocks in the Judah-dominated biblical text should also be considered as northern "artifacts" that migrated to the south, possibly in the late eighth century B.C.E. (see also Schniedewind 2004; Dietrich 2007, 248).

All this indicates a major population shift in the hill country over a short period of time in the second half of the eighth century. The only possible reason for this is the fall of the northern kingdom and resettlement of Israelite groups from the area of southern Samaria, including Bethel, in Jerusalem and Judah. Judah was consequently transformed from an isolated, clan-based homogeneous society into a mixed Judahite-Israelite kingdom under Assyrian domination. This, in turn, brought about the rise of pan-Israelite ideas in Judah. The emergence of biblical Israel as a concept was therefore the result of the fall of the kingdom of Israel.

7.2. THE RISE OF THE CONCEPT OF BIBLICAL ISRAEL

Two concepts made up the core of the pan-Israelite idea: the centrality of the Davidic dynasty and the Jerusalem temple for all Hebrews. Two texts more than others are crucial for understanding the emergence of the biblical concept of Israel as representing not only one kingdom but the entire "nation," northerners and southerners alike. These are the "History of David's Rise to Power" (1 Sam 16:14–2 Sam 5) and the "Succession History" (2 Sam 9–20 + 1 Kgs 1–2; see, e.g., Rost 1982 [original 1926]; von Rad 1966, 176–204 [original 1944]; de Pury and Römer 2000).

It is obvious that these stories contain some early, pre-Deuteronomistic memories, such as the portrayal of Gath as the most important city in Philistia and the existence of the small Aramaic kingdoms of Geshur and Maacah on the periphery of Damascus. As indicated above, Gath was destroyed in the second half of the ninth century B.C.E. and never recovered (Maeir 2004, 2012); indeed, it is not mentioned in late-monarchic biblical sources and in seventh-century Assyrian records (Schniedewind 1998). In the eighth century B.C.E., Geshur and Maacah had already been incorporated into the kingdom of Damascus.

Both the History of David's Rise and the Succession History contain information about the Saulides—the first north Israelite dynasty—and neither is entirely complimentary to King David. They include hinted allegations against the founder of the Jerusalem dynasty for cooperating with the Philistines, betraying his fellow Israelites, being responsible for the death of the first king of Israel, being liable for the death of other key figures related to Saul, and being guilty of other murders and wrongdoings. It is significant that most of the accusations deal with themes related to the Saulides and the north.

It seems that the orally transmitted History of David's Rise and the Succession History were first put in writing in the late eighth century B.C.E. (Finkelstein and Silberman 2006b; Na'aman 2009) by an author who composed his work against the background of the demographic changes that took place in Judah. This author took advantage of the fact that after 720 B.C.E. the term "Israel" became vacant territorially and politically.

Traditionally, the History of David's Rise and the Succession History were conceived by scholars as pro-Davidic legitimacy stories. McCarter (1980a) and Halpern (2001) suggested that much of the material was written in real time or close to the time of the founders of the Jerusalem dynasty, as an apologia. The History of David's Rise aimed, in their opinion, at countering bitter northern allegations against King David, vindicating him of any wrongdoing, and explaining "what really happened" according to the point of view of the Davidic dynasty. In the case of the Succession History, the apologia was needed in order to explain why Solomon, who was not the first or even second in the line of succession to the throne, came to reign after David.

However, the apologia theory fails to deal with a crucial issue: taking into consideration the fact that writing is not in evidence in Judah before around 800 B.C.E. (in other words, the apologia could not have been written in the tenth century), the question is: Why were the northern negative traditions on David preserved at all in the final Judahite composition? After all, a late eighth-century author could have eliminated this material and accomplished results similar to those of the author of the books of Chronicles several centuries later. The question therefore remains: What were the circumstances that forced the author (or authors) to preserve these northern anti-Judah traditions in a Judahite composition?

The fundamental criterion in searching the historical background for the authorship of the History of David's Rise and the Succession History should therefore be: What is the period that best fits a compilation of a saga that takes into account northern traditions about the founder of the Jerusalem dynasty? In what period did the author write, and what made him, certainly a Judahite, need to counter these traditions with an apologia? Why could he not simply ignore these stories altogether? These texts cannot be dated too late, because it is quite obvious that they went through a Deuteronomistic redaction in the late seventh century (for pre-Deuteronomistic materials in Samuel, see Halpern 2001, 57–72). The only chronological time span left for their initial composition is thus the second half of the eighth century and the first half of the seventh century B.C.E. When one considers the broader historical situation, the most reasonable period for the initial composition of these blocks is the late eighth century B.C.E., after the fall of the north, when the population of Judah swelled dramatically to include a large number of Israelite refugees.

As noted above, the results of the archaeological surveys carried out in the highlands show that the Israelites who came to Judah in the late eighth century originated mainly from the southern part of the hill country of Israel, as this area demonstrates a demographic decline in post-720 times. The people who resettled in Judah must have brought with them traditions that praised the Saulide dynasty that had ruled their territory and antagonistic traditions regarding the founder of the dynasty in Jerusalem. They must also have been intimately associated with the temple of YHWH at Bethel, located close to their home towns, where many of the north Israelite texts must have been put into writing.

The pre-Deuteronomistic Saul and David cycles represent Judah's way of handling this situation. The northern traditions that were cherished by what was now a significant part of the population of Judah needed to be absorbed, not ignored. The author did not eliminate them, because he needed to cater to the large northern population in Judah (also Schniedewind 2004, 78, 191). The texts were included in the Judahite story but at the same time were addressed in such a way as to attempt to vindicate David from almost all serious wrongdoing. The author incorporated the northern and southern traditions but subjected them to his main ideological goals: to promote the Davidic kings as the only legitimate rulers over all Israel and the Jerusalem temple as the only legitimate cult-place for all *Bene Israel*.

By doing so, the author advanced a pan-Israelite idea, though at this stage, still under Assyrian domination, this pan-Israelism was an ideology *within*, directed toward the mixed population inside Judah. The full-fledged pan-Israelite ideology—an appeal to those living in the ex-Israelite territories in the north to join the nation—came only later, probably in the days of Josiah in the late seventh century B.C.E., after the withdrawal of Assyria from the region. The ideological construct of a great united monarchy that ostensibly ruled from Jerusalem over all Israelites—in the north and south—is a product of this period. It was needed in order to provide "historical" legitimacy to the Jerusalem claim for dominance over all Hebrew territories and all Hebrew people—in both the north and south. Evidently, another side of the same coin was the need to downplay the importance of the northern kingdom of Israel, which was historically the more important of the two Hebrew kingdoms.

Downplaying the significance of the north, in fact, disparaging it and appropriating the term *Israel*, was especially crucial—both in the end days of Judah and in Persian period Yehud and Hellenistic Judea—in view of the settlement continuity and demographic prosperity around Shechem and in northern Samaria. There a competing Israel, made up of the descendants of the kingdom of Israel and deportees from the east, now known as Samaritans, with their temple on Mount Gerizim, continued to thrive for centuries.[2]

---

2. The Samaritans are beyond the scope of this book. For current research, see Anderson 2002; Stern and Eshel 2002; Magen 2004, 2008; Kartreit 2009; Mor and Reiterer 2010.

CONCLUDING REMARKS: LONG-TERM HISTORY VERSUS THE UNIQUENESS OF ISRAEL

Archaeological work in the highlands and the northern valleys in the last three decades, in excavations and surveys, makes it possible to delineate the full story of the northern kingdom, a story that is poorly told in the Bible and ideologically twisted in order to serve the goals of Judah at a time when Israel was no more.

1. It's All about Timing

This book is established on several pillars of modern archaeological research. The most essential is the new understanding of the chronology of the Iron Age, both relative and absolute. The development of a precise and minute study of the ceramic typology of the Iron Age leads to the division of the four hundred years between circa 1130 and 730 B.C.E. into five phases. This also stands in the heart of achieving a better and more accurate absolute chronology for the Iron Age. A change in the dating of the Iron Age strata in the Levant is dictated by radiocarbon results as well as by historical and material culture considerations. In the main, the new chronological scheme decrees lower dates for the Iron I and the Iron IIA.

The resulting chronological system has revolutionized the historical reconstruction of ancient Israel: it sheds light on the last days of the "New Canaan" phenomenon in the northern valleys in the late Iron I, pulls the carpet from under the idea of a great tenth-century united monarchy that ruled from Jerusalem over the entire territory between Dan and Beer-sheba, helps us understand that the two Hebrew kingdoms grew in parallel rather than from a single formative entity, "shifts" monuments in the north from the tenth to the ninth century and by doing so helps to acknowledge the greatness of the northern kingdom in the days of the Omride dynasty, opens the way for the study of territorial expansion and retraction in the history of Israel, and reveals the power of the kingdom of Damascus under Hazael in the late ninth century and the impact of this kingdom on the history of Israel.

2. Long-Term History

From a territorio-political perspective, the history of the northern part of the central hill country in the centuries that cover the Late Bronze, Iron I, and Iron IIA is a classic case of *la longue durée*, the French *Annales* School phrase for long-term history. This phenomenon was influenced by the special character of the geography of the region, its economy, and its population. This territory forms a rugged hill country that is, at the same time, not isolated but rather open to the lowland areas around it, and that is well connected to the highlands area to the east, across the Jordan. It was inhabited by a relatively large number of sedentary people with a meaningful pastoral component in the population, a combination that gave it special strength. It also featured significant output of secondary products of its orchards, especially olive oil, which presented it with an advantage in trade with neighboring arid regions that lacked this basic, important commodity.

These parameters led to the continuous rise of territorial entities in this region that were governed by strongmen who resembled in their policies the conduct of the Apiru of the Late Bronze Age—unruly gangs made up of mercenaries and uprooted elements who lived on the margins of organized society. The first such entity that is hinted at is the "Land of Shechem" mentioned in the Khu Sobek Stela of the Twelfth Egyptian Dynasty in the Middle Bronze Age, and the first fully recorded one is the Shechem highlands entity of Labayu and his sons in the Amarna period in the fourteenth century B.C.E. The story of Abimelech in the book of Judges may preserve a vague memory of an Iron I entity that was also centered in Shechem or its vicinity, and the rise of the kingdom of Jeroboam I is certainly another example in the same area. The only such polity in the northern part of the central hill country that had not been ruled from the area of Shechem is the Gibeon/Gibeah entity of the late Iron I. This territorial formation is hinted at by the itinerary of the Sheshonq I campaign and by biblical memories about the rule of the house of Saul.

These early kingdoms were formative hill-country territorial entities that were ruled from modest towns with no evidence of fortifications or monumental public building activity. Time and again they attempted to expand to the lowlands to their north and west. Their goal was to take over the fertile Jezreel Valley, the breadbasket of the country; to control the international military and trade routes that passed along the coastal plain, the Jezreel Valley, and Transjordan; and to establish for themselves a port on the Mediterranean coast, which could give them the necessary link to Meditarranean trade. The expansionist nature of highlands polity in the Levant was written in their genetic code, as demonstrated by similar cases in neighboring highlands territories in different periods. I refer to the kingdom of Amurru in Mount Lebanon in the Late Bronze Age, which expanded to the Orontes Valley and the coast and at a certain point took over the coastal city of Sumur; the Hasmonean state in the late Hellenistic period, which, early in its history, took over Gezer on the coastal plain and the port of Jaffa; the polity of Fakhr ed-Din in the Chouf Mountains in Lebanon circa 1600 C.E.; and the Bedouin "state" of Dahr el-Umar in the Lower Galilee in the eighteenth century C.E., which managed to take over the port of Acco. At least in their early days, all of these entities ruled from modest towns or villages with no monuments and no fortifications.

The rise of these territorial entities characterized periods of weakening imperial rule or intermediate periods with no strong power in the region. In times of imperial rule in the Levant, these expansion attempts ultimately failed and ended with the demise of the strongmen or ruling family. This was so with Labayu of Shechem in the Late Bronze Age, who was killed by agents of the Egyptian administration; the Gibeon/Gibeah entity that, as a result of its policies in the lowlands, faced the Sheshonq I campaign; and Dahr el-Umar, who was finally defeated by the Ottoman government. Success in these expansion endeavors was possible only when the entity in question served as an agent of an imperial rule or in the absence of a strong power. This was the case of the early days of the northern kingdom, possibly under the Egyptian umbrella, in the late tenth century B.C.E., and the Hasmonean state that emerged as a result of successful maneuvers between contending Hellenistic powers of its time.

The absence of a strong power ruling directly in the region in the first half of the ninth century enabled the northern kingdom to take the great leap forward and consolidate itself as a major regional player. This was accompanied by continuous territorial expansion to lands that had never before been ruled from the central highlands: Moab, the northeastern Gilead, the mountainous Galilee, and the upper Jordan Valley. It was also accompanied by the construction of an elaborate capital, Samaria, and by impressive monumental building activities in administrative centers and forts on the borders of the kingdom.

The emergence of the northern kingdom was therefore a twofold process: it was part of long-term developments in the highlands, which had started no later than the Late Bronze Age, and it was the immediate outcome of the specific circumstances of the ninth and early eighth centuries B.C.E. The rise of a strong regional power that ruled over vast territories with a variegated population was unique in the history of the southern Levant—the only such phenomenon in recorded history.

3. ISRAEL AND JUDAH

The diplomatic, economic, and territorial history of the Levant in the ninth and eighth centuries B.C.E. was dictated by the balance between three powers: Israel's and Damascus's struggle for hegemony, under the influence of the Assyrian Empire. Damascus must have been the stronger of the two regional kingdoms, but periods of Assyrian pressure west of the Euphrates opened the way for Israelite territorial expansion. Later, Assyrian imperial policy of military expansionism devoured both Damascus and the northern kingdom. In parallel, the decision in Assyria to spare Judah and use it as a vassal and buffer kingdom gave birth to the rise of Jerusalem as a major player on the stage of the Levant. It also initiated in Judah economic processes that promoted, in turn, population growth, urbanism, advanced administration, scribal activity, and reflections on the historical and cultural role of the kingdom among the Hebrews. This, in turn, brought about the beginning of compilation of biblical texts. From this perspective, the Bible can be described as a product of Assyrian imperialism.

Archaeological and historical research point to the cultural, economic, and military dominance of Israel over Judah. Almost every significant process in Israel can be dated several decades and sometime a century before it took place in Judah; in certain fields, such as monumental public construction, Judah never reached the level of Israel. An important example for the precedence of Israel is the case of scribal activity and compilation of elaborate "historical" texts.

Assembling all available data for scribal activity in Israel and Judah reveals no evidence of writing before approximately 800 B.C.E. In fact, it shows that meaningful writing in Israel began in the first half of the eighth century, while in Judah it commenced only in the late eighth and more so in the seventh century B.C.E. Past ideas regarding the date of compilation of biblical texts were based on the testimony of the Bible and hence fell prey to circular reasoning. Recent archaeological and biblical research has made it clear that no biblical text could have been written before circa 800 B.C.E. in Israel and about a century later in Judah. This means that the earliest northern texts, such as the core of the Jacob cycle in Genesis, were probably put in writing in the first half of the eighth century, during the period of prosperity of Israel, especially under the long reign of Jeroboam II. This indicates, in turn, that ninth-century B.C.E. and earlier memories could have been preserved and transmitted only in oral form.

When it comes to the compilation of texts, two important factors make a clear distinction between Israel and Judah. The first is the special nature of the northern kingdom: the varied population, the rule over different types of geographical units, and, as a result, the rise of successive dynasties. The second is the fact that Israel was erased from the face of the earth right at the beginning of direct Assyrian rule that changed the history, economy, and material culture of the Levant. Needless to say, we know very little about the scope of the compilation of texts in the north in the eighth century B.C.E., but from the little that we can grasp it seems that the northern texts dealt with regional, local traditions and were written in different places, at least in the capital Samaria and in the temples of Bethel and Penuel. This is very different from the compilation of texts in Jerusalem—and Jerusalem only—as early as the late eighth century and certainly in the late seventh century. The authors in Judah attempted to present an overall, broad vision regarding temple, dynasty, and the role of Judah in the story of ancient Israel—and this took place when the northern kingdom no longer existed.

It was only the fall of the northern kingdom and the move of a large number of Israelites to Judah that brought about the rise of pan-Israelite ideology in the south. The new vision promoted the idea of the supremacy and sole legitimacy of the Davidic dynasty and the Jerusalem temple among the mix of Judahites and Israelites that now constituted the population of Judah. Still later, with the withdrawal of Assyria, this ideology was expanded to include all people and territories that were once ruled by the two Hebrew kingdoms. As part of this ideological process, and in competition with the remaining Israelites, the Samaritans, and their temple at Mount Gerizim, the term *Israel* was transformed from the name of the kingdom to a concept of a future unified nation living under a Davidic king and worshiping in the Jerusalem temple. The short, two-century-long history of the kingdom of Israel gave birth, then, to the millennia-long concept of the people of Israel.

This said, the crucial role of the latter concept, in both Christianity and Judaism for centuries and up to the present, must not overshadow the history and culture of the first Israel: the Forgotten Kingdom.

WORKS CITED

Abu Husayn, A.-R. 1985. *Provincial Leaderships in Syria 1575–1650.* Beirut: American University of Beirut.

Adams, M. J., I. Finkelstein, and D. Ussishkin. Forthcoming. The Great Temple of Early Bronze I Megiddo. *AJA.*

Ahituv, S., E. Eshel, and Z. Meshel. 2012. The Inscriptions. Pages 73–142 in Z. Meshel, *Kuntillet 'Ajrud (Horvat Teman): An Iron Age II Religious Site on the Judah-Sinai Border.* Jerusalem: Israel Exploration Society.

Albertz, R. 2001. Exodus: Liberation History against Charter Myths. Pages 128–43 in *Religious Identity and the Invention of Tradition: Papers Read at a NOSTER Conference in Soesterberg, January 4–6, 1999.* Edited by J. W. van Henten and A. W. J. Hautepen. Assen: Van Gorcum.

Albright, W. F. 1924. *Excavations and Results at Tell el-Ful (Gibeah of Saul).* AASOR 4. New Haven: American Schools of Oriental Research.

———. 1931. The Site of Tirzah and the Topography of Western Manasseh. *Journal of the Palestine Oriental Society* 11:241–51.

———. 1936. The Song of Deborah in the Light of Archaeology. *BASOR* 62:26–31.

———. 1960. *The Archaeology of Palestine.* Harmondsworth, U.K.: Penguin.

Alt, A. 1925a. Judas Gaue unter Josia. *PJb* 21:100–116.

———. 1925b. *Die Landnahme der Israeliten in Palästina.* Reformationsprogramm der Universität Leipzig. Leipzig: Druckerei der Werkgemeinschaft.

Anderson, R. T. 2002. *The Keepers: An Introduction to the History and Culture of the Samaritans.* Peabody, Mass.: Hendrickson.

Arie, E. 2006. The Iron Age I Pottery: Levels K-5 and K-4 and an Intra-site Spatial Analysis of the Pottery from Stratum VIA. Pages 191–298 in Finkelstein, Ussishkin, and Halpern 2006.

———. 2008. Reconstructing the Iron Age II Strata at Tel Dan: Archaeological and Historical Implications. *Tel Aviv* 35:6–64.

———. 2011. "In the Land of the Valley": Settlement, Social and Cultural Processes in the Jezreel Valley from the End of the Late Bronze Age to the Formation of the Monarchy [Hebrew]. Ph.D. diss., Tel Aviv University.

———. 2013. The Late Bronze III and Iron I Pottery. Pages 475–667 in Megiddo V: The 2004–2008 Seasons. Edited by I. Finkelstein, D. Ussishkin, and E. H. Cline. Monograph Series of the Institute of Archaeology Tel Aviv University 31. Tel Aviv: Emery and Claire Yass Publications in Archaeology.

Arnold, P. M. 1990. Gibeah: The Search for a Biblical City. Sheffield: JSOT Press.

Ash, P. S. 1999. David, Solomon and Egypt: A Reassessment. JSOTSup 297. Sheffield: Sheffield Academic Press.

Assmann, J. 1998. Moses the Egyptian: The Memory of Egypt in Western Monotheism. Cambridge: Harvard University Press.

Avigad, N. 1983. Discovering Jerusalem. Nashville: Thomas Nelson.

Ayalon, E. 1995. The Iron Age II Pottery Assemblage from Horvat Teiman (Kuntillet ʿAjrud). Tel Aviv 22:141–205.

Aznar, C. A. 2005. Exchange Networks in the Southern Levant during the Iron Age II: A Study of Pottery Origin and Distribution. Ph.D. diss., Harvard University.

Ballard, R. D., L. E. Stager, D. Master, D. Yoerger, D. Mondell, L. L. Whitcomb, H. Singh, and D. Piechota. 2002. Iron Age Shipwrecks in Deep Water off Ashkelon, Israel. AJA 106:151–68.

Beck, P. 1982. The Drawings from Horvat Teiman (Kuntillet ʿAjrud). Tel Aviv 9:3–68.

———. 1994. The Cult Stands from Taanach: Aspects of the Iconographic Tradition of Early Iron Age Cult Objects in Palestine. Pages 352–81 in From Nomadism to Monarchy: Archaeological and Historical Aspects of Early Israel. Edited by I. Finkelstein and N. Naʾaman. Jerusalem: Yad Izhak Ben-Zvi.

———. 2000. The Art of Palestine during the Iron Age II: Local Traditions and External Influences (10th–8th Centuries BCE). Pages 165–183 in Images as Media: Sources for the Culture History of the Near East and the Eastern Mediterranean (1st Millennium BCE). Edited by C. Uehlinger. OBO 175. Fribourg: Editions universitaires Fribourg; Göttingen: Vandenhoeck & Ruprecht.

Becking, B. 1992. The Fall of Samaria: An Historical and Archaeological Study. SHANE 2. Leiden: Brill.

Ben-Ami, D. 2004. The Casement Fort at Tel Harashim in Upper Galilee. *Tel Aviv* 31:194–208.

Ben-Dor Evian, S. 2011. Shishak's Karnak Relief—More Than Just Name-Rings. Pages 11–22 in *Egypt, Canaan and Israel: History, Imperialism, Ideology and Literature*. Edited by S. Bar, D. Kahn, and J. J. Shirley. Leiden: Brill.

Ben-Tor, A. 2000. Hazor and Chronology of Northern Israel: A Reply to Israel Finkelstein. *BASOR* 317:9–15.

———. 2008. Hazor. *NEAEHL* 5:1769–76.

Bernett, M., and O. Keel. 1998 *Mond, Stier und Kult am Stadttor: Die Stele von Betsaida (et-Tell)*. Fribourg: Universitatsverlag.

Berlejung, A. 2009. Twisting Traditions: Programmatic Absence-Theology for the Northern Kingdom in 1 Kgs 12:26–33* (The "Sin of Jeroboam"). *JNSL* 35:1–42.

Bietak, M. 1987. Comments on the "Exodus." Pages 163–71 in *Egypt, Israel, Sinai: Archaeological and Historical Relationships in the Biblical Period*. Edited by A. F. Rainey. Tel Aviv: Tel Aviv University.

Biran, A. 1994. *Biblical Dan*. Jerusalem: Israel Exploration Society.

Biran, A., and J. Naveh. 1995. The Tel Dan Inscription: A New Fragment. *IEJ* 45:1–18.

Blenkinsopp, J. 1974. Did Saul Make Gibeon His Capital? *VT* 24:1–7.

———. 2003. Bethel in the Neo-Babylonian period. Pages 93–107 in *Judah and the Judeans in the Neo-Babylonian Period*. Edited by O. Lipschits and J. Blenkinsopp. Winona Lake, Ind.: Eisenbrauns.

Bloch, M. 1952. *Apologie pour l'histoire, ou, Metier d'historien*. Paris: Colin.

Blum, E. 2009. Hosea 12 und die Pentateuchüberlieferungen. Pages 291–321 in *Die Erzväter in der biblischen Tradition: Festschrift für Matthias Köckert*. Edited by A. C. Hagedorn and H. Pfeiffer. Berlin: de Gruyter.

———. 2012a. Der historische Mose und die Frühgeschichte Israels. *HBAI* 1:37–63.

———. 2012b. The Jacob Tradition. Pages 181–212 in *The Book of Genesis: Composition, Reception, and Interpretation*. Edited by C. A. Evans, J. N. Lohr and D. L. Petersen. Leiden: Brill.

Boaretto, E., I. Finkelstein, and R. Shahack-Gross. 2010. Radiocarbon Results from the Iron IIA Site of Atar Haroa in the Negev Highlands and Their Archaeological and Historical Implications. *Radiocarbon* 52:1–12.

Bordreuil, P., and F. Briquel-Chatonnet. 2000. *Le temps de la Bible*. Paris : Fayard.

Braudel, F. 1958. La longue durée. *Annales Economies Sociétés Civilisations* 13:725–53.

Briend, J. 1981. Jeroboam II, sauveur d'Israel. Pages 41–50 in *Mélanges bibliques et orientaux en l'honneur de M. Henri Cazelles.* Edited by A. Caquot and M. Delcor. AOAT 212. Kevelaer: Butzon & Bercker; Neukirchen-Vluyn: Neukirchener.

———. 1996. Tell el-Far'ah et son identification ancienne. Pages 5–14 in P. Amiet, J. Briend, L. Courtois, and J.-B. Dumortier, *Tell el-Far'ah: Histoire, glyptique et céramologie.* OBO 14. Fribourg: Editions universitaires Fribourg; Göttingen: Vandenhoeck & Ruprecht.

Briquel-Chatonnet, F. 1992. *Les relations entre les cités de la côte phénicienne et les royaumes d'Israël et de Juda.* Leuven: Peeters.

———. 2010. Le royaume de Tyr et son voisin Israël: Quelques réflexions sur les premiers échanges. Pages 31–36 in *Carthage et les autochtones de son empire du temps de Zama.* Coordinated by A. Ferjaoui. Tunis: Institut national du patrimoine.

Broshi, M. 1974. The Expansion of Jerusalem in the Reigns of Hezekiah and Manasseh. *IEJ* 24:21–26.

Broshi, M., and I. Finkelstein. 1992. The Population of Palestine in Iron Age II. *BASOR* 287:47–60.

Buhl, M.-L., and S. Holm-Nielsen. 1969. *Shiloh: The Danish Excavations at Tall Sailūn, Palestine in 1926, 1929, 1932 and 1963.* Copenhagen: Nationalmuseet.

Bunimovitz, S. 1994. The Problem of Human Resources in Late Bronze Age Palestine and Its Socioeconomic Implications. *UF* 26:1–20.

Burke, A. 2008. *"Walled up to Heaven": The Evolution of Middle Bronze Age Fortification Strategies in the Levant.* Winona Lake, Ind.: Eisenbrauns.

Callaway, J. A. 1976. Excavating Ai (et-Tell): 1964–1972. *BA* 39:18–30.

Callaway, J. A., and R. E. Cooley. 1971. A Salvage Excavation at Raddana, in Bireh. *BASOR* 201:9–19.

Cantrell, D. O. 2006. Stables Issues. Pages 630–42 in Finkelstein, Ussishkin, and Halpern 2006.

———. 2011. *The Horsemen of Israel: Horses and Chariotry in Monarchic Israel (Ninth-Eighth Centuries B.C.E.).* Winona Lake, Ind.: Eisenbrauns.

Cantrell, D. O., and I. Finkelstein. 2006. A Kingdom for a Horse: The Megiddo Stables and Eighth Century Israel. Pages 643–65 in Finkelstein, Ussishkin, and Halpern 2006.

Carr, D. M. 2012. The Moses Story: Literary Historical Reflections. *HBAI* 1:7–36.

Chambon, A. 1984. *Tell el-Far'ah I, l'âge du Fer.* Éditions Recherche sur les Civilisations. Mémoire 31. Paris: Éditions Recherche sur les civilisations.

———. 1993. Far'ah, Tell el- (North). *NEAEHL* 2:433–440.

Cline, E. H. 2006. Area L (The 1998–2000 Seasons). Pages 104–23 in Finkelstein, Ussishkin, and Halpern 2006.

———. 2011. Whole Lotta Shakin' Going On: The Possible Destruction by Earthquake of Stratum VIA at Megiddo. Pages 55–70 in *The Fire Signals of Lachish: Studies in the Archaeology and History of Israel in the Late Bronze Age, Iron Age, and Persian Period in Honor of David Ussishkin.* Edited by I. Finkelstein and N. Na'aman. Winona Lake, Ind.: Eisenbrauns.

Cogan, M. 1992. Chronology. *ABD* 1:1002–11.

Cohen, A. 1973. *Palestine in the 18th Century: Patterns of Government and Administration.* Jerusalem: Magnes.

Cross, F. M. 1973. *Canaanite Myth and Hebrew Epic.* Cambridge: Harvard University Press.

Crowfoot, J. W., K. M. Kenyon, and E. L. Sukenik. 1942. *Samaria-Sebaste I: The Buildings at Samaria.* London: Palestine Exploration Fund.

Dagan, Y. 1992. The Shephelah during the Period of the Monarchy in Light of Archaeological Excavations and Surveys [Hebrew]. M.A. thesis, Tel Aviv University.

———. 2009. Khirbet Qeiyafa in the Judean Shephelah: Some Considerations. *Tel Aviv* 36:68–81.

Daviau, P. M. M. 2006a. Hirbet el-Mudēyine in Its Landscape, Iron Age Towns, Forts and Shrines. *ZDPV* 122:14–30.

———. 2006b. The Wadi ath-Thamad Project, 2006. *Liber Annuus* 56:566–68.

Daviau, P. M. M., and P. E. Dion. 2002. Economy-Related Finds from Khirbat al-Mudayna (Wadi ath-Thamad, Jordan). *BASOR* 328:31–48.

Daviau, P. M. M., and M. Steiner. 2000. A Moabite Sanctuary at Khirbat al-Mudayna. *BASOR* 320:1–21.

Davies, P. R. 2007a. *The Origins of Biblical Israel.* New York: T&T Clark.

———. 2007b. The Trouble with Benjamin. Pages 93–111 in *Reflection and Refraction: Studies in Biblical Historiography in Honour of A. Graeme Auld.* Edited by R. Rezetko, T. H. Lim, and W. B. Aucker. Leiden: Brill.

Dearman, J. A. 1984. The Location of Jahaz. *ZDPV* 100:122–26.

———. 1989a. Historical Reconstruction and the Mesha Inscription. Pages 155–210 in Dearman 1989b.

———, ed. 1989b. *Studies in the Mesha Inscription and Moab*. Atlanta: Scholars Press.

Dessel, J. P. 1999. Tell "Ein Zippori and the Lower Galilee in the Late Bronze and Iron Ages: A Village Perspective. Pages 1–32 in *Galilee through the Centuries*. Edited by E. M. Meyers. Winona Lake, Ind.: Eisenbrauns.

Dever, W. G. 1997. Archaeology and the "Age of Solomon": A Case Study in Archaeology and Historiography. Pages 217–51 in *The Age of Solomon: Scholarship at the Turn of the Millennium*. Edited by L. K. Handy. Leiden: Brill.

———. 2003. *Who Were the Early Israelites and Where Did They Come From?* Grand Rapids: Eerdmans.

Dever, W. G., D. H. Lance, R. G. Bullard, D. P. Cole, A. M. Furshpan, J. S. Holladay, J. D. Seger, and R. B. Wright. 1971. Further Excavations at Gezer, 1967–1971. *BA* 34:94–132.

Diakonoff, I. M. 1992. The Naval Power and Trade of Tyre. *IEJ* 42:168–93.

Dietrich, W. 2007. *The Early Monarchy in Israel: The Tenth Century B.C.E.* Translated by Joachim Vette. Biblical Encyclopedia 3. Atlanta: Society of Biblical Literature.

Dion, P.-E. 1997. *Les Araméens à l'âge du Fer: Histoire politique et structures sociales*. Paris: Gabalda.

Dozeman, T. B. 1989. *God on the Mountain: A Study of Redaction, Theology and Canon in Exodus 19–24*. SBLMS 37. Atlanta: Scholars Press.

———. Hosea and the Wilderness Wandering Tradition. Pages 55–70 in *Rethinking the Foundations: Historiography in the Ancient World and in the Bible, Essays in Honour of John Van Seters*. Edited by S. L. McKenzie and T. Römer. Berlin: de Gruyter.

Dozeman, T. B., and K. Schmid, eds. 2006. *A Farewell to the Yahwist? The Composition of the Pentateuch in Recent European Interpretation*. SBLSymS 34. Atlanta: Society of Biblical Literature.

Dozeman, T.B., K. Schmid, and B. J. Schwartz, eds. 2011. *The Pentateuch: International Perspectives on Current Research*. Tübingen: Mohr Siebeck.

Edelman, D. 1985. The "Ashurites" of Eshbaal's State (2 Sam. 2.9). *PEQ* 117:85–91.

———. 1988. Saul's Journey through Mt. Ephraim and Samuel's Ramah (1 Sam. 9:4–5, 10:2–5). *ZDPV* 104:44–58.

——. 1992. Saul. *ABD* 5:989–99.

——. 1996. Saul ben Kish in History and Tradition. Pages 142–59 in *The Origins of the Ancient Israelite States.* Edited by V. Fritz and P. R. Davies. Sheffield: Sheffield Academic Press.

Eitam, D. 1979. Olive Presses of the Israelite Period. *Tel Aviv* 6:146–55.

Eliyahu-Behar, A., N. Yahalom-Mack, Y. Gadot, and I. Finkelstein. 2013. Metalworking in Area K: A Reevaluation. Pages 1271–84 in *Megiddo V: The 2004–2008 Seasons.* Edited by I. Finkelstein, D. Ussishkin, and E. H. Cline. Monograph Series of the Institute of Archaeology Tel Aviv University 31. Tel Aviv: Emery and Claire Yass Publications in Archaeology.

Eliyahu-Behar, A., N. Yahalom-Mack, Y. Gadot, and I. Finkelstein. Forthcoming. Iron Smelting and Smithing in Urban Centers in Israel during the Iron Age. *JAS.*

Fantalkin, A. 2008. The Appearance of Rock-Cut Bench Tombs in Iron Age Judah as a Reflection of State Formation. Pages 17–44 in *Bene Israel: Studies in the Archaeology of Israel and the Levant during the Bronze and Iron Ages in Honour of Israel Finkelstein.* Edited by A. Fantalkin and A. Yassur-Landau. CHANE 31. Leiden: Brill.

Fantalkin, A., and I. Finkelstein. 2006. The Sheshonq I Campaign and the 8th-Century BCE Earthquake—More on the Archaeology and History of the South in the Iron I-IIA. *Tel Aviv* 33:18–42.

Faust, A. 2006. *Israel's Ethnogenesis: Settlement, Interaction, Expansion and Resistance.* London: Equinox.

——. 2010. The Large Stone Structure in the City of David. *ZDPV* 124:116–30.

Faust, A., and H. Katz. 2012. Survey, Shovel Tests and Excavations at Tel 'Eton: On Methodology and Site History. *Tel Aviv* 39:158–85.

Finkelstein, I. 1981. The Shephelah of Israel. *Tel Aviv* 8:84–94.

——. 1988. *The Archaeology of the Israelite Settlement.* Jerusalem: Israel Exploration Society.

——. 1995. The Great Transformation: The "Conquest" of the Highlands Frontiers and the Rise of the Territorial States. Pages 349–65 in *The Archaeology of Society in the Holy Land.* Edited by T. E. Levy. New York: Facts on File.

——. 1996a. The Archaeology of the United Monarchy: An Alternative View. *Levant* 28:177–87.

——. 1996b. The Stratigraphy and Chronology of Megiddo and Bethshan in the 12–11th Centuries B.C.E. *Tel Aviv* 23:170–84.

————. 1996c. The Territorio-Political System of Canaan in the Late Bronze Age. *UF* 28:221–55.

————. 1997. Pots and People Revisited: Ethnic Boundaries in the Iron Age I. Pages 216–237 in *The Archaeology of Israel: Constructing the Past, Interpreting the Present*. Edited by N. A. Silberman and D. Small. JSOTSup 237. Sheffield: Sheffield Academic Press.

————. 1999a. Hazor and the North in the Iron Age: A Low Chronology Perspective. *BASOR* 314:55–70.

————. 1999b. State Formation in Israel and Judah: A Contrast in Context, A Contrast in Trajectory. *NEA* 62:35–52.

————. 2000. Omride Architecture. *ZDPV* 116:114–38.

————. 2002a. The Campaign of Shoshenq I to Palestine: A Guide to the 10th Century BCE Polity. *ZDPV* 118:109–35.

————. 2002b. The Philistine in the Bible: A Late-Monarchic Perspective. *JSOT* 27:131–67.

————. 2003. City States and States: Polity Dynamics in the 10th–9th Centuries B.C.E. Pages 75–83 in *Symbiosis, Symbolism and the Power of the Past: Canaan, Ancient Israel, and their Neighbors*. Edited by W. G. Dever and S. Gitin. Winona Lake, Ind.: Eisenbrauns.

————. 2006a. The Last Labayu: King Saul and the Expansion of the First North Israelite Territorial Entity. Pages 171–77 in *Essays on Ancient Israel in Its Near Eastern Context: A Tribute to Nadav Na'aman*. Edited by Y. Amit, E. Ben Zvi, I. Finkelstein, and O. Lipschits. Winona Lake, Ind.: Eisenbrauns.

————. 2006b. Shechem in the Late Bronze Age. Pages 349–56 in *Timelines: Studies in Honour of Manfred Bietak*. Edited by E. Czerny, I. Hein, H. Hunger, D. Melman, and A. Schwab. Leuven: Peeters.

————. 2010. A Great United Monarchy? Archaeological and Historical Perspectives. Pages 3–28 in *One God—One Cult—One Nation: Archaeological and Biblical Perspectives*. Edited by R. G. Kratz and H. Spieckermann. Berlin: de Gruyter.

————. 2011a. The "Large Stone Structure" in Jerusalem: Reality versus Yearning. *ZDPV* 127:1–10.

————. 2011b. Observations on the Layout of Iron Age Samaria. *Tel Aviv* 38:194–207.

————. 2011c. Saul, Benjamin and the Emergence of "Biblical Israel": An Alternative View. *ZAW* 123:348–67.

————. 2011d. Tell el-Ful Revisited: The Assyrian and Hellenistic Periods (with a New Identification). *PEQ* 143:106–18.

———. 2011e. Tell el-Umeiri in the Iron I: Facts and Fiction. Pages 113–128 in *The Fire Signals of Lachish, Studies on the Archaeology and History of Israel in the Late Bronze Age, Iron Age and Persian Period in Honor of David Ussishkin*. Edited by I. Finkelstein and N. Na'aman. Winona Lake, Ind.: Eisenbrauns.

———. 2012. The Great Wall of Tell en-Nasbeh (Mizpah), The First Fortifications in Judah and 1 Kings 15: 16–22. *VT* 62:14–28.

———. Forthcoming. The Wilderness Narrative and Itineraries: What, How and When Did Biblical Author Know about the Southern Deserts. In *Out of Egypt: Israel's Exodus between Text and Memory, History and Imagination*. Edited by T. E. Levy.

Finkelstein, I., S. Bunimovitz, and Z. Lederman. 1993. *Shiloh: The Archaeology of a Biblical Site*. Monograph Series of the Institute of Archaeology Tel Aviv University 10. Tel Aviv: Institute of Archaeology of Tel Aviv University.

Finkelstein, I., B. Halpern, G. Lehmann, and H. M. Niemann. 2006. The Megiddo Hinterland Project. Pages 705–76 in Finkelstein, Ussishkin, and Halpern 2006.

Finkelstein, I., Z. Herzog, L. Singer-Avitz, and D. Ussishkin. 2007. Has the Palace of King David in Jerusalem Been Found? *Tel Aviv* 34:142–64.

Finkelstein, I., I. Koch, and O. Lipschits. 2011. The Mound on the Mount: A Solution to the "Problem with Jerusalem." *JHS* 11. Online: http://www.jhsonline.org/Articles/article_159.pdf.

———. 2012. The Biblical Gilead: Observations on Identifications, Geographic Divisions and Territorial History. *UF* 43:131–59.

Finkelstein, I., and O. Lipschits. 2010. Omride Architecture in Moab: Jahaz and Ataroth. *ZDPV* 126:29–42.

———. 2011. The Genesis of Moab. *Levant* 43:139–52.

Finkelstein, I., O. Lipschits, and O. Sergi. 2013. Tell er-Rumeith in Northern Jordan: Some Archaeological and Historical Observations. *Semitica* 55:7–23.

Finkelstein, I., and Y. Magen. 1993. *Archaeological Survey of the Hill Country of Benjamin*. Jerusalem: Israel Antiquities Authority.

Finkelstein, I., and N. Na'aman. 2005. Shechem of the Amarna Period and the Rise of the Northern Kingdom of Israel. *IEJ* 55:172–93.

Finkelstein, I., and E. Piasetzky. 2006. The Iron I-IIA in the Highlands and beyond: [14]C Anchors, Pottery Phases and the Shoshenq I Campaign. *Levant* 38:45–61.

———. 2008. The Date of Kuntillet 'Ajrud: The ^{14}C Perspective. *Tel Aviv* 35:175–85.

———. 2009. Radiocarbon-Dated Destruction Layers: A Skeleton for Iron Age Chronology in the Levant. *Oxford Journal of Archaeology* 28:255–74.

———. 2010. Radiocarbon Dating the Iron Age in the Levant: A Bayesian Model for Six Ceramic Phases and Six Transitions. *Antiquity* 84:374–85.

———. 2011. The Iron Age Chronology Debate: Is the Gap Narrowing? *NEA* 74:50–54.

Finkelstein, I., and B. Sass. Forthcoming. The West Semitic Alphabet: Late Bronze to Iron IIB. *HBAI.*

Finkelstein, I., B. Sass, and L. Singer-Avitz. 2008. Writing in Iron IIA Philistia in the Light of the Tel Zayit Abecedary. *ZDPV* 124:1–14.

Finkelstein, I., and N. A. Silberman. 2001. *The Bible Unearthed: Archaeology's New Vision of Ancient Israel and the Origin of its Sacred Texts.* New York: Free Press.

———. 2006a. *David and Solomon: In Search of the Bible's Sacred Kings and the Roots of Western Tradition.* New York: Free Press.

———. 2006b. Temple and Dynasty: Hezekiah, the Remaking of Judah and the Rise of the Pan-Israelite Ideology. *JSOT* 30:259–85.

Finkelstein, I., and L. Singer-Avitz. 2009. Reevaluating Bethel. *ZDPV* 125:33–48.

Finkelstein, I., D. Ussishkin, and B. Halpern, eds. 2006. *Megiddo IV: The 1998–2002 Seasons.* Monograph Series of the Institute of Archaeology Tel Aviv University 24. Tel Aviv: Emery and Claire Yass Publications in Archaeology.

Finkelstein, I., E. Zapassky, Y. Gadot, D. Master, L. E. Stager, and I. Benenson. 2011. Phoenician "Torpedo" Amphoras and Egypt: Standardization of Volume Based on Linear Dimensions. *Egypt and the Levant* 21:249–59.

Fleming, D. E. 2012. *The Legacy of Israel in Judah's Bible: History, Politics, and the Reinscribing of Tradition.* Cambridge: Cambridge University Press.

Frankel, R. 2006. Two Installations for the Production of Olive Oil. Pages 618–29 in Finkelstein, Ussishkin, and Halpern 2006.

Frankenstein, S. 1979. The Phoenicians in the Far West: A Function of Neo-Assyrian Imperialism. Pages 263–94 in *Power and Propaganda: A Symposium on Ancient Empires.* Edited by M. T. Larsen. Studies in Assyriology 7. Copenhagen: Akademisk forlag.

Franklin, N. 2004. Samaria: From the Bedrock to the Omride Palace. *Levant* 36:189–202.

Frick, F. S. 2000. *Tell Taannek 1963–1968 IV/2: The Iron Age Cultic Structure.* Birzeit: Palestinian Institute of Archaeology, Excavations and Surveys.

Gal, Z., and Y. Alexandre. 2000. *Horbat Rosh Zayit: An Iron Age Storage Fort and Village.* IAA Reports 8. Jerusalem: Israel Antiquities Authority.

Galil. G. 2009. The Hebrew Inscription from Khirbet Qeiyafa/Netafim. *UF* 41:193–242.

Galpaz, P. 1991. The Reign of Jeroboam and the Extent of Egyptian Influence. *BN* 60:13–19.

Garfinkel, Y., and S. Ganor. 2009. *Khirbet Qeiyafa 1: Excavation Report 2007–2008.* Jerusalem: Israel Antiquities Authority.

Gersht, D. 2006. The Flint Assemblage from Area K. Pages 343–52 in Finkelstein, Ussishkin, and Halpern 2006.

Geus, C. H. J. de. 1976. *The Tribes of Israel: An Investigation into Some of the Presupostions of Martin Noth's Amphictyony Hypothesis.* Assen: Van Gorcum.

Geva, H. 2003. Western Jerusalem at the End of the First Temple Period in Light of the Excavations in the Jewish Quarter. Pages 183–208 in *Jerusalem in Bible and Archaeology: The First Temple Period.* Edited by A. G. Vaughn and A. E. Killebrew. SBLSymS 18. Atlanta: Society of Biblical Literature.

Gilboa, A. 2005. Sea Peoples and Phoenicians along the Southern Phoenician Coast—A Reconciliation: An Interpretation of Šikila (*SKL*) Material Culture. *BASOR* 337:47–78.

Gilboa, A., and I. Sharon. 2003. An Archaeological Contribution to the Early Iron Age Chronological Debate: Alternative Chronologies for Phoenicia and Their Effects on the Levant, Cyprus, and Greece. *BASOR* 332:7–80.

Glass, J., Y. Goren, S. Bunimovitz, and I. Finkelstein. 1993. Petrographic Analysis of Middle Bronze Age III, Late Bronze Age and Iron Age I Ceramic Assemblages. Pages 271–277 in Finkelstein, Bunimovitz, and Lederman 1993.

Glueck, N. 1934. *Explorations in Eastern Palestine.* AASOR 14. New Haven: American Schools of Oriental Research.

———. 1943. Ramoth-gilead. *BASOR* 92:10–16.

Goren, Y., I. Finkelstein, and N. Na'aman. 2003. The Expansion of the Kingdom of Amurru according to the Petrographic Investigation of the Amarna Tablets. *BASOR* 329:2–11.

———. 2004. *Inscribed in Clay: Provenance Study of the Amarna Letters and other Ancient Near Eastern Texts*. Monograph Series of the Institute of Archaeology, Tel Aviv University 23. Tel Aviv: Emery and Claire Yass Publications in Archaeology.

Grabbe, L., ed. 2007. *Ahab Agonistes: The Rise and Fall of the Omri Dynasty*. London: T&T Clark.

Guillaume, P. 2004. *Waiting for Josiah: The Judges*. JSOTSup 385. London: T&T Clark.

Haggi, A. 2006. Phoenician Atlit and Its Newly Excavated Harbour: A Reassessment. *Tel Aviv* 33:43–60.

Halpern, B. 1993. The Exodus and the Israelite Historian. *EI* 24:89*–96*.

———. 2001. *David's Secret Demons: Messiah, Murderer, Traitor, King*. Grand Rapids: Eerdmans.

Handy, L. K. 1997. On the Dating and Dates of Solomon's Reign. Pages 96–105 in *The Age of Solomon: Scholarship at the Turn of the Millennium*. Edited by L. K. Handy. Leiden: Brill.

Harrison, T. P. 2004. *Megiddo 3: Final Report on the Stratum VI Excavations*. Oriental Institute Publications 127. Chicago: Oriental Institute of the University of Chicago.

Hasegawa, S., and Paz, Y. 2009. Tel 'En Gev: Preliminary Report. *Excavations and Surveys in Israel* 121. Online: http://www.hadashot-esi.org.il/report_detail_eng.asp?id=1013&mag_id=115.

Hauptmann, A. 2007. *The Archaeometallurgy of Copper: Evidence from Faynan, Jordan*. Berlin: Springer.

Helck, W. 1971. *Die Beziehungen Ägyptens zu Vorderasien im 3. und 2. Jahrtausend v. Chr.* Ägyptologische Abhandlungen 5. Wiesbaden: Harrassowitz.

Hellwing, S., M. Sadeh, and V. Kishon. 1993. Faunal Remains. Pages 309–50 in *Shiloh: The Archaeology of a Biblical Site*. Edited by I. Finkelstein. Monograph Series of the Institute of Archaeology Tel Aviv University 10. Tel Aviv: Institute of Archaeology of Tel Aviv University.

Hendel, R. 2001. The Exodus in Biblical Memory. *JBL* 120: 601–8.

Herr, L. G., and D. R. Clark. 2009. From the Stone Age to the Middle Ages in Jordan: Digging up Tall al-'Umayri. *NEA* 72:68–97.

Herzog, Z., and L. Singer-Avitz. 2004. Redefining the Centre: The Emergence of State in Judah. *Tel Aviv* 31:209–44.

———. 2006. Sub-dividing the Iron IIA in Northern Israel: A Suggested Solution to the Chronological Debate. Tel Aviv 33:163–95.

Hesse, B. 1990. Pig Lovers and Pig Haters: Patterns of Palestinian Pork Production. *Journal of Ethnobiology* 10:195–225.

Hoffman, Y. 1989. A North Israelite Typological Myth and a Judaean Historical Tradition: The Exodus in Hosea and Amos. *VT* 39:169–82.

———. 1998. The Exodus-Tradition and Reality: The Status of the Exodus Tradition in Ancient Israel. Pages 193–202 in *Jerusalem Studies in Egyptology*. Edited by I. Shirun-Grumach. Wiesbaden: Harrassowitz.

Hoffmann, H. D. 1980. *Reform und Reformen: Untersuchungen zu einem Grundthema der deuteronomistischen Geschichtsschreibung*. Zurich: Theologischer Verlag.

Hoffmeier, J. K. 2005. *Ancient Israel in Sinai: The Evidence for the Authenticity of the Wilderness Tradition*. Oxford: Oxford University Press.

Humbert, J.-B. 1993. Keisan, Tell. *NEAEHL* 3:862–67.

Hutton, J. M. 2009. *The Transjordanian Palimpsest: The Overwritten Texts of Personal Exile and Transformation in the Deuteronomistic History*. Berlin: de Gruyter.

Ilan, D. 1999. Northeastern Israel in the Iron Age I: Cultural, Socioeconomic and Political Perspectives. Ph.D. diss., Tel Aviv University.

Isser, S. 2003. *The Sword of Goliath: David in Heroic Literature*. SBLSBL 6. Atlanta: Society of Biblical Literature.

Jasmin, M. 2005. Les conditions d'émergence de la route de l'encens à la fin du IIe millénaire avant notre ère. *Syria* 82:49–62.

Ji, C.-H. 2002. The Iron Age Temple at Khirbat "Ataruz. Paper presented at the American Schools of Oriental Research Annual Meeting in Toronto, November 2002.

Kartreit, M. 2009. *The Origin of the Samaritans*. Leiden: Brill.

Keel, O. 2010. *Corpus der Stempelsiegel-Amulette aus Palästina/Israel: Von den Anfangen bis zur Perserzeit*. OBO Series archaeologica 31. Fribourg: Academic Press.

Keel, O., and C. Uehlinger, 1998. *Gods, Goddesses and Images of Gods in Ancient Israel*. Minneapolis: Fortress.

Kempinski, A. 1989. *Megiddo: A City State and Royal Centre in North Israel*. Munich: Beck.

Kenyon, K. M. 1942. The Summit Buildings and Constructions. Pages 91–139 in J. W. Crowfoot, K. M. Kenyon, and E. L. Sukenik, *The Buildings at Samaria*. London: Palestine Exploration Fund.

———. 1971. *Royal Cities of the Old Testament*. New York: Schocken.

Kitchen, K. A. 1986. *The Third Intermediate Period in Egypt (1100–650 BC)*. Warminster: Aris & Phillips.

———. 1998. Egyptians and Hebrews, from Raamses to Jericho. Pages 65–131 in *The Origin of Early Israel—Current Debate*. Edited by E. Oren. Beer-Sheva 12. Beer-sheba: Ben-Gurion University of the Negev Press.

———. 2002. Hazor and Egypt: An Egyptological and Ancient Near Eastern Perspective. *SJOT* 16:309–13.

Knauf E. A. 1991. King Solomon's Copper Supply. Pages 167–86 in *Phoenicia and the Bible*. Edited by E. Lipiński. Leuven: Peeters.

———. 1995. Edom: The Social and Economic History. Pages 93–117 in *You Shall Not Abhor an Edomite for He Is Your Brother: Edom and Seir in History and Tradition*. Edited by D. Vikander Edelman. ABS 3. Atlanta: Scholars Press.

———. 1997. Le roi est mort, vive le roi! A Biblical Argument for the Historicity of Solomon. Pages 81–95 in *The Age of Solomon: Scholarship at the Turn of the Millennium*. Edited by L. K. Handy. Leiden: Brill.

———. 2001a. The Mist of Ramthalon, Or: How Ramoth-gilead Disappeared from the Archaeological Record. *BN* 110:33–36.

———. 2001b. Saul, David, and the Philistines: From Geography to History. *BN* 109:15–18.

———. 2006. Bethel: The Israelite Impact on Judean Language and Literature. Pages 291–349 in *Judah and the Judeans in the Persian Period*. Edited by O. Lipschits and M. Oeming. Winona Lake, Ind.: Eisenbrauns.

Koch, I. 2012. The Geopolitical Organization of the Judean Shephelah during the Iron Age I-IIA (1150–800 BCE) [Hebrew]. *Cathedra* 143:45–64.

Kochavi, M. 1989. The Identification of Zeredah, Home of Jeroboam son of Nebat, King of Israel [Hebrew]. *EI* 20:198–201.

Köckert, M. 2010. YHWH in the Northern and Southern Kingdom. Pages 357–94 in *One God—One Cult—One Nation: Archaeological and Biblical Perspectives*. Edited by R. G. Kratz and H. Spieckermann. Berlin: de Gruyter.

Kratz, R. G. 2005. *The Composition of the Narrative Books of the Old Testament*. London: T&T Clark.

Kuan, J. K. 2001. Samsi-ilu and the Realpolitic of Israel and Aram Damascus in the Eighth Century BCE. Pages 135–51 in *The Land That I Will Show You: Essays in the History and Archaeology of the Ancient Near*

East in Honor of J. Maxwell Miller. Edited by J. A. Dearman and M. P. Graham. JSOTSup 343. Sheffield: Sheffield Academic Press.

Lamon, R. S., and G.M. Shipton. 1939. *Megiddo I: Seasons of 1925–34, Strata I–V.* Chicago: University of Chicago Press.

Lapp, N. L. 1993. Rumeith, Tell er-. *NEAEHL* 4:1291–93.

Lapp, P. 1963. Chronique archéologique: Tell er-Rumeith. *RB* 70:406–11.

Lederman, Z. 1999. An Early Iron Age Village at Khirbet Raddana: The Excavations of Joseph A. Callaway. Ph.D. diss., Harvard University.

Lemaire, A. 1977. *Inscriptions hébraïques 1: Les ostraca.* Paris: Cerf.

———. 1981. Galaad et Makîr. *VT* 31:39–61.

———. 1984. Date et origine des inscriptions hebraïques et pheniciennes de Kuntillet ʿAjrud. *Studi Epigrafici e Linguistici* 1:131–43.

———. 1991. Hazaël de Damas, roi d'Aram. Pages 91–108 in *Marchands, Diplomates et Empereurs.* Edited by D. Charpin and F. Joannès. Paris: Editions Recherche sur les civilisations.

———. 1993. Joas de Samarie, Barhadad de Damas, Zakkur de Hamat. La Syrie-Palestine vers 800 av. J.-C. *EI* 24:148*–157*.

———. 2007. West Semitic Inscriptions and Ninth-Century BCE Ancient Israel. Pages 279–303 in *Understanding the History of Ancient Israel.* Edited by H. G. M. Williamson. Proceedings of the British Academy 143. Oxford: Oxford University Press.

———. 2012. New Perspectives on the Trade between Judah and South Arabia. Pages 93–110 in *New Inscriptions and Seals Relating to the Biblical World.* Edited by M. Lubetski. SBLABS 19. Atlanta: Society of Biblical Literature.

Lemche, N. P. 1977. The Greek "Amphictyony"—Could It Be a Prototype for the Israelite Society in the Period of the Judges? *JSOT* 4:48–59.

———. 1989. Mysteriet om det forsvundne tempel. *Svensk exegetisk årsbok* 54:118–26.

Levy, T. E., R. B. Adams, M. Najjar, A. Hauptmann, J. D. Anderson, B. Brandl, M. A. Robinson, and T. Higham. 2004. Reassessing the Chronology of Biblical Edom: New Excavations and ^{14}C Dates from Khirbat en-Nahas (Jordan). *Antiquity* 78:865–79.

Lipiński, E. 2000. *The Aramaeans: Their Ancient History, Culture, Religion.* Leuven: Peeters.

———. 2006. *On the Skirts of Canaan in the Iron Age: Historical and Topographical Research.* OLA 153. Leuven: Peeters.

Liverani, M. 1992. Early Caravan Trade between South-Arabia and Mesopotamia. *Yemen* 1:111–15.

———. 2005. *Israel's History and the History of Israel*. Translated by Chiara Peri and Philip R. Davies. London: Equinox.

Loud, G. 1948. *Megiddo II: Seasons of 1935–39*. Chicago: University of Chicago Press.

Maeir, A.M. 1997. The Material Culture of the Central Jordan Valley during the Middle Bronze II Period: Pottery and Settlement Pattern, Vol. II: Appendices, Bibliography and Illusterations. Ph.D. diss., The Hebrew University, Jerusalem.

———. 2004. The Historical Background and Dating of Amos VI 2: An Archaeological Perspective from Tell es-Safi/Gath. *VT* 54:319–34.

———. 2012. Tell es-Safi/Gath Archaeological Project 1996–2010: Introduction, Overview and Synopsis of Results. Pages 1–89 in vol. 1 of *Tell es-Safi/Gath I: The 1996–2005 Seasons*. Edited by A. M. Maeir. Ägypten und Altes Testament 69. Wiesbaden: Harrassowitz.

Magen, I. 2004. *The Aramaic, Hebrew and Samaritan Inscriptions*. Vol. 1 of *Mount Gerizim Excavations*. Jerusalem: Israel Antiquities Authority.

———. 2008. *A Temple City*. Vol. 2 of *Mount Gerizim Excavations*. Jerusalem: Israel Antiquities Authority.

Mallet, J. 1987–1988. *Tell el-Far'ah II, le Bronze Moyen*. Éditions Recherche sur les Civilisations 66. Paris: Éditions Recherche sur les Civilisations.

Marfoe, L. 1979. The Integrative Transformation: Patterns of Sociopolitical Organization in Southern Syria. *BASOR* 234:1–42.

Mastin, B.A. 2011. Who Built and Who Used the Buildings at Kuntillet 'Ajrud? Pages 69–85 in *On Stone and Scroll: Essays in Honour of Graham Ivor Davies*. Edited by J. K. Aitkin, K. J. Dell, and B. A. Mastin. Berlin: de Gruyter.

Mattingly, G. L., and J. H. Pace. 2007. Crossing Jordan by the Way of the Karak Plateau. Pages 153–59 in *Crossing Jordan: North American Contributions to the Archaeology of Jordan*. Edited by T. E. Levy, M. P. M. Daviau, R. W. Younker, and M. Shaer. London: Equinox.

Mazar, A. 1981. Giloh: An Early Israelite Settlement Site near Jerusalem. *IEJ* 31:1–36.

———. 2006. Jerusalem in the 10th Century B.C.E.: The Glass Half Full. Pages 255–72 in *Essays on Ancient Israel in Its Near Eastern Context: A Tribute to Nadav Na'aman*. Edited by Y. Amit, E. Ben Zvi, I. Finkelstein, and O. Lipschits. Winona Lake, Ind.: Eisenbrauns.

———. 2009. Introduction and Overview. Pages 1–32 in *The 13th–11th Century BCE Strata in Areas N and S*. Vol. 3 of *Excavations at Tel Beth-*

shean 1989–1996. Edited by N. Panitz-Cohen and A. Mazar. Jerusalem: Israel Exploration Society.

———. 2010. Archaeology and the Biblical Narrative: The Case of the United Monarchy. Pages 29–58 in *One God—One Cult—One Nation: Archaeological and Biblical Perspectives*. Edited by R. G. Kratz and H. Spieckermann. Berlin: de Gruyter.

Mazar, A., and S. Ahituv. 2011. Inscriptions from Tel Rehov and Their Contribution to the Study of Writing and Literacy during the Iron Age IIA [Hebrew]. *EI* 30:300–316.

Mazar, A., H. J. Bruins, N. Panitz-Cohen, and J. van der Plicht. 2005. Ladder of Time at Tel Rehov: Stratigraphy, Archaeological Context, Pottery and Radiocarbon Dates. Pages 193–255 in *The Bible and Radiocarbon Dating: Archaeology, Text and Science*. Edited by T. E. Levy and T. Higham. London: Equinox.

Mazar, B. 1957. Pharaoh Shishak's Campaign to the Land of Israel. Pages 57–66 in *Volume du congrès: Strasbourg, 1956*. Edited by P. A. H. de Boer. VTSup 4. Leiden: Brill.

———. 1993. En Gev, Excavations on the Mound. *NEAEHL* 2:409–11.

Mazar, B., A. Biran, M. Dothan, and I. Dunayevsky. 1964. 'Ein Gev Excavations in 1961. *IEJ* 14:1–49.

Mazar, E. 2009. *The Palace of King David, Excavations at the Summit of the City of David, Preliminary Report of Seasons 2005–2007*. Jerusalem: Shoham Academic Research and Publication.

McCarter, P. K., Jr. 1980a. The Apology of David. *JBL* 99:489–504.

———. 1980b. *1 Samuel*. AB 8. Garden City, N.Y.: Doubleday.

———. 1994. The Books of Samuel. Pages 260–80 in *The History of Israel's Tradition: The Heritage of Martin Noth*. Edited by S. L. McKenzie and M. P. Graham. Sheffield: Sheffield Academic Press.

Meshel, Z. 1994. The "Aharoni Fortress" near Quseima and the "Israelite Fortresses" in the Negev. *BASOR* 294:39–67.

———. 2012. *Kuntillet 'Ajrud (Ḥorvat Teman): An Iron Age II Religious Site on the Judah-Sinai Border*. Jerusalem: Israel Exploration Society.

Meshel, Z., and R. Cohen. 1980. Refed and Hatira: Two Iron Age Fortresses in the Northern Negev. *Tel Aviv* 7:70–81.

Millard, A. 2011. The Ostracon from the Days of David Found at Khirbet Qeiyafa. *Tyndale Bulletin* 61:1–13.

Miller, M. J. 1966. The Elisha Cycle and the Accounts of the Omride Wars. *JBL* 85:441–54.

———. 1975. Geba/Gibeah of Benjamin. *VT* 25:145–66.

————. 1997. Separating the Solomon of History from the Solomon of Legend. Pages 1–24 in *The Age of Solomon: Scholarship at the Turn of the Millennium.* Edited by L. K. Handy. Leiden: Brill.

Miller, M. J., and J. H. Hayes. 1986. *A History of Ancient Israel and Judah.* Philadelphia: Westminster.

Misgav, H., Y. Garfinkel, and S. Ganor. 2009. The Ostracon. Pages 243–57 in Y. Garfinkel and S. Ganor, *Excavation Report 2007–2008.* Vol. 1 of *Khirbet Qeiyafa.* Jerusalem: Israel Exploration Society.

Mor, M., and F. V. Reiterer, eds. 2010. *Samaritans: Past and Present.* Berlin: de Gruyter.

Moran, W. L. 1992. *The Amarna Letters.* Baltimore: Johns Hopkins University Press.

Mullen, T. E. 1992. Crime and Punishment: The Sins of the King and the Despoliation of the Treasuries. *CBQ* 54:231–48.

Münger, S., J. Zangenberg, and J. Pakkala. 2011. Kinneret—An Urban Center at the Crossroads: Excavations on Iron IB Tel Kinrot at the Lake of Galilee. *NEA* 74:68–90.

Musil, A. 1907. *Moab: Topographischer Reisebericht.* Vol. 1 of *Arabia Petraea.* Vienna: Hölder.

Myers, E. A. 2010. *The Ituraeans and the Roman Near East.* Cambridge: Cambridge University Press.

Na'aman, N. 1975. The Political Disposition and Historical Development of Eretz Israel according to the Amarna Letters [Hebrew]. Ph.D. diss., Tel Aviv University.

————. 1990.The Kingdom of Ishbaal. *BN* 54:33–37.

————. 1991. The Kingdom of Judah under Josiah. *Tel Aviv* 18:3–71.

————. 1995. Rezin of Damascus and the Land of Gilead. *ZDPV* 111:105–17.

————. 1997a. Historical and Literary Notes on the Excavations of Tel Jezreel. *Tel Aviv* 24:122–28.

————. 1997b. King Mesha and the Foundation of the Moabite Monarchy. *IEJ* 47:83–92.

————. 1997c. The Network of Canaanite Kingdoms and the City of Ashdod. *UF* 29:599–626.

————. 2000. Three Notes on the Aramaic Inscription from Tel Dan. *IEJ* 50:92–104.

————. 2001. Solomon's District List (1 Kings 4:7–19) and the Assyrian Province System in Palestine. *UF* 33:419–36.

———. 2002a. The Abandonment of Cult Places in the Kingdoms of Israel and Judah as Acts of Cult Reform. *UF* 34:585–602.

———. 2002b. *The Past That Shaped the Present: The Creation of Biblical Historiography in the Late First Temple Period and after the Downfall* [Hebrew]. Jerusalem: Ornah Hes.

———. 2006. *Ancient Israel's History and Historiography: The First Temple Period.* Winona Lake, Ind.: Eisenbrauns.

———. 2007. Royal Inscription versus Prophetic Story: Mesha's Rebellion according to Biblical and Moabite Historiography. Pages 145–83 in Grabbe 2007.

———. 2008a. In Search of the Ancient Name of Khirbet Qeiyafa. *JHS* 8. Online: http://www.jhsonline.org/Articles/article_98.pdf.

———. 2008b. Shaaraim —The Gateway to the Kingdom of Judah. *JHS* 8. Online: http://www.jhsonline.org/Articles/article_101.pdf.

———. 2009. Saul, Benjamin and the Emergence of "Biblical Israel." *ZAW* 121:211–24, 335–49.

———. 2011a. The Exodus Story: Between Historical Memory and Historiographical Composition. *Journal of Ancient Near Eastern Religions* 11:39–69.

———. 2011b. A Hidden Anti-Samaritan Polemic in the Story of Abimelech and Shechem (Judges 9). *Biblische Zeitschrift* 55: 1–20.

———. 2012a. The Inscriptions of Kuntillet 'Ajrud through the Lens of Historical Research. *UF* 43:1–43.

———. 2012b. Khirbet Qeiyafa in Context. *UF* 42:497–526.

Negbi, O. 1974. The Continuity of the Canaanite Bronzework of the Late Bronze Age into the Early Iron Age. *Tel Aviv* 1:159–72.

Nelson, R. D. 1981. Josiah in the Book of Joshua. *JBL* 100:531–40.

Niemann, H. M. 1997. The Socio-political Shadow Cast by the Biblical Solomon. Pages 252–299 in *The Age of Solomon: Scholarship at the Turn of the Millennium.* Edited by L. K. Handy. Leiden: Brill.

———. 2007. Royal Samaria—Capital or Residence? Or: The Foundation of the City of Samaria by Sargon II. Pages 187–207 in *Ahab Agonistes: The Rise and Fall of the Omri Dynasty.* Edited by L. L. Grabbe. European Seminar in Historical Methodology 6. London: T&T Clark.

———. 2008. A New Look at the Samaria Ostraca: The King-Clan Relationship. *Tel Aviv* 35:249–66.

———. 2012. Observations on the Layout of Iron Age Samaria: A Reply to Israel Finkelstein. *UF* 43:325–34.

Noth, M. 1940. Der Wallfahrtsweg zum Sinai (Nu 33). *PJb* 36:5–28.

———. 1966. *Das System der zwölf Stämme Israels*. Darmstadt: Wissenschaftliche Buchgesellschaft.

———. 1968. *Numbers: A Commentary*. Translated by James D. Martin. OTL. Philadelphia: Westminster.

———. 1981. *The Deuteronomistic History*. JSOTSup 15. Sheffield: Sheffield Academic Press.

Ofer, A. 1994. "All the Hill Country of Judah": From a Settlement Fringe to a Prosperous Monarchy. Pages 92–121 in *From Nomadism to Monarchy: Archaeological and Historical Aspects of Early Israel*. Edited by I. Finkelstein and N. Na'aman. Jerusalem: Yad Izhak Ben-Zvi.

Ornan, T. Forthcoming. The Drawings from Kuntillet 'Ajrud Reconsidered [Hebrew]. In S. Ahituv, E. Eshel, Z. Meshel, and T. Ornan, *To Yahweh Teiman and His Ashera, the Inscriptions and Drawings from Kuntillet 'Ajrud*. Jerusalem.

Ortiz, S., and S. Wolf. 2012. The Iron Age City of Gezer. *NEA* 75:4–19.

Otto, E. 2000. Mose und das Gesetz: Die Mose-Figur als Gegenentwurf Politischer Theologie zur neuassyrischen Königsideologie im 7 Jh. v. Chr. Pages 43–83 in *Mose: Ägypten und das Alte Testament*. Edited by E. Otto. Stuttgart: Verlag Katholisches Bibelwerk.

Pakkala, J. 2008. Jeroboam without Bulls. *ZAW* 120:501–25.

Pritchard, J. B. 1963. *The Bronze Age Cemetery at Gibeon*. Philadelphia: University of Pennsylvania.

———. 1964. *Winery, Defenses, and Soundings at Gibeon*. Philadelphia: University of Pennsylvania.

Puech, É. 2010. L'Ostracon de Khirbet Qeyafa et les débuts de la royauté en Israël. *RB* 117:162–84.

Pury, A. de. 1975. *Promesse divine et légende cultuelle dans le cycle de Jacob*. Paris: Gabalda.

———. 1991. Le cycle de Jacob comme légende autonome des origines d'Israël. Pages 78–96 in *Congress Volume: Leuven, 1989*. Edited by J. A. Emerton. VTSup 43. Leiden: Brill.

———. 2001. Situer le cycle de Jacob: Quelques réflexions, vingt-cinq ans plus tard. Pages 213–41 in *Studies in the Book of Genesis: Literature, Redaction and History*. Edited by A. Wénin. Leuven: Leuven University Press.

———. 2006. The Jacob Story and the Beginning of the Formation of the Pentateuch. Pages 51–72 in *A Farewell to the Yahwist? The Composition of the Pentateuch in Recent European Interpretation*. Edited by T.

B. Dozeman and K. Schmid. SBLSymS 34. Atlanta: Society of Biblical Literature.

Pury, A. de, and T. Römer, eds. 2000. *Die Sogenannte Thronfolgegeschichte Davids: neue Einsichten und Anfragen.* OBO 176. Fribourg: Universitätsverlag; Göttingen: Vandenhoeck & Ruprecht.

Rad, G. von. 1966. *The Problem of the Hexateuch and Other Essays.* Edinburgh: Oliver & Boyd. Originally published in German in 1944 in the *Archiv für Kulturgeschichte* 32:1–42.

Rafiq, A. K. 1966. *The Province of Damascus, 1723–1783.* Beirut: Khayats.

Redford, D. B. 1987. An Egyptological Perspective on the Exodus Narrative. Pages 137–61 in *Egypt, Israel, Sinai: Archaeological and Historical Relationships in the Biblical Period.* Edited by A. F. Rainey. Tel Aviv: Tel Aviv University.

———. 1992. *Egypt, Canaan and Israel in Ancient Times.* Princeton: Princeton University Press.

Reich, R., and E. Shukron. 2003. The Urban Development of Jerusalem in the Late Eight Century B.C.E. Pages 209–18 in *Jerusalem in Bible and Archaeology: The First Temple Period.* Edited by A. G. Vaughn and A. E. Killebrew. SBLSymS 18. Atlanta: Society of Biblical Literature.

Reisner, G. A., C. S. Fisher, and D. G. Lyon. 1924. *Harvard Excavations at Samaria, 1908–1910.* Cambridge: Harvard University Press.

Reviv, H. 1966. The Government of Shechem in the El-Amarna Period and in the Days of Abimelech. *IEJ* 16:252–57.

Richter, W. 1966. *Traditionsgeschichtliche Untersuchungen zum Richterbuch.* Bonn: Hanstein.

Riklin, S. 1997. An Iron IIB Site in Bet Arye [Hebrew]. *Atiqot* 32:7–20.

Rollston, C. 2011. The Khirbet Qeiyafa Ostracon: Methodological Musings and Caveats. *Tel Aviv* 38:67–82.

Römer, T. 1998. Why Would the Deuteronomist Tell about the Sacrifice of Jephthah's Daughter? *JSOT* 23:727–38.

———. 2002. *Moïse: "Lui que Yahvé a connu face à face."* Paris: Gallimard.

———. 2003. La construction d'une "vie de Moïse" dans la Bible hébraïque et chez quelques auteurs hellénistiques. *Revue de l'Institut Catholique de Paris* 85:13–30.

———. 2007. *The So-Called Deuteronomistic History: A Sociological, Historical, and Literary Introduction.* London: T&T Clark.

Römer, T., and A. de Pury. 2000. Deuteronomistic Historiography (DH): History of Research and Debated Issues. Pages 24–141 in *Israel Constructs Its History: Deuteronomistic Historiography in Recent Research.*

Edited by A. de Pury, T. Römer, and J.-D. Macchi. Sheffield: Sheffield Academic Press.

Römer, T., and K. Schmid. 2007. *Les Dernières Rédactions du Pentateuque, de l'Hexateuque et de l'Ennéateuque.* Leuven: Peeters.

Rost, L. 1982. *The Succession to the Throne of David.* Sheffield: Almond. Originally published in 1926 as *Die Überlieferung von der Thronnachfolge Davids.*

Routledge, B. 2004. *Moab in the Iron Age: Hegemony, Polity, Archaeology.* Philadelphia: University of Pennsylvania Press.

———. 2008. Thinking "Globally" and Analyzing "Locally": South-Central Jordan in Transition. Pages 145–76 in *The Archaeology.* Vol. 1 of *Israel in Transition: From Late Bronze II to Iron IIa (c.1250–850 B.C.E.).* Edited by L. Grabbe. New York: T&T Clark.

Sass, B. 2005. *The Alphabet at the Turn of the Millennium.* Tel Aviv: Emery and Claire Yass Publications in Archaeology.

Schenker, A. 2000. Jeroboam and the Division of the Kingdom in the Ancient Septuagint: LXX 3 Kingdoms 12.24 A-Z, MT 1 Kings 11–12; 14 and the Deuteronomistic History. Pages 214–57 in *Israel Constructs Its History: Deuteronomistic Historiography in Recent Research.* Edited by A. de Pury, T. Römer, and J.-D. Macchi. Sheffield: Sheffield Academic Press.

———. 2008. Jeroboam's Rise and Fall in the Hebrew and Greek Bible. *JSJ* 39:367–73.

Schley, D. G. 1989. *Shiloh: A Biblical City in Tradition and History.* JSOTSup 63. Sheffield: JSOT Press.

Schmid, K. 2012a. Genesis and Exodus as Two Formerly Independent Traditions of Origins for Ancient Israel. *Bib* 93:187–208.

Schmid, K. 2012a. *The Old Testament: A Literary History.* Minneapolis: Fortress.

Schniedewind, W. M. 1996. The Tel Dan Stele: New Light on Aramaic and Jehu's Revolt. *BASOR* 302:82–86.

———. 1998. The Geopolitical History of Philistine Gath. *BASOR* 309:69–77.

———. 2004. *How the Bible Became a Book: The Textualization of Ancient Israel.* Cambridge: Cambridge University Press.

———. 2006. The Search for Gibeah: Notes on the Historical Geography of Central Benjamin. Pages 711–22 in *"I Will Speak the Riddles of Ancient Times": Archaeological and Historical Studies in Honor of*

Amihai Mazar. Edited by A. M. Maeir and P. de Miroschedji. Winona Lake, Ind.: Eisenbrauns.

Sharon, I., A. Gilboa, T. A. J. Jull, and E. Boaretto. 2007. Report on the First Stage of the Iron Age Dating Project in Israel: Supporting A Low Chronology. *Radiocarbon* 49:1–46.

Shiloh, Y. 1987. South Arabian Inscriptions from the City of David, Jerusalem. *PEQ* 119:9–18.

Singer-Avitz, L. 2010. The Relative Chronology of Khirbet Qeiyafa. *Tel Aviv* 37:79–83.

Smend, R. 1995. Mose als geschichtliche Gestalt. *Historische Zeitschrift* 260:1–19.

Stager, L. E. 1990. Shemer's Estate. *BASOR* 277/278:93–107.

Stern, E. 2000. *Dor, Ruler of the Seas: Nineteen Years of Excavations at the Israelite-Phoenician Harbor Town on the Carmel Coast*. Jerusalem: Israel Exploration Society.

Stern, E., and H. Eshel, eds. 2002. *The Samaritans* [Hebrew]. Jerusalem: Yad Ben-Zwi.

Sweeney, M. A. 2007. A Reassessment of the Masoretic and Septuagint Versions of the Jeroboam Narratives in 1 Kings/3 Kingdoms 11–14. *JSJ* 38:165–95.

Talshir, Z. 1993. *The Alternative Story of the Division of the Kingdom*. Jerusalem Biblical Studies 6. Jerusalem: Simor.

Tappy, R. E. 1992. *Early Iron Age through the Ninth Century BCE*. Vol. 1 of *The Archaeology of Israelite Samaria*. Atlanta: Scholars Press.

Thareani, Y. 2011. *Tel 'Aroer: The Iron Age II Caravan Town and the Hellenistic-Early Roman Settlement*. Jerusalem: Nelson Glueck School of Biblical Archaeology.

Timm, S. 1982. *Die Dynastie Omri*. Göttingen: Vandenhoeck & Ruprecht.

Toffolo, M. B., E. Arie, M. A. S. Martin, E. Boaretto, and I. Finkelstein. Forthcoming. The Absolute Chronology of Megiddo, Israel in the Late Bronze and Iron Ages: High-Resolution Radiocarbon Dating. *Radiocarbon*.

Toorn, K. van der. 1993. Saul and the Rise of the Israelite State Religioin. *VT* 43:519–42.

———. 1996. *Family Religion in Babylonia, Syria and Israel: Continuity and Change in the Forms of Religious Life*. Leiden: Brill.

Ussishkin, D. 1990: Notes on Megiddo, Gezer, Ashdod, and Tel Batash in the Tenth to Ninth Centuries B.C. *BASOR* 277/278:71–91.

———. 1995. The Destruction of Megiddo at the End of the Late Bronze Age and Its Historical Significance. *Tel Aviv* 22:240–67.

Ussishkin, D., and J. Woodhead. 1992. Excavations at Tel Jezreel 1990–1991: Preliminary Report. *Tel Aviv* 19:3–56.

———. 1994. Excavations at Tel Jezreel 1992–1993: Second Preliminary Report. *Levant* 26:1–71.

———. 1997. Excavations at Tel Jezreel 1994–1996: Third Preliminary Report. *Tel Aviv* 24:6–72.

Uziel, J., and A. Maeir. 2005. Scratching the High Surface of Gath: Implications of the Tell es-Safi/Gath Surface Survey. *Tel Aviv* 32:50–75.

Van Seters, J. 1983. *In Search of History: Historiography in the Ancient World and the Origins of Biblical History.* New Haven: Yale University Press.

———. 2001. The Geography of the Exodus. Pages 255–76 in *The Land That I Will Show You: Essays in the History and Archaeology of the Ancient Near East in Honor of J. Maxwell Miller.* Edited by J. A. Dearman and M. P. Graham. JSOTSup 343. Sheffield: Sheffield Academic Press..

———. 1990. Joshua's Campaign of Canaan and Near Eastern Historiography. *SJOT* 4.2:1–12.

Vaux, R. de. 1941. Notes d'histoire et de topographie transjordaniennes. *RB* 49:16–47.

———. 1951. La troisième campagne de fouilles à Tell el-Farʿah, près Naplouse, rapport préliminaire. *RB* 58:393–430, 566–90.

———. 1952. La quatrième campagne de fouilles à Tell el-Farʿah, près Naplouse, rapport préliminaire. *RB* 59:551–83.

———. 1956. The Excavations at Tell el-Farʿah and the Site of Ancient Tirzah. *PEQ* 88:125–40.

———. 1957. Les fouilles à Tell el-Farʿah, près Naplouse, sixième campagne: Rapport préliminaire. *RB* 64:552–80.

———. 1961. Les fouilles à Tell el-Farʿah, rapport préliminaire sur les 7ᵉ, 8ᵉ, 9ᵉ campagnes, 1958–1960. *RB* 68:557–92.

———. 1967. Tirzah. Pages 371–83 in *Archaeology and Old Testament Study.* Edited by D. W. Thomas. Oxford: Clarendon.

Vaux, R. de, and A.M. Stève. 1947. La première campagne de fouilles à Tell el-Farʿah, près Naplouse, rapport préliminaire. *RB* 54:394–433, 573–89.

———. 1948. La seconde campagne de fouilles à Tell el-Farʿah, près Naplouse, rapport préliminaire. *RB* 55:544–80.

Veldhuijzen, H. A., and T. Rehren. 2007. Slags and the City: Early Iron Production at Tell Hammeh, Jordan and Tel Beth-Shemesh, Israel. Pages 89–201 in *Metals and Mines: Studies in Archaeometallurgy.* Edited by S. La Niece, D. R. Hook, and P. T. Craddock. London: Archetype Publications in association with The British Museum.

Vieweger, D., and J. Häser. 2007. Tall Zira'a: Five Thousand Years of Palestinian History on a Single-Settlement Mound. *NEA* 70:147–67.

Watzinger, K. 1929. *Tell el-Mutesellim II: Die Funde.* Leipzig: Haupt.

Wente E. F. 1976. Review of K. A. Kitchen, *The Third Intermediate Period in Egypt. JNES* 35:275–78.

Westermann, C. 1986. *Genesis 12–36: A Commentary.* Translated by John J. Scullion. Minneapolis: Augsburg.

White, M. 1997. *The Elijah Legends and Jehu's Coup.* BJS 311. Atlanta: Scholars Press.

Williamson, H. G. M. 1996. Tel Jezreel and the Dynasty of Omri. *PEQ* 128:41–51.

Wolff, H. W. 1982. *Hosea: A Commentary on the Book of the Prophet Hosea.* Philadelphia: Fortress.

Würthwein, E. 1994. Abimelech und der Untergang Sichems—Studies zu Jdc 9. Pages 12–28 in *Studien zum deuteronomistischen Geschichtswerk.* Edited by E. Würthwein. BZAW 227. Berlin: de Gruyter.

Yadin, Y. 1958. Solomon's City Wall and Gate at Gezer. *IEJ* 8:80–86.

———. 1970. Megiddo of the Kings of Israel. *BA* 33:66–96.

———. 1972. *Hazor: The Head of All Those Kingdoms: Joshua 11:10; With a Chapter on Israelite Meggido.* The Schweich Lectures of the British Academy. London: Oxford University Press.

Yadin, Y., Y. Aharoni, R. Amiran, T. Dothan, I. Dunayevsky, and J. Perrot. 1960. *Hazor II: An Account of the Second Season of Excavations, 1956.* Jerusalem: Magnes.

Younger, K. L. 2007. Neo-Assyrian and Israelite History in the Ninth Century: The Role of Shalmaneser III. Pages 243–77 in *Understanding the History of Ancient Israel.* Edited by H. G. M. Williamson. Proceedings of the British Academy 143. Oxford: Oxford University Press.

Zertal, A. 1994. "To the Land of the Perizzites and the Giants": On the Israelite Settlement in the Hill Country of Manasseh. Pages 47–69 in *From Nomadism to Monarchy: Archaeological and Historical Aspects of Early Israel.* Edited by I. Finkelstein and N. Na'aman. Jerusalem: Yad Izhak Ben-Zvi..

Zimhoni, O. 2004a. The Pottery of Levels V and IV and Its Archaeologi-
    cal and Chronological Implications. Pages 1643–1788 in D. Ussish-
    kin, *The Renewed Archaeological Excavations at Lachish (1973–1994)*.
    Monograph Series of the Institute of Archaeology Tel Aviv University
    22. Tel Aviv: Tel Aviv University, Institute of Archaeology.
———. 2004b. The Pottery of Levels III and II. Pages 1789–1899 in D.
    Ussishkin, *The Renewed Archaeological Excavations at Lachish (1973–
    1994)*. Monograph Series of the Institute of Archaeology Tel Aviv Uni-
    versity 22. Tel Aviv: Tel Aviv University, Institute of Archaeology.

INDEX OF PLACE NAMES

Index of Personal Names

Lightning Source UK Ltd.
Milton Keynes UK
UKOW04f1338290216

269298UK00002B/627/P